THE

COMPLETE IDIOT'S GUIDE® TO

Teaching Music on Your Own

by Karen Berger

ALPHA

A member of Penguin Group (USA) Inc.

This book is dedicated, with love, to David Hodge, who has been my partner in every part of this grand adventure of teaching, writing, and making music.

ALPHA BOOKS

Published by the Penguin Group

Penguin Group (USA) Inc., 375 Hudson Street, New York, New York 10014, USA

Penguin Group (Canada), 90 Eglinton Avenue East, Suite 700, Toronto, Ontario M4P 2Y3, Canada (a division of Pearson Penguin Canada Inc.)

Penguin Books Ltd., 80 Strand, London WC2R 0RL, England

Penguin Ireland, 25 St. Stephen's Green, Dublin 2, Ireland (a division of Penguin Books Ltd.)

Penguin Group (Australia), 250 Camberwell Road, Camberwell, Victoria 3124, Australia (a division of Pearson Australia Group Pty. Ltd.)

Penguin Books India Pvt. Ltd., 11 Community Centre, Panchsheel Park, New Delhi—110 017, India

Penguin Group (NZ), 67 Apollo Drive, Rosedale, North Shore, Auckland 1311, New Zealand (a division of Pearson New Zealand Ltd.)

Penguin Books (South Africa) (Pty.) Ltd., 24 Sturdee Avenue, Rosebank, Johannesburg 2196, South Africa

Penguin Books Ltd., Registered Offices: 80 Strand, London WC2R 0RL, England

International Standard Book Number: 978-1-59257-961-7
Library of Congress Catalog Card Number: 2009934672

12 11 10   8 7 6 5 4 3 2 1

Interpretation of the printing code: The rightmost number of the first series of numbers is the year of the book's printing; the rightmost number of the second series of numbers is the number of the book's printing. For example, a printing code of 10-1 shows that the first printing occurred in 2010.

Printed in the United States of America

Note: This publication contains the opinions and ideas of its author. It is intended to provide helpful and informative material on the subject matter covered. It is sold with the understanding that the author and publisher are not engaged in rendering professional services in the book. If the reader requires personal assistance or advice, a competent professional should be consulted.

The author and publisher specifically disclaim any responsibility for any liability, loss, or risk, personal or otherwise, which is incurred as a consequence, directly or indirectly, of the use and application of any of the contents of this book.

Most Alpha books are available at special quantity discounts for bulk purchases for sales promotions, premiums, fund-raising, or educational use. Special books, or book excerpts, can also be created to fit specific needs.

For details, write: Special Markets, Alpha Books, 375 Hudson Street, New York, NY 10014.

Publisher: *Marie Butler-Knight*
Editorial Director: *Mike Sanders*
Senior Managing Editor: *Billy Fields*
Acquisitions Editor: *Karyn Gerhard*
Development Editor: *Julie Coffin*
Senior Production Editor: *Megan Douglass*
Copy Editor: *Krista Hansing Editorial Services, Inc.*

Cartoonist: *Steve Barr*
Cover Designer: *Bill Thomas*
Book Designer: *Trina Wurst*
Indexer: *Brad Herriman*
Layout: *Brian Massey*
Proofreader: *Laura Caddell*

Contents at a Glance

Contents

Introduction

How would you like to have a career in which you determine your own hours, can schedule vacations when you want them, manage everything yourself, meet scores of people of all ages and walks of life in your community, and spend your working hours sharing the art that you love?

Sounds too good to be true? Not if you were one of the smart, or lucky, ones who took music lessons, made time to practice, and eventually got good enough at your instrument that you now feel qualified to teach.

Of course, other things come into play. Running an independent music studio means more than being able to play an instrument, and it requires more than hanging out a shingle and waiting for eager and willing students to pour through the door of your studio. You'll need to cope with pricing, scheduling, insurance, zoning laws, advertising and marketing, student relations (and parent relations, too), professional development, continuing education, recital management—oh, and teaching, too.

Look at this book as a friendly guide from teachers who have been on this road before you. I designed this book to help you start your studio with a bang and run it successfully.

How to Use This Book

The Complete Idiot's Guide to Teaching Music on Your Own has four parts. Each addresses a different facet of teaching music and running your own studio.

Part 1, "Getting Started," covers the initial basics, beginning with a review of the skills needed to be a successful music teacher. Don't worry, I've got you covered. If your business skills aren't quite up to snuff or you need to brush up a little on your pedagogy and teaching skills, I tell you some of the basics—and suggest ways to get help when and if you need it.

In **Part 2, "The Business of Running a Successful Studio,"** I discuss the nitty-gritty business issues. True, if you had wanted to be an accountant, a lawyer, a bill collector, a marketing vice president, a public relations executive, or an insurance agent, you'd be following a different career path. But you need to have your business ducks in a row, and I help you put them there.

Part 3, "The Teacher-Student Relationship," focuses on the heart of the matter: your students. Who are they and what do you need to know about them? Preschool students, school-age students, and adults all have unique goals and challenges. In this part, I cover interviewing students, teaching them as they move through various ages and levels, and working with them when things don't go exactly as planned.

Finally, in **Part 4, "A Career That Grows and Changes,"** I talk about managing your career so it lasts a lifetime. Today's music teacher has more resources than have ever been available. From evaluating modern pedagogy to continuing your professional development, from understanding new digital tools to bringing your students' musical performances to your community, I cover the ongoing issues that keep you and your studio vibrant and energetic.

Extras

This book also contains dozens of sidebars that include tips, warnings, interesting bits and pieces of information, and quotations from teachers all over North America. You'll find four kinds of sidebars:

> **Out of Tune**
>
> These sidebars highlight various mistakes that new teachers might make—and the consequences.

> **Wise Words**
>
> The wise words you'll find in these sidebars include quotations from musicians and music teachers all over North America.

> **Facts and Stats**
>
> The music world is filled with fascinating bits and pieces of information. These sidebars provide interesting insight into your new career.

> **Take Note**
>
> These sidebars give quick and easy advice. They are intended to give specific examples of—and solutions for—issues described in the text.

Acknowledgments

I would like to thank the many people who have contributed to this book.

First, to my agent, Marilyn Allen, and to my editor, Karyn Gerhard, who is not only a sharp and smart editor, but a pianist, too—how lucky could I get?

Thanks also to the team at Alpha-Penguin: Development Editor Julie Coffin, Production Editor Megan Douglass, Copy Editor Krista Hansing, and other behind-the-scenes professionals, as well as Marie Butler-Knight, Publisher.

I'd also like to thank the many music teachers who contributed ideas and quotations to this book, including Rebecca Brown, Kevin Coan, Debra Culver, Sarah Crandall Dunkirk, Jennifer Foxx, Sue Garratt, Susanne Gravel, Julie Gunvalson, Sandra Layman, D'Net Layton, Shelagh McKibbon, Karen Monroe, Carol Montparker, Alice Peterson, Robyn Pfeifer, Marci Pittman, Sallie Ritchie, Saundra Robinson, Anne-Marie Scott, Vickie Steenhoek, Gretchen B. Taylor, Libby Wiebel, and Janna Williamson.

And finally, and most of all, thanks to David Hodge, who is not only my partner in teaching music and everything else, but who served as a sounding board for ideas and took care of so many home-front chores, even as he was working on his own book.

Trademarks

All terms mentioned in this book that are known to be or are suspected of being trademarks or service marks have been appropriately capitalized. Alpha Books and Penguin Group (USA) Inc. cannot attest to the accuracy of this information. Use of a term in this book should not be regarded as affecting the validity of any trademark or service mark.

Part 1

Getting Started

The world of the private music teacher starts with the home studio and expands beyond it to teaching in myriad venues, from colleges to preschools, music stores to community centers, not to mention in students' homes.

By learning where to look for music teaching opportunities, you'll get an idea of the many directions you might take your career. You'll also learn about the skills required to get started: the ability to play an instrument, a knowledge of teaching methodology, and business skills.

Chapter 1

What It Takes to Teach

In This Chapter

- ◆ The musical skills required to be a successful music teacher
- ◆ Pedagogy and the art of teaching
- ◆ Business skills for running a home music studio
- ◆ Getting started

Bob is a former concert pianist who teaches group lessons in his home. Martha has a degree in music and teaches in after-school programs. Susan is a massage therapist who also gigs as a guitarist; she teaches two days a week at the local music store. Bill is a recording engineer and would-be rock performer who offers lessons in songwriting, recording engineering, and beginning guitar. Caroline has a degree in classical music; she turned to teaching after burning out in her first career as a magazine editor. Daniel splits his time between teaching and performing African drumming. Kris doesn't have a degree in anything, but teaches groups of beginning adult guitar students at the local community college. Lisa teaches piano and violin in students' homes.

Music teaching is as varied as the people who do it. Music teachers range from educators trained in music pedagogy, to talented performers, to hobbyists who simply play and want to share their music on a part-time basis.

What does it take to be a good music teacher? And what does it take to make it a career? Accreditation is not required, and there is no single accepted curriculum. You aren't required to have a college degree, a teaching degree, or, for that matter, any degree at all. Teaching and learning music are personal endeavors, and no single set of criteria determines who may or may not become a private music teacher.

Still, no doubt some teachers enjoy more success than others, both financially and as teachers. They have full studios, they have high rates of student retention, and some of their students even go on to major in music and become teachers or performers themselves. These are the instructors whose names always come up when parents are looking for teachers for their kids. What do they have, or do, that is so special? Do they have concert-level technique? The patience of Job? An advanced degree? Years of experience? Special teacher training? Let's see if we can shed some light on the answers to these questions.

Music Skills Required for Teaching Music

First things first. To teach an instrument, you have to be able to play an instrument. But how well? It doesn't take a concert pianist to show a 6-year-old how to play "Chopsticks." Yet it's also true that the better musician you are, the more you bring to the lesson, even if the student is "only" a 6-year-old. The more advanced you are, the more advanced your students can become while studying with you. When students are able to play concert-level repertoire, it can be argued that they need a concert-level teacher. What is most important is that the teacher's technical and performance skills are sufficient to demonstrate the music being taught.

Musicianship for the Successful Teacher

In addition to performance and technical skills, the ideal music teacher knows a great deal about music theory, harmonization, arranging, different music styles, improvisation, recording, and music history. You should be able to make up an accompaniment on the fly and help a student figure out a song by ear. You need to be familiar with a wide range of styles (some of which may go beyond your own initial training in music). Being able to demonstrate a blues scale to a bored teenager, tell an interesting and inspirational story about a famous composer (or rock star who maybe studied at Juilliard), and show a student how to arrange a song three different ways are the types of skills that help teachers connect with students. It is also helpful for instrumental musicians to have basic piano skills, so they can accompany an instrumental or vocal student when necessary.

Most students take music lessons not to be concert artists, but to express themselves. For one student, this may lead to an interest in classical composition; another student may veer off to jazz improvisation. Yet a third student might form a rock band. The successful teacher has the skills to go beyond the traditional lesson books, to explore these ideas and styles, and then to pull it all together in a course of study that engages the student while teaching necessary skills. Being able to play just slightly better than the student is not enough.

> **Wise Words** _____
>
> I always loved music; who so has skill in this art is of good temperament, fitted for all things. We must teach music in schools; a schoolmaster ought to have skill in music, or I would not regard him.
>
> —Martin Luther, sixteenth-century theologian and composer

How Much Performing Experience Is Enough?

Music teachers need to have solid skills, but they don't have to be concert-level players. In fact, this may be counterproductive, especially when teaching beginners. The skills required to voice a perfect four-part fugue and leave the listener hanging on the fermata before the final chord are not the same as the skills required to coax a young child into putting the right finger on the right note. Many high-level performers become bored with teaching at the beginning levels.

However, some performing experience is a definite plus for teachers. For one thing, teachers who have never prepared pieces for public performance are at a disadvantage when it comes to preparing students for their first auditions, competitions, and recitals. All performers have a "toolbox," so to speak, of tricks and skills picked up through years of practice and performance—for example, how to memorize a piece, what to do during a memory lapse, and how to help a member of your ensemble who has lost his or her place in the piece. The stories you tell your students of your own past triumphs and disasters also can be inspiring, fascinating, and illuminating, as well as practical and educational.

If your own background includes a lot of ensemble playing, you may remember what worked and what didn't work when you first started "playing out." If you participated in competitions, you have gleaned some tricks about dealing with the snide comments from another competitor or the blank faces of the judges. Finally, if you currently perform in your community, you may have the opportunity not only to inspire students by your own example, but also to involve them in your performances.

The bottom-line answer to the question is that although you don't have to be a virtuoso performer to teach, the more you bring to the lesson from your own experience, the more flexibility you have to take on different kinds of students.

Music Degrees: Necessary or Not?

A music degree is rarely a requirement to teach private music lessons, although having one can certainly help the new teacher establish a reputation. Sometimes community-based music schools require that faculty members have at least a Bachelor's degree in music, although it might be a degree in performance, music education, music technology, or history and theory. But quite honestly, most parents don't think to ask.

Whether or not you actually have a music degree, if you plan to teach beyond the beginner level, you should certainly have the kinds of musicianship skills taught in most university music programs. You also need to be familiar with the entry requirements for university music programs, in case you have a student who plans to continue studying music or music education.

This means you'll need a solid knowledge of your instrument's standard repertoire, including etudes and method books, along with a firm grasp of standard technique, including fingering. You should also know what the typical freshman-level classes in music theory, ear training, and music history cover, and be able to help prepare your students so they don't feel lost when confronted with these courses of study.

Pedagogy and Interpersonal Skills

If parents aren't asking about your music education, what do they care about? They care about whether you can teach. They care about whether their kids will like you. They care about whether you are pleasant and easy to work with.

Pedagogy is the art of teaching—the art of presenting skills so the student is able to understand, copy, and internalize them. Teaching music requires more than being able to play an instrument and demonstrate how to perform a set of skills.

Music is a multidimensional undertaking. It's an aural activity, a visual activity, an intellectual activity, a physical activity—and, ultimately, when it all comes together, an emotional activity. All of these factors have to work together for the student to learn to play and to enjoy playing. But each student takes in and processes information differently.

One of the most important lessons a new music teacher learns is that you can't teach all students the way you were taught. In fact, quite the contrary. Most music teachers have an affinity for music and learned quickly. If you like music enough to want to teach it, you probably liked your lessons (at least, most of the time) and practiced regularly (at least, some of the time), and you probably moved ahead at a satisfying pace. While not all music teachers are concert-level performers, it is safe to say that, as a group, they learned to play their instruments more easily than the average child. Most people pursue skills and subjects they are good at; music teachers are no exception.

> **Wise Words**
>
> Teaching music is not my main purpose. I want to make good citizens. If children hear fine music from the day of their birth and learn to play it, they develop sensitivity, discipline, and endurance. They get a beautiful heart.
>
> —Shinichi Suzuki, founder of the Suzuki method

But the typical music student won't grow up to be a musician or a music teacher. Average students may not learn as quickly, or in the same way, as you did. They may have different problems. They will most likely have different musical tastes. Thus, they can't be taught the same way you were taught. They may need reinforcement, games, supplemental exercises, or a completely different approach.

The skilled teacher learns how to teach to each student's strengths while bolstering the weaknesses. Studying pedagogy gives teachers information on which kinds of methods and approaches might help various students solve different problems. Pedagogy also suggests alternatives for when the "standard" techniques don't seem to be working.

> **Wise Words**
>
> It is much more important who the singing master at Kisvárda (a small town) is than who the director of the Opera House is, because a poor director will fail. (Often even a good one.) But a bad teacher may kill off the love of music for thirty years from thirty classes of pupils. (1929)
>
> —Zoltán Kodály (1882–1967), music educator and composer

Basic Pedagogy Skills

If you've never taught, consider the following questions. If they leave you scratching your head, it may be time to take a pedagogy course, read a book, or join a music teacher's association.

- What is the first thing you will want to teach a young child who shows up for his first-ever music lesson? What will that child leave the lesson having learned?

- How will you teach the child to find notes on her instrument? Each instrument is different. Learning notes on the piano is very visual. Learning notes on a wind instrument involves different fingerings. Learning notes on a string instrument involves first "making" the note, then playing it, and then correcting the intonation.

- Will you teach note reading immediately? If not, how will you build up to it?

- How will you teach note reading? Do mnemonics such as "every good boy does fine" really work? What are some other choices (landmarks, intervals, skips, and steps), and which are appropriate for your instrument?

- How will you teach rhythm? Fast notes first, or slow notes first? What about dotted quarter notes and compound time?

- Will you require students to count out loud, tap rhythms, or keep time by tapping their feet?

- When will you introduce the idea of key signatures and scales? Why?

- When and how will you introduce theory, ear training, harmonization, and improvisation?

- What are the standard teaching methods on your instrument? Which are currently most popular with today's teachers?

- Are you familiar with the standard fingerings of chords, arpeggios, and scales, as well as the standard etudes and exercises on your instrument? Do you know how to alter them for small hands?

- What are the "student savers" for your instrument (repertoire that can revive flagging interest and provide inspiration)?

These are just some of the questions that an experienced teacher can answer, and a few of them are questions that will present themselves when your very first student walks in the door.

If you don't know the answers, don't despair! Working with your instrument's leading method books will help get you started. You might also consider taking a music education class at a local college, or even asking a more experienced teacher (maybe your own teacher, if you still live in the same community) if you can sit in on some lessons. In Chapter 18, we discuss continuing education and filling in the gaps in more detail.

Take Note _____

If you've never taught, go to a music store and ask for the most popular one or two beginner method books for your instrument. Go through them page by page to learn the order in which subjects and concepts are taught. You'll probably find that today's methods are quite a bit different from the methods used when you were learning. And you'll be reminded of elements of music education that you have most likely forgotten.

Remember, teaching is not a fallback job for performers. It requires its own special skills. Not every musician is a good or "natural" teacher.

The Personal Touch

All the technique and training in the world won't help you teach if students don't enjoy coming to their lessons and spending one-on-one time with you. Part of the art of teaching is the art of seducing students into learning. Learning to play an instrument even moderately well is a long-term process. The teacher needs to be able to inspire the student (and the student's parents) to stick with it, even when the student is complaining about practice and the parent doesn't want to be "the bad guy," even when it's softball season (and soccer and skiing and basketball season) or when it seems that progress has ground to a halt.

Wise Words _____

As you begin teaching, you might think that you will never forget each student. But you will. Twenty years from now, you just might get a phone call from someone who says, "Remember me? I have a 7-year-old child and I would like you to teach!" So take a picture of each child at the very first piano lesson and the last lesson, and put them in an album, including names and dates. The photo album will help you remember the student, and you will be able to show their child a picture of their mom or dad at their first piano lesson.

—Shelagh McKibbon, music teacher, Ontario, Canada

The personal relationship between student and teacher is an important one. It's important that you see your student as a complete little person, with all the complexities and intricacies of any other person. Ask him how his week was. Ask if anything interesting has happened. Students will usually say "No," and you can feign surprise and say "Come on, *something* interesting must have happened in a whole week!"

Chances are, you'll find out about the new kitten, or Grandma's visit, or camping in the rain, or a whole host of trivia. These conversations help put your students at ease.

Setting Expectations

You'll also need to decide how to establish expectations and requirements, and how to reward students when they do well—and how to correct them when they don't. In part, this means understanding your priorities as a teacher. Many teachers frequently start their studios with aspirations to share the joy of music, be friends with their students, and maintain high standards.

Then reality interferes. The first group of students a teacher gets is often quite random: people might respond to your ads in the local paper or pick up your studio brochure in the Main Street piano shop. Over time, the students who aren't willing to practice—or who get frustrated too easily, or who don't have necessary support from parents, or are too busy for regular lesson attendance—will drop out, leaving you with a higher percentage of students who practice regularly, can cope with frustration, have the support of parents, and attend lessons without fail. These student families will become the basis of referrals, and as people often refer others like themselves, you may find yourself with a group of students that is better matched to your teaching than the random group who first wandered in the door.

As you gain more experience, you may become more skilled at interviewing prospective students (see Chapter 10). With a little experience, your expectations will become more clear (perhaps more realistic), and you will be better able to communicate them to students and parents as well.

Patience, Patience, Patience

Perhaps above all, patience is the most important characteristic of a good music teacher. Patience is the ability to repeat the same instructions 10 times in a row without sounding critical or mean or bored. It is the ability to sound enthusiastic at yet another too-fast and too-sloppy rendition of the piccolo solo in "Stars and Stripes Forever," yet another bombastic rendition of "Stairway to Heaven," yet another butchering of the lovely but constantly tormented "Für Elise."

And let there be no mistake: it also takes patience to deal with parents who consistently forget to bring their checks, who make excuses for their child's lack of practice, who miss lessons at the last minute and want unlimited make-ups, or who don't support the student's musical progress by enforcing a regular practice schedule.

Hand in hand with patience is judgment—the ability to determine whether a student is not progressing because she is not practicing, concentrating, or following directions, or because the information is not getting through to the student in a way that she can understand. If the former, a firm hand may be required to set the student on the right path. If the latter, the teacher must exercise yet more patience in going through the instructions again. Also required is the creativity to try to alter those instructions and try another approach.

It takes judgment to know whether a student is really trying and patience to work through the problems, especially because so many of the problems are the same, student after student. But this patience is the greatest gift we can give our students. Students can't become freely creative if they feel their teacher is an ogre standing over their shoulder ready to bark and bite.

Business Skills

The business of teaching music is relatively straightforward—people pay you to teach music lessons. And there is a great demand for your skills. Parents routinely reply in surveys that music education is important to their children. However, budgets for school music programs have been relentlessly cut in the last decade.

Private music teachers are filling the gaps and are finding that because parents prioritize arts education, and because music teachers work for many families, their jobs and incomes are relatively protected, even in difficult economic times. But to make a living as a music teacher, you need to treat your studio as a business.

Facts and Stats

The No Child Left Behind Act has been blamed for cuts in music education programs across the country because schools focus on math and reading, the most tested subjects. Yet note these statistics, according to a 2003 nationwide Gallup survey:

- Ninety-five percent of Americans consider music to be a crucial part of a child's education.
- Eighty-eight percent believe learning music helps teach children discipline.
- Eighty percent believe that studying music makes participants smarter.
- Seventy-eight percent believe that learning a musical instrument helps students perform better in other subjects.

Given the cuts in school music programs nationwide, those attitudes and beliefs mean a bigger market for private music teachers.

Most experienced teachers agree that one of the most important things a teacher can do to stay sane is to develop a studio policy that sets forth the terms of the student-teacher business relationship. Setting fees is covered in Chapter 5; writing and implementing a studio policy is covered in detail in Chapter 7.

In addition to thinking through, writing, and enforcing your studio policy, you need advertising and public relations skills (covered in Chapter 9), especially when you are starting out. And you need to consider legal issues such as required business licenses, zoning, accounting, and business insurance (see Chapter 6).

What Is Your Business Plan?

At the outset, it may seem like overkill to worry about business issues such as refund policies or make-ups. The new teacher is mostly concerned with getting students in the door and what to do with them once they get there.

A formal business plan—the type of plan that you might have to provide to the bank if you were asking for a loan to open a music retail shop, for example—is probably not necessary for the single-teacher music studio. The single-teacher studio doesn't employ others, keep (much) inventory, or require (usually) a separate building or expensive start-up investments in equipment.

But it's a good idea to spare at least a few thoughts for your overall business goals. Here are some questions to consider:

- How much of your income do you hope to make by teaching music?

- How much of your time will you devote to teaching?

- How many students would you like to teach?

- What levels and ages of students do you plan to attract?

- Beyond music lessons, would you like to offer other programs? What expenses and income are involved?

- What kinds of near-term expenses are you likely to have (electronic equipment, sheet music, instruments)?

After your studio catches on and you gain more students, policies may be hard to change. People quickly get used to the way you do things, so you might as well learn from the mistakes and experiences of other teachers as you think about how to run your studio.

> ## Out of Tune
> Don't quit your day job! It takes most people about two years to fill up a new studio, and that is with aggressive marketing. This is because word of mouth, the prime marketing tool, takes time to build. When you're starting, work around your day job by teaching evenings and perhaps on weekends. This will help build a student base that's big enough that you can confidently make the move to teaching full-time.

Recordkeeping

Bookkeeping is a fairly simple chore for music teachers, and Chapter 6 discusses it in detail. A studio's records should include a schedule and an attendance sheet for each student, which includes entries for both attendance and fees paid. Mark these down as soon as they come in, or you will likely forget who has paid for how many lessons. Remember that all income—whether it comes by cash or check—is taxable.

Additionally, you'll need to keep track of teaching-related expenses for tax purposes—and for your own information. To put it all together, you'll need either an accountant or the ability to work a computer tax program. In either case, a tax professional, or the Help menu within your tax program, can provide tips and advice about what records to keep, how to organize them, and so on. Chapter 6 also is a good place to start.

Managing Space and Time

The prime teaching hours for many music teachers are the hours that most of the world has "off." Music teachers give lessons to children after school, and to adults in the evenings after work. Many teachers also work on weekends; some give early-morning lessons as well. And of course, there are always a few seniors and home-schoolers who want to come smack in the middle of the day.

Fitting the odd hours of a music teacher's schedule into personal and family life is a constant challenge, especially for parents of young children. Issues include not only scheduling, but also space: Where will you teach where your students won't be tripping over your children and vice versa? If your young children require supervision, who will provide it while you are teaching? How will you separate your family life from your work life?

Working with student families on scheduling issues will also be a challenge. It's not uncommon for children to be involved in several sports and after-school programs. Parents frequently request scheduling changes, and missed lessons and requests for unlimited or extra "make-up" lessons are one of the biggest problems for teachers, especially those with busy studios (who don't have time in their schedules to rear-range lessons).

The upshot of this is that it can be difficult for music teachers who have their own families to carve out teaching schedules that meet their own needs as well as student families' needs. I discuss some scheduling and management strategies in Chapter 8.

Managing Irregular Paychecks

Imagine that you have 15 students—just the right number to fit your schedule and your income needs. But during any given week, two students forget to bring pay-ment, one student is sick, and another cancels a lesson because of a soccer conflict. That's four students who don't pay you this week. What does that do to your weekly budget? As you can see, a music teacher's income is not as stable as the income of a schoolteacher or an office worker. But neither is it as variable as the income of a commissioned sales representative, for example. In Chapter 5, we talk about ways to price and schedule payments that eliminate some of the ebbs and flows of the music teacher's weekly and monthly income.

No matter how rigorous a studio policy may be, and no matter how clear a teacher is about policies and payments, students do drop out, miss lessons, change teachers, and take summer vacations—very often with little or no advance notice to the music teacher. As a result, one skill a music teacher must have is the ability to plan budgets with a little leeway in them. Another skill—or virtue, perhaps—is having the disci-pline to keep money on hand for the inevitable downturns in income that happen in the summer, when fewer students take lessons, or in those rare cases when a cluster of students stops lessons at the same time.

The Least You Need to Know

- Teaching music privately doesn't require a college music degree, but it does require solid musical skills.

- The study of pedagogy—the art of teaching—shows teachers how to communi-cate their skills to students, who learn music in very different ways.

- Teaching requires space, an instrument, and teaching material.

- Running a music studio requires a few basic business skills, including marketing and advertising, billing, collecting payments, managing student relations, and budgeting.

The Home Studio

In This Chapter

◆ The advantages and disadvantages of teaching at home

◆ The business and legal issues of owning and operating a home-based teaching studio

◆ Planning a home studio that meets your teaching requirements

◆ Determining the equipment you need

The traditional private home teaching studio is the gold standard for private music lessons. Can you imagine it? A fantastically outfitted home studio, with a collection of instruments, computer programs and learning stations, a keyboard (or maybe a grand piano), a separate entrance for students, a waiting room, and enough recording equipment to produce a professional-sounding CD.

But most teachers don't start out with such a collection of equipment and amenities. In fact, although it's nice to have great workspace and state-of-the-art teaching tools, it isn't necessary. Teaching boils down to a teacher, a student, an instrument, and a whole lot of effort. Everything else is secondary. So don't postpone hanging out your shingle because you don't feel you have the perfect studio!

Pros and Cons of the Home Studio

For teachers, the advantages of a home studio are obvious. Working at home means no commuting and more control over your schedule. Teachers at home can either schedule students back to back or factor in time between students for breaks or non-teaching work. Plus, if students cancel, teachers can use the time for household chores or business paperwork.

Teachers working at home also have more control over their environment. No TV is blaring in the next room. Piano teachers in home studios can teach on good instruments, which is important for students to experience. And all teachers at home have their teaching materials close at hand, meaning that if little Johnny expresses an interest in playing "Star Wars," you can grab a copy from your sheet music library and give it to him while the interest is strong. In addition, if you use computer learning stations, recording equipment, and CD players, those are right at your disposal whenever you need them.

Financial Issues for the Home Teacher

For most teachers, home teaching offers financial advantages. For one thing, commuting costs—gas, car wear and tear, parking, and tolls, not to mention the time spent sitting in traffic—are zero.

Another advantage is that all student tuition goes to you, the teacher. If you rent studio space or you teach in association with a retail music store, for example, you'll have rent and/or commissions to pay out of your students' fees.

The cost of start-up equipment is fairly minimal. You probably already have an instrument, a metronome, a music stand, a computer, and some recording and listening equipment. This isn't to say that you won't want to expand or upgrade, but if you're already a musician, you probably have the basics you need to teach.

In addition, there is a financial advantage in terms of deducting business expenses for tax purposes. Chapter 6 discusses business expenses, but you should also consult an accountant about the specifics of your situation. In general, teachers can deduct a portion of home expenses (such as rent, heat, electricity, and housecleaning) that are directly related to your studio space.

Location, Location, Location

The location of your home can be an advantage or a disadvantage in terms of attracting students. In different parts of the country, people have very different ideas about how far is "too far" to go for a music lesson. In some communities, people balk at trips of more than 10 minutes; in other communities, it's common for students to commute half an hour or more (sometimes quite a bit more) for a lesson.

Although many families are willing to make some effort to get to a teacher they like, the amount of that effort varies. Being near a main thoroughfare, near a school, or near a main shopping area (where parents can run errands during a child's lesson) is certainly an advantage. In a snowbound area, being close to a main thoroughfare is also important because main roads are the first to be plowed after a storm.

Competition from other piano teachers in your location is also a factor, but that's more a matter of luck than anything you have any control over. There's nothing to stop another piano teacher from moving in next door. In some communities, good music teachers have waiting lists; in others, teachers are constantly advertising to get students. Being aware of who those other teachers are and what they offer may give you some ideas for how to present yourself and what programs to offer. For example, if another teacher is a jazz virtuoso and you teach the classics, you might emphasize your own specialty. And you might even come to a mutual agreement with the other teacher to refer appropriate students to each other.

If you are located in a tiny town that happens to have a coterie of qualified teachers, you may find that starting a home studio is a slow process. One solution is to combine teaching at home one or two days a week with being a traveling teacher (read more about this in Chapter 3). As time passes and your studio matures, you'll learn which strategy works better for you.

Neighborly Relations

Another consideration for home-based teachers is the proximity of neighbors. Are you cheek-by-jowl with the next house, or do you live in an area with 1-acre zoning? Some neighbors welcome having a stay-at-home music teacher next door, feeling that it adds stability to the neighborhood. But some neighbors find it unendurable to listen to beginning musicians pounding out scales all afternoon and evening.

Out of Tune

Don't wait until you've started and equipped a studio before thinking about sound issues! Retroactive soundproofing is expensive and often involves structural work. If your studio is going to bother the neighbors, better to find out before you spend a lot of money on it. Some ways to mitigate the noise level include adding carpets, curtains, and upholstered furniture. Add bookshelves for your sheet music and teaching books, which will also help absorb sound. Face amps and piano soundboards away from the neighbor's. You can even staple cardboard egg cartons to a wall to absorb sound.

The issue of neighbors involves an element of luck, but there are some things you can do. First, consider the placement of your studio. If neighbors can't hear the violins, they probably won't complain about them. Does the room you intend to teach in face the neighbor's family room? Will they have to hear an endless succession of beginning violinists while they are eating dinner and watching TV? Will you be teaching early in the morning, just as the shift-worker who lives next door is trying to get some sleep? Sometimes the solution is as simple as choosing a different room for your studio. Or it may be as complex as building a soundproof addition over your garage.

Parking and traffic can also be sore spots with neighbors, especially if your students are constantly using the neighbor's driveway as a turn-around. Ask neighbors to let you know about any problems, and respond to them courteously and promptly. Make the effort to talk directly to the parents—or whoever is driving—instead of expecting children to convey to their parents messages about the neighbor's driveway or the issue about sitting in the car with the radio playing too loudly.

Legal Issues That Affect Home Teaching

Before you can even think about opening up your studio for business, you must address legal and insurance issues. Indeed, in some communities—especially in co-ops, condominiums, apartments, and planned developments—zoning laws or covenants restrict what you can and can't do in your home. In some communities, home-based businesses are regulated, and sometimes businesses that involve student or client traffic are prohibited or require special permits.

Zoning Laws

Zoning laws control who may do what with a piece of property. In many residential areas, uses are regulated. In most suburbs, for example, you generally are not allowed to operate a tattoo parlor in the garage in back of your home.

Music studios, of course, are generally regarded more benignly than tattoo parlors, but jurisdictions vary enormously, even within a region. One town may allow private teaching anywhere in town. Another may permit it, but only if you apply for a special permit or business license (which can be a simple fill-out-a-form-and-pay-a-fee transaction, or a drawn-out process involving public notices and hearings, not to mention the possibility of being denied). Yet a third town might allow music teaching in its rural areas but require a permit for studios located in the middle of the downtown area. A fourth may limit the number of students you may have at any one time or the hours you may teach.

If you already live in the community in which you plan to teach, you'll need to learn the rules and follow them; if necessary, you'll have to apply for a permit. If you are moving into a new community and intend to teach at home, make absolutely certain that you will have the right to conduct your business there. You don't want to face a situation in which you have invested in a house and the local authorities deny you permission to teach in it.

If you think you are in the clear, be certain that you read the bylaws yourself, or, even better, have your attorney look at them. Small-town bylaws can be dense, imprecise, and hard to understand. But your livelihood might depend on getting this right, especially if neighbors complain. Good communications and efforts to be considerate can help win over neighbors—at least, most of the time. And in those rare cases in which conflict can't be easily resolved, if you've complied with your town's bylaws or other covenants, you'll know you have the law on your side.

Out of Tune

In some communities, you need a special permit to run a business or teach in your home, but you are not allowed to apply for the permit until you actually own the property. That's a serious catch-22; be sure to discuss the issue with your attorney before buying a house where permits are required, but where community officials can't guarantee that permits will be granted. Unless the rules are very clear and straightforward (and they often are not), it would be worth considering a house in a neighboring community that does not have the same restrictions.

Co-ops, Condominiums, and Apartment Buildings

In co-ops, condominiums, and apartment buildings, where people live close together, bylaws and leases may impose even more rigid regulations or prohibit home teaching altogether. It's impossible to hide a music teaching business. Neighbors will notice the hourly pick-ups and drop-offs of young children clutching instrument cases and music books, and you will most certainly be heard (especially if you teach trumpet or rock 'n' roll drumming). Before you hang out a shingle, you need to find out what is and is not permitted.

> **Wise Words** _____
>
> When I taught in an apartment, I ended up selling my wonderful 85-year-old piano and buying an electronic piano. At the time, it was the right thing to do. I could control the volume (or wear earphones) and I didn't need to pay to have it tuned (money was very tight!). But the students still had an in-tune piano to play. The other reason was that the keyboard was much easier to move and we knew we would have several more major moves before we settled down permanently. I still miss that wonderful old piano but am grateful that I was able to keep teaching in the apartment and that my own children have a very good ear because they always played on an in-tune instrument.
>
> —Anne-Marie Scott, music teacher, Knoxville, Tennessee

If you already live in the co-op, condo, or apartment building and want to teach there, you are bound by the rules in place, and there's very little chance that a condo board or landlord will bend those rules. If they did it for you, they'd have to do it for everyone, and the fact is, like it or not, music teaching is noisy and involves a flow of traffic.

If you are looking for a city home, where most of the housing stock is in multiple-family dwellings, this is a question you need to ask. Some configurations are more workable than others. In cities, one option might be living in a town home. For instance, you might rent two floors, to put a floor between your studio and the next neighbor. Or you might find a townhouse with a separate garage with finished work-space overhead. Some older townhouses also come with carriage houses in the back. A two-family home might work, too, if the other family doesn't object. Don't take the landlord's word for it; ask the family.

Business Insurance

Simple homeowner's insurance policies do not cover home-based businesses. In fact, they specifically exclude business uses, which means that if a student sets fire to your piano and the fire burns down the house, your insurance won't cover it.

True, student-set fires are not on the "10 most common disasters" list for music teachers, but if you want to be insured for when Suzie spills her thermos of grape juice into your $30,000 Steinway, or when her little brother stuffs up your toilet with paper towels, or when her grandmother slips on the ice in front of your house and breaks her hip, you have to purchase a separate business rider that covers business activities.

Indeed, most insurance companies insist on a business rider for your home studio. An insurance company could cancel your personal insurance if it finds out you are working uninsured in your home. (Note to teachers in small towns: everyone, including the local insurance agent, knows everyone else's business. You won't be able to "stay under the radar," and you shouldn't try. The consequences of being uninsured are too dire.) I cover the specifics of a home business policy in Chapter 7.

Home Studio Requirements

Most teachers start by carving out a studio from their current home, perhaps using a den or a basement as teaching space. Others might add on to a residence (perhaps finishing a basement or converting that unused space over the garage). Of course, if the start of your music teaching career coincides with a move, you will be able to consider your studio space needs while looking for a home to rent or buy.

Regardless of whether you are renting, buying, remodeling, moving, or making do with your old family room, you have a few practicalities to consider.

Teaching Space

The most important consideration is the room in which you will teach. Ideally, of course, it will be a well-lit, well-ventilated space, perhaps with a glorious view and a fireplace. Not everyone is so lucky, of course. You may end up in the basement, or off in the unused former bedroom of a grown child. Even so, with a little creativity, your teaching space can be comfortable and welcoming.

First things first: the student needs to be able to learn without constant interruptions. Family members continuously popping in with questions and demands reflects on your professionalism and interferes with the learning process. If you have young children, you will need a door. You may also need an adult or teenaged helper on the other side of it who can keep things under control while you work. You also need to be sure that the sounds of everyday family life, such as arguments between the kids, music blaring, and video game sound effects, are not disruptive.

Wise Words

In my own studio, within arm's reach, are art books and music reference books of any given period or subject that will enhance my understanding of music literature; I also read from certain collections of composers' letters if I think they will serve to enlighten. I have gone about the business, over the past many years, of consciously surrounding myself with paintings, pottery, and books that help to put me (and I hope my students) in a sensitized, peaceful, receptive, and fertile state of mind. What seems to count a lot to me is not only the availability of reference material, but a harmonious space, with every corner balanced in form, color, and design.

—Carol Montparker, pianist, teacher, and author of *A Pianist's Landscape*; Huntington, Long Island

How you carve studio space out of your preexisting home will vary, according to the layout of your house, who else lives there and is present during teaching hours, and your personality.

There might be an obvious place for your studio—perhaps a separate wing or a walk-out basement with its own entrance, waiting room, and bathroom. If you live alone or with another adult who is off at work during most of your teaching hours, you might choose to use your living room or a cozy den as a teaching studio.

Personality also comes into play. Some teachers prefer a physical separation between their work lives and their personal space, which means having the teaching space in a separate, enclosed room or on another floor entirely. (For teachers with young children, this becomes less a matter of preference than a requirement.) Some possible separate studio areas include a den with a door, an unused guest room, a sunroom, or a basement space—anywhere out of the flow of normal family traffic.

You also need to consider where waiting parents will stay. Some teachers of young students prefer (or insist) that parents attend the lesson so they can supervise practice. Some parents want to watch the lessons; some don't. When teenaged students are involved, this is less of an issue because most teenagers make it clear that they do not want the parent hanging around. Sometimes parents bring young siblings to lessons. This can be disruptive for many reasons, regardless of the ages of the siblings. You can cover some of these issues in a studio policy, but studio policy or not, you need to be prepared for families to show up and set themselves down somewhere while you are teaching.

You also need space for your computer and office equipment, including a photocopy machine, which should be near your teaching area. In most cases, the office area can occupy a small corner of your teaching space.

Finally, you need space for enough good chairs for student ensembles, music stands, instruments, music storage, a white board, and off–bench games.

Instruments and Teaching Materials

Which instruments you use for teaching depends on what instrument you play, what you already have on hand, and how you feel, for instance, about a 6-year-old relentlessly kicking at the pedal lyre of your grand piano.

Many teachers end up with a collection of instruments. Guitarists may have acoustics, classicals, electric, and jazz hollow-bodies, along with basses, mandolins, baritone guitars, and maybe even a ukulele or two. Percussionists tend to have collections of weird and wonderful instruments (which they need to keep an eye on, especially if their students' younger siblings invade the studio).

Wise Words

My mother-in-law moved into a retirement home and gave me her piano. The addition of a second piano in my studio opened up a whole new world of possibilities: two-piano duets, my being able to play along with the student in the same octave, and, most importantly it has alleviated back and shoulder problems from reaching to demonstrate.

—Susanne Gravel, music teacher, Oakville, Ontario, Canada

It's a nice sentiment that young music students should be exposed to good instruments—until they start banging on them, plucking too hard, kicking at them, or picking at the wood finish. With pianos, organs, and drum sets and amplification equipment, the student receiving instruction in a home studio will use the teacher's instruments and equipment. All other music students (violinists, clarinetists, flutists, and so on) will bring their own instruments. Although strict lecturing about the value of fine instruments and the respect they need to be shown may work, constant vigilance is also needed when introducing a young child to an instrument.

If you'd prefer to have a more relaxed approach, you may want to limit the use of your fine piano to students who are ready to treat it properly, and teach the beginners on a sturdier, more replaceable instrument. It's just plain safer that way. Although we want to expose students to good instruments, we don't want the instruments destroyed in the process. Nor do we want to convey an overly restrictive "look but don't touch" demeanor. Better to just put the Stradivarius out of reach.

In addition to a primary instrument, you may want percussion toys (useful for rhythm games). A piano teacher who can pluck out a few guitar chords might keep a guitar around to play duets with students. And all instrumental teachers benefit from having a piano, or at least an 88-key electronic keyboard, in their studios for accompanying students and teaching music theory.

Finally, you'll need a small collection of teaching materials, which, in addition to your sheet music, might include a metronome, blank manuscript paper, aids such as a white board, materials for off-bench games, and stickers.

Storage Space

Music teachers need storage space for instruments and teaching supplies. Be aware that instruments—especially small, portable instruments such as drums, percussion toys, or small stringed instruments—are kid magnets. Where you place them in your studio may have less to do with aesthetics than with practicality. Keep fragile instruments and anything you don't want plucked and played with out of reach.

Other space hogs include additional electronic equipment you frequently use in teaching, keyboards, computer workstations, recording equipment, a sound system, and amplifiers.

Sheet music storage is another constant challenge for serious musicians and music teachers. Conventional bookshelves aren't well suited to the standard music book, which is a floppy, large-format paperback. Stacking isn't a solution; it's more a promise that you will never, ever be able to find the piece of music you're looking for. And don't even get most music teachers started on the subject of filing and organizing, or you'll be arguing all day. Do you organize by composer? By style? By period? By level? Do you separate the music you play from music you might share with your students?

Out of Tune

Wooden instruments such as pianos, violins, and guitars are extremely sensitive and require climate control for both temperature and humidity. No instruments should be stored next to heat vents or in direct sunlight. In humid weather, pianos should be in a dehumidified space. In dry weather, pianos should be in a humidified space. Humidification and dehumidification systems are also available for installation in the piano itself. Various sizes of specialty humidifiers are also available for stringed instruments.

If you have a high-end budget, some specialty manufacturers custom-build beautiful wooden cabinets with shallow wide drawers that are designed for the typical size of a sheet music score. But if you don't happen to have several thousand dollars lying around, try a cheaper solution. Anyone with basic carpentry skills can build a basic cabinet with sheet music–size cubbyholes. For the nonhandy, plastic cabinets from an office supply store work well. It's effective to keep a supply of your primary method books in a cabinet, with each level in a different drawer. Or use plastic magazine racks—the larger sizes are good for music scores—lined up on a bookshelf.

The Ideal Studio Wish List

Whether you're buying a home, remodeling, or making do, the following wish list may guide your planning and decision-making.

- Adequate space for teaching, ensembles, instrument storage, sheet music storage, computer and teacher's desk, and computer or keyboard learning stations for students

- Separate entrance

- Waiting area for parents, siblings, or students who come early or must wait to be picked up

- "Public" bathroom

- Soundproofing or sound mitigation

- Climate control to ensure comfort for you and your students—and also appropriate temperature and humidity for instruments

- Good lighting

- Plenty of electrical outlets (always more than you think you need) and a good power supply

Real life being what it is, most teachers don't have ideal studios complete with every single item on their wish list. (Indeed, every teacher's wish list probably differs from every other teacher's.) But with a warm, welcoming space free of distractions, you'll have the setting in which the real work of making music can begin.

Parking

From the sublime to the prosaic. Parking is an important issue, especially in cities and crowded suburbs with limited street parking. Your students won't want to park two blocks away and haul a cello through the snow to get to your house. And if you live in a condominium complex with limited guest parking (and the neighbor's kid always takes the spot you were hoping to use for your students), you may need to negotiate with the neighbors, make an arrangement with a local business or church, or park your own car elsewhere during studio times so that your students have a place to park.

The Least You Need to Know

- ◆ In choosing home studio space, consider your family's needs and select a space that is separate from family members' everyday lives.

- ◆ Local zoning regulations may limit or even prohibit business activities in a residential area. Be aware of rules and regulations before you start your studio.

- ◆ Rules for co-op, condominium, and apartment dwellers frequently prohibit home businesses. Studios are more likely to be permitted in privately owned townhouses and duplexes.

- ◆ Homeowner's insurance does not cover your home studio. Get a business rider that covers business property and liability.

Chapter **3**

The Traveling Teacher

In This Chapter

♦ The challenges and benefits of traveling to teach in students' homes

♦ Different kinds of music teaching jobs—and how to get them

♦ The pros and cons of teaching in community music schools, for-profit music studios, and music stores

♦ The financial and practical implications of working outside the home

Many private teachers work in home studios full time, but others choose to work outside their homes. Sometimes it's not a matter of choice. Zoning laws or leases may not allow home businesses, or the teacher's family situation may be incompatible with at-home work. And sometimes the teacher just isn't able to fill a home studio.

Many opportunities are available to teachers willing to teach in someone else's space, whether it's a music school, a music store, an after-school program, or a private home where several families of homeschoolers take turns having music lessons. These can be excellent opportunities for people new to a community, teachers just starting their businesses, or teachers who are uncertain of how to advertise.

In most cases, traveling teachers are self-employed. Either they are paid directly by student families or they work for a studio or store as private contractors. In some cases, however, a school or store hires teachers as hourly employees.

It's also entirely possible to work at home a certain number of days a week and work outside the home for the other days. Many teachers feel that this gives them the best of both worlds.

Teaching in Students' Homes

A teacher who is willing to travel to students' homes offers a valuable and much-desired service. In some localities, teaching in students' homes is common; in others, it isn't practical.

For example, in up-scale communities, people may be accustomed to having their masseuses, physical fitness trainers, and nutritionists come to their homes. Music teachers, as "service providers," may be expected to follow suit. On the other hand, in very rural areas where towns are 15 or 20 miles apart, traveling teachers have to charge so much to make up for the travel time and gas that in-home lessons aren't feasible.

Teaching Space and the Traveling Teacher

It is crucial that you meet the family in their home before you accept the job. The most important consideration is where you will be expected to teach. Students at home need the same distraction-free learning environment that you would offer in a home studio, without the interference of televisions, sibling chatter, and family traffic. Discussing the necessity of a distraction-free environment for teaching up front establishes it as a priority. Taking a look at the teaching space when you visit will answer the question of whether the teaching space allotted to you is adequate. Of course, if you're teaching piano, you won't have a choice—you'll be teaching where the piano is.

Out of Tune

Don't ever teach in a student's bedroom or behind a closed door, even if that's where the parent suggests you teach. Musical teaching often requires physical contact as a teacher positions or repositions a student's hands, arms, shoulders, neck, or what have you. To avoid even a hint of impropriety, and to protect both teacher and student, teach in a space removed from the flow of family traffic but open to at least occasional observation from a parent.

Most accomplished teachers have fine instruments, but you don't want to be hauling a $4,000 guitar to student homes every day, not to mention leaving it in a hot (or freezing) car while you run errands between lessons. You'll need an acceptable teaching-quality instrument—not a bargain-basement factory second, perhaps, but something you don't mind exposing to a little travel wear.

You'll also need to consider how to haul around multiple instruments, for instance, if you happen to teach banjo, bass, guitar, and mandolin all on the same day. And then there are amplifiers and perhaps a CD player (if you use one in your teaching and you can't count on one being available in each home where you need it). Many teachers find that they simply have to teach a bit differently when they are traveling because they don't have their studio at their fingertips.

 Take Note

Be sure your instruments are insured not only when they are on your property, but also when you are taking them to and from lessons. Instruments should be listed on a rider to your business insurance policy, and they need to be covered for theft and damage when you are away from home.

When Your Car Becomes Your Office

Organization is one of the challenges of a traveling music teacher's existence. In your home studio, you might have complete sets of etudes and scales, not to mention extra copies of all the literature series you commonly use. But when you're traveling, it always seems that you've just given away the last copy of something.

Pack a "survival box" of important items so that you always have them available and don't have to pack and unpack constantly. The box should include teaching material supplies such as a lightweight music stand, lights, and items particular to your instrument (valve oil, extra strings, capos, picks, electronic pick-ups, tuners).

In addition to sheet music and any musical supplies you carry, be sure to have a cell phone with you so you can take calls regarding cancellations (or make calls regarding delays), a calendar so you can immediately make changes to your schedule if you need to, business cards, and a list of the contact numbers of the students you are traveling to visit.

Wise Words _____

The most important tool I have for teaching in students' homes is my big shoulder bag. In there, I keep any music I'll need to give to students that week: supplementary books/sheets at various levels, some sight reading material, a clipboard with a stack of assignment sheets, some staff paper, and blank paper. I also have a pencil box with mechanical pencils (no need for a sharpener), gel pens, ballpoint pens, a Sharpie (for labeling books), a metronome/tuner, Post-It notes, sticky tabs for marking pages, stickers, flash cards, game pieces, and crayons (the 'twistable' ones don't melt if I have to leave my bag in the car). Finally, I have a three-ring binder with the lesson plans I'll need for the month.

—Libby Wiebel, music teacher, singer, songwriter; Washington, D.C.

Practical and Financial Considerations

It's a worthwhile goal to try to schedule lessons to minimize travel time between students' homes, but it isn't always possible. You might be thinking that on Mondays you'll go to one neighborhood and on Tuesdays you'll go to another, but some of your students in the first neighborhood will have soccer on Mondays, while a student in the second neighborhood might have an attendance-required Chinese sword dancing class on Tuesdays.

Even if you can schedule your lessons to minimize travel time between student's homes, you'll probably spend at least 45 minutes for every half-hour you teach, and sometimes more. Your fees (see Chapter 5) should reflect your travel time as well as your teaching time. You must also take into consideration parking fees, toll road fees, and gasoline expenses. You'll have to decide whether you charge all of your at-home students the same or whether you increase the price for a student who is a significant number of miles farther away than other students.

Cancellations are a common problem for all music teachers, whether they teach in a home studio or on the road. But cancelled lessons, especially last-minute cancellations, are particularly problematic if you have a series of on-the-road lessons. Depending on where the students live and how you are scheduled, you could be left sitting in your car with nothing to do. (Of course, you might also be lucky enough to be able to use the extra time to do some shopping or errands, but that assumes your students live in a place where you can do these chores.) Traveling teachers need to be very clear about their policies and explain them to students at the beginning of the relationship. Do you charge a student for a lesson if there is a last-minute cancellation? Do you forgive *some* last-minute cancellations, depending on the circumstances? You'll see guidance in Chapter 7 on studio policies regarding cancellations, make-ups, and payment.

Finally, traveling teachers incur some expenses that in-home teachers don't. There are different ways of accounting for these, so keep detailed daily records of business-related travel and expenses, including mileage, parking, tolls, car repair, and insurance, and turn them over to your accountant at year end.

Music Schools and Studios

Music schools come in two basic flavors: nonprofits, which are usually run as community-based schools, and for-profit enterprises, in which an owner makes a profit from the school's business activities. In addition to private lessons, schools might offer in-depth programs such as master classes, concerts, guest speakers, theory classes, jam classes, group classes, and ensemble and performance opportunities (which may range from rock bands to full-fledged orchestras). Some of these programs offer teachers an additional opportunity to teach.

How They Work, and How You Work with Them

Typically, a teacher applies for a faculty position at this type of school or studio and, once accepted, agrees to be available certain hours each week. The music school schedules lessons during those times, collects the money, and pays the teacher.

The school provides marketing, scheduling, and billing; a facility to teach in; and, where appropriate, instruments such as pianos or organs, as well as instrument maintenance for school-owned instruments. Sometimes support services such as photocopying and message taking are included. Many schools also have a recital facility, and some have libraries and rental instruments.

Different schools have different contracts for teachers specifying how they will be paid, what the school supplies, and what teachers supply. School policies also usually cover such issues as student cancellations and end-of-year early termination—endemic problems that leave holes in teacher schedules and pocketbooks. Be sure you understand what the school's policy is so you know what to do when you drive half an hour only to find out that the student cancelled five minutes before the start of the lesson. Will you be paid, or are you expected to make up the student's missed lesson out of your own time? The school's policies may not be the same as those you apply in your home studio, so be sure you know the rules.

Facts and Stats

The National Association of Community Schools of the Arts (NACSA) has 400 member schools in 45 states. According to the NACSA:

♦ These schools serve more than one million students through direct instruction.

♦ Enrollments range from less than 100 to more than 7,000.

♦ More than 16,000 professional artists are employed as teachers at these schools.

♦ More than 50 percent of these schools offer multidisciplinary instruction, with music being by far the most popular course of study: 70 percent of NACSA schools offer music, followed by dance (27 percent), theater/drama (26 percent), and visual arts and crafts (27 percent).

All of this means jobs for music teachers.

Compensation

Teachers at music schools are generally paid by the hour, and only for the hours they actually teach. So if you have a lesson from 1 to 2 P.M., and then a lesson from 2:30 to 3 P.M., you'll be paid for the hour and a half you actually teach, and not the half hour you had to sit in between lessons. Depending on the popularity of your instrument and the school's ability to market and schedule lessons (not to mention your own reputation and draw as a teacher), you could have a lot of unpaid time blocks. Many teachers practice their own music during these times or do paperwork. But too much free time during what should be income-earning hours is a potential problem.

Typically, the school collects fees from parents and then pays a portion to the teacher. The exact percentages vary, but expect the amount paid to teachers to hover around 65 percent of the tuition money collected. The problem is that, in any given community, parents are generally willing to pay only so much for a music lesson, and it doesn't much matter to the parent whether the lesson takes place in a school or in a private home studio. A music school may offer some additional benefits, such as degreed teachers, a library, and a recital hall, but parents will mostly consider the convenience of the location and the price. For the teacher, this means that a qualified private teacher working in a home studio down the street is probably charging about the same per-lesson fee as a music school charges. The difference is that the private teacher keeps it all, whereas the school music teacher gets only about 65 percent.

Teachers can be compensated either as independent contractors or as employees. There probably isn't a big difference in terms of your paycheck. True, employees have taxes withheld from their paychecks, but independent contractors must pay quarterly estimated taxes; either way, the government gets its cut. Employees get a Social Security advantage because a music school must pay half of the Social Security tax, whereas independent contractors pay the full amount of their Social Security tax. On the other hand, private contractors are allowed more tax deductions, including transportation expenses, than are employees. The differences tend to balance out. However, there is a difference in how your accountant (and the IRS) will see and treat the two different types of income and related deductions.

Take Note

The music school's hourly rate may sound better than it really is when you take into account door-to-door travel time both ways, plus the total hours you have to be at the school, including all those 15-minute in-between lesson periods they couldn't schedule a student for. Let's assume you are getting paid for 5 hours of lessons and have to be at the school for 6½ hours because there's an hour in the middle they couldn't fill, and two 15-minute holes. Assuming an hour-long round-trip commute, you're spending 7½ hours to be paid for 5. And that doesn't count gas and wear and tear on your car.

It is an unfortunate fact of life that most teachers at music schools do not receive health insurance benefits. Though teachers in colleges and universities are considered full-time employees while teaching only 15 to 20 or so hours a week (because their other work hours are assumed to be used for class and lesson planning, practice, office hours, and research), teachers at community music schools are usually treated like hourly workers and have to teach a full 40 hours to qualify for health insurance. Considering the lesson preparation time involved, this is an impossible task. In a recent poll of nearly 100 piano teachers, only 18 percent taught 25 to 29 hours a week; a mere 4 percent taught 30 to 39 hours a week. No one taught 40 hours.

Benefits of Working at a Music School

Though there is certainly a financial downside to teaching at a music school (for example, the commute and lack of control over schedules), there is also an upside. Music schools offer some important benefits that make them a viable and valuable option for some teachers, especially for one or two days a week.

First of all, if you are new to a community, you should realize that even if you are experienced and qualified, it may take a year or two to build your studio—and longer if there is a glut of teachers in your area. If you've managed to fill half your studio at home, it might be worth teaching at a school one or two afternoons a week. It's a good way to network with other teachers and music professionals as well, which can lead to ensemble opportunities, playing gigs, and references down the road, even when you no longer teach at the school.

Music school positions are also good choices for teachers of less common instruments because the schools tend to attract students from the surrounding region. Let's say you live on a remote road in an out-of-the-way small town. You might not be able to fill your studio with French horn players, but if you're willing to travel half an hour to the bigger town with a music school, you might find a studio full of students waiting for you. This is win-win for everyone. And your full schedule compensates for the fact that the school takes a percent of the tuition fee.

There's also the cachet that comes with being on a faculty. You aren't merely some guy who plays drums. Rather, you're on the percussion faculty at XYZ Music School. Additionally, music schools may offer faculty such benefits as reduced prices on concert tickets, access to pedagogy workshops, access to a music library, and chances to perform (and a venue to perform in), as well as additional resources for their students.

Out of Tune

It's common for music schools to have a noncompete clause that prohibits teachers from "stealing" the school's students during the teacher's employ, or when the teacher leaves the school. This is one of those clauses that is easier signed than followed. Students are not, after all, merely economic units; they are human beings with whom you have an intense and sometimes long-standing personal relationship. You may have some difficulties if you decide to leave the employ of the music school and have to leave your students behind.

Finally, many teachers like the collegiality of working in a music school a couple days a week. It balances the long hours spent working one-on-one with students. Getting out of the house can be an important benefit as well. It's nice to be able to trade war stories (and share suggestions) around the water cooler with some colleagues.

How to Get the Gig

Networking is always useful, particularly if you can get an introduction to a school's director. In smaller communities, the executive director of a music school is likely to be involved with the chamber of commerce, the local arts council, various community groups, and possibly a church. Try to make an appointment to meet with the director. Be prepared to deliver a resumé (and a CD, if you have one).

> **Wise Words** _____
>
> As the owner of a music school, I am often contacted by job seekers through the e-mail address on my website. One way of getting a position is by offering to substitute teach when the school needs help. This provides the opportunity to show your assets, and puts you in a prime position for future hiring because the owner or director of the school has already had the opportunity to see how well you work with students. When looking for new teachers, I look for a genuine interest in teaching children; excitement about learning new things and supporting other teachers in the studio; the ability to listen, share, and be flexible; and good communication skills.
>
> —Robyn Pfeifer, owner, Pfeifer MusicWerks Studio; Portland, Oregon

Be aware that most community music schools aren't looking for top-drawer classical performers as much as they are looking for personable teachers who will be able to keep students happy and their studios full. So be sure to highlight your teaching experience, as well as any community music activities you've participated in and any ancillary programs (such as adult guitar workshops, chamber music coaching, or jazz improvisation classes,) you can offer.

Other Venues for the Traveling Teacher

Many other opportunities exist for teachers willing to work outside their home. Some of them work on terms similar to those of a music school, with an organization or business basically getting a cut of the teacher's earnings in return for a place to teach and ancillary services. In some cases, the teacher may get all the income. The following list isn't exhaustive, but it gives you a starting place for options that may exist, or that you may be able to create, in your community.

Music Stores

Many music stores offer private lessons, usually in small studios in the back of the store. It just makes sense. These businesses sell instruments, and buyers are constantly asking for referrals to teachers. If a music store has the space, adding lessons to the mix is just good business sense.

Generally, teaching at a music store isn't very different from teaching at a music school, although you probably wouldn't say that you are "on faculty." Most often, you'll be hired as an independent contractor, and the music store will handle billing, collecting money from students, and paying you. You might have an assigned afternoon to come in, and the store will schedule lessons for you. Sometimes the school will give teaching slot preference to staffers (the retail sales staff tend to be musicians). If you have any interest in working at a music store, combining retail work with teaching might be a good path for you.

Out of Tune

Be careful about a conflict of interest when dealing with a music store. Many music stores offer teachers discounts or cash finders' fees for referring students who buy instruments, and the amounts can be quite high if you're talking about a $10,000 piano. If you teach at a music store, the pressure to refer students may be palpable. As a teacher, you need to maintain objectivity and act in the students' best interest.

As with a music school, the store provides studio space and sometimes instruments. (In fact, they may be happy to let students try various instruments during lessons, hoping that the student likes one so much that he or she buys it.) There will probably be an unspoken (or possibly spoken) assumption that you will recommend that students buy sheet music, additional instruments, and supplies at the store. This is fine, as long as you believe that the store offers good merchandise at a fair price. The store may offer you a discount on merchandise.

Teaching at a music store can fill gaps in your home studio schedule or provide a teaching venue for those who can't teach at home. In addition, working at a music store often puts you in the heart of the local music community. If you're looking for gigs or people to play with, working at a music store might introduce you to the local talent and a potential ensemble or bandmates.

In terms of compensation, your actual hourly rate will probably be less than you would earn at home, and you will need to accept and adhere to the store's policies regarding make-ups, no-shows, snow days, and last-minute cancellations. You'll have to determine whether the store's conveniences outweigh the lower hourly rate.

To get the gig, show up with a resumé and be dressed in a professional manner. You don't have to wear a suit and tie, but if it's a piano shop with high-end instruments, you might want to look like someone who belongs in the store. At a hip guitar shop that caters to the rock 'n' roll crowd, casual dress is certainly okay. Just remember that you're not auditioning for a slot in a punk band; you're looking to be some kid's music teacher.

Lots of people wander in and out of music stores every week, so it will take a while to get your name on the radar as someone who is a working teacher. Don't be discouraged if you don't hit a home run your first time at bat; you're in this for the long haul.

Keep the music store on your weekly rounds. Send students there (and make sure your students tell them you sent them). Buy stuff, even if it's only some strings one week and a capo the next. Attend the gig of the guy behind the counter or buy his CD (guaranteed, he'll have a CD for sale).

Private and Public Schools

Whether private music teachers can give music lessons in public schools varies from region to region. In some areas, local laws or policies prohibit commercial private activity (which includes private music teaching) on public school property.

Private schools, of course, don't have this restriction, so the only question is whether you can sell your services to the principal or music director and, thence, the students—or, more accurately, their tuition-paying parents.

How you will be paid varies. Most often, the school provides the instrument (if necessary) and teaching space, and teachers are paid directly by the parents. Sometimes schools charge teachers a fee; sometimes they don't charge teachers at all because they consider the music lessons an enrichment activity for the kids or a welcome addition to their after-school offerings. The advantage of this arrangement is that it puts the teachers where the kids are. It especially benefits children whose parents work full-time and who might not otherwise be able to schedule after-school lessons.

In some cases, lessons can even be offered during the school day. Some (rare) schools allow children to be pulled out of class for a half-hour music lesson. This situation reduces the problems of make-ups caused by after-school conflicts, and it gives teachers work during the impossible-to-fill school-day hours.

Getting these gigs is difficult and often involves being in the right place at the right time with the right idea to share with the right person. Sometimes a music director will put word out that he's looking for a drum teacher for one afternoon a week, and you'll hear about it from your friend the guitar teacher, who got word from the local music store. But more often, you'll need to initiate contact.

To start the ball rolling, you'll want to get to know the teachers who work in the private school music department, perhaps the principal, and maybe the director of after-school programs. Research the school. The website and school publications should tell you what programs are available, so when you draw up your proposal, you can make it fit the existing structure for enrichment activities. Also be sure that what you're offering doesn't conflict or compete with what's already being offered. Your offer to coach a jazz ensemble after school, followed by a private lesson for each member, might not be welcomed if the school already has a jazz program and instrumental lessons are already in place.

Write an introductory letter, and then follow up with a phone call. Ask if you can send a proposal, and be sure it's addressed to the right person.

Other Music Teachers

Music teaching tends to be a fairly solitary business, but sometimes there are opportunities for teachers to work with and for each other. In some communities (generally, places where there are a lot of arts venues and teachers), some teachers may form a cooperative and share studio space and perhaps some secretarial or clerical support. This works well for teachers who don't have space of their own, and it also works well for teachers interested in working with ensembles and other instruments.

Working for another music teacher is a less common way to enter the teaching business, but it's a good way to get started if you don't have much experience. Or you might find a teacher whose studio is full and who is looking for someone to whom to refer additional students. Word-of-mouth may also tell you when an older teacher might be cutting back or retiring, in which case there may soon be a studio full of students looking for a new teacher. There is no sure path to finding these opportunities, but one thing is certain—you won't find them sitting at home. Networking with other teachers (see Chapter 9) will pay you back time and again.

At first, you may be working as an unpaid apprentice, but you might also find a teacher who runs group lessons or classes for young children and needs someone to assist—or to take over some of the classes.

Subcontracting Services

Subcontracting services are another way new teachers might be able to build up a studio. Basically, the service maintains a screened list of music teachers. The service drums up students through door-to-door flyers, telephone book ads, Internet marketing, and other advertising and marketing efforts. Prospective students contact the service, which probably has a name like "Pleasant County Music Teachers," and, based on the student's instrument and music education goals, the service assigns a teacher from its stable of independent contractors. Usually, the student and teacher arrange the scheduling. Often teachers are expected to travel to students' homes. The teacher bills the service, and the service bills the student. These services are more prevalent in cities and suburbs than in rural areas, where word-of-mouth is more important. As with teaching at a music school or in a music store, the downside with a subcontracting service is that the service keeps a hefty percentage as a commission. And unlike a music school or store, it doesn't provide space, recital halls, instruments, contacts, colleagues, discounts, or cachet.

The upside is that these services work well for teachers who are new to the communities in which they want to teach. For example, a city-based teacher who lives in a neighborhood where suburban students aren't likely to travel for music lessons might want to teach in the suburbs, where higher-paying work is available. However, it can be difficult for city-based teachers to figure out "how things work" in the suburbs—where to advertise, how to find students, and so on. A subcontracting service acts as an intermediary, or agent, between teacher and student.

As with schools and studios, you'll have to read the fine print covering the service's make-up, cancellation, and noncompete policies.

To get the gig, you'll first need to know of the service. You might find out through word-of-mouth, through neighborhood flyers, or through ads in the local papers. These operations are small mom-and-pop businesses; feel free to call and introduce yourself. Most services require at least a resumé, and possibly a CD (to prove you can play) or an interview. They're in the business of referring teachers, so they have to be choosy.

The Least You Need to Know

- In some communities, music teachers typically commute to students' homes to teach; in other communities, this may not be workable due to distance and travel expenses.

- Opportunities for the independent music teacher include music schools and studios, music stores, and private and public schools.

- Teachers who travel to teach need to consider additional expenses and studio policy issues.

- Teaching outside the home may incur more expenses or bring in less income—or both, but there are other benefits.

Chapter 4

Group Lessons

In This Chapter

- ◆ Deciding whether group teaching is for you
- ◆ The different kinds of group lessons
- ◆ Maximizing the student's experience in a group lesson
- ◆ Common group teaching challenges

Music education has been handed down from one teacher to one student for centuries, and there's a reason for that: it works. Every student learns differently, and part of the music teacher's art is to figure out, from among the many different ways to explain how to make a Csharpminor7flat5 chord, which approach will work for each particular student. Trying to do this in a group can be frustrating, ineffective, and often impossible.

However, music is also a communal activity, most often performed not by soloists, but by groups. So it only makes sense that it should also be taught in groups, at least some of the time. Most school band and orchestra students start in group lessons and then advance to private lessons if and when they show aptitude and interest. Partner and parent/child lessons can work wonders to motivate students who enjoy making music together. So can group lessons for adults, especially guitar players or singers. Indeed, group lessons may be the only way some students ever get a musical education.

The communal aspects of music are especially important when teaching a nonsolo instrument. Although a pianist or a guitarist can play in solitary splendor for hours on end, a tuba player or a violist needs musical company to experience and hear the instrument in the context of a full arrangement.

Pros and Cons of Group Lessons

Some teachers enjoy teaching groups. Some teachers would rather herd cats. Some teachers thrive on teaching preschoolers but shudder at the thought of taking on a group of adults, and vice versa. Some instruments seem better suited to group lessons than others. Let's explore the options and possibilities a bit.

Are Group Lessons for You?

What kind of teacher does well with group lessons? The answer depends on the teacher—and the group. The successful teacher of young children's and beginner groups may have to be more of a teacher than a musician. The opposite may be true when coaching advanced students and groups of adults.

Not everyone is cut out to teach group lessons. Teaching groups requires its own set of teaching skills and approaches, as well as a lot of planning and creativity. Lesson plans and activities need to be choreographed for the ages and levels of the students. The teacher has to be able to rein in each member of the class from wandering down his own particular path of learning. The group teacher must be able to corral all the members of the class and lead them down a common learning highway.

Group teaching can vary enormously. You may teach your primary instrument to groups of two or more students; coach ensembles, bands, and jam classes; or provide theory and performance instruction. Group teaching can mean working with very accomplished adults and teens. Or it can mean playing games with preschoolers or teaching a group piano class to 8- and 9-year-olds.

Take Note

A few well-established music education programs offer teacher training. Classes range from seminars to online training. For instance, the Suzuki program, which involves both private lessons and group lessons, offers an introductory one-day teacher-training course called "Every Child Can." Kindermusik offers online training. Taking a course is a small investment in continuing education, and it can help you find out if this kind of teaching appeals to you.

When considering the idea of group lessons, it helps to consider the many options and narrow your choices to a specific scenario or two. Focus on the types of musical experiences you would be comfortable sharing and the types of student groups with which you feel you interact best. Take your own learning and playing experiences into consideration. For example, if you play regularly in small ensembles, you might try coaching an ensemble. Group teaching is certainly not for everyone, but teaching some kinds of group classes might be a pleasant surprise.

Then again, maybe not. Do not underestimate the skills and patience required to work with a group of students. You might get your feet wet with a single small group teaching situation. See how that goes, and then you can either add more group situations or eliminate group teaching from your schedule completely.

Advantages of Group Lessons

For a teacher, one advantage of group lessons is that because they appeal disproportionately to young children and to adults (and not to school-aged children), they may well take place during the day (for preschool children) or later in the evening (for adults). If you're looking to expand your teaching day, this can be a good way to do it. (And, of course, very young children grow up into school-aged students who need lessons.)

 Wise Words _____

I teach groups …

… because I love to be with a group of people.

… because I enjoy connecting people with similar interests.

… because I believe that making music socially enriches one's life.

… because I want more private students.

… because I am maxed out with prep for individual lessons but need more income.

… because I am aware of the health benefits of making music with others in a relaxed setting.

… because I think that learning piano with others encourages students to reach beyond what they perceive as their limitations.

… because it is an affordable way to offer lessons to less-served communities.

… because people and music are two of my favorite things, and I love combining them!

—Alice Peterson, music teacher, Westbrook, Maine

Another advantage for the teacher may be compensation. I talk about pricing group lessons in Chapter 5. For now, it's enough to note that the teacher's per-hour rate is generally higher for groups than for individuals, although some of that is cancelled out by the fact that group lessons take more preparation time (and, some might argue, recovery time).

From a student's perspective, there are two key advantages to group lessons. The first is price, which depends on the venue and the size of the group, but which will always be lower per hour than private lessons. This makes group lessons affordable for some students who might not otherwise be able to afford music lessons.

The second advantage is the social nature of group lessons. Interestingly, this seems to be most important to very young children (who often learn more by taking cues from each other and by playing games than by following an adult's directions) and to adults (who are reassured that they aren't the only fumble-fingered person in the room, and who develop relationships with other students). The social nature of the class also adds an element of group goofiness and camaraderie.

Disadvantages of Group Lessons

The primary disadvantage of group lessons is that classes are rarely made up of students of similar ability. Unless the teacher is a master at the craft of managing groups, group lessons tend to penalize faster students who are ready to move on. And they frustrate slower students who get left behind.

This is probably why group lessons work so much better for very young children and adults. Preschoolers can be successfully taught in groups of pre-instrumental classes where they learn to count, move to rhythm, and identify pitches going up and down. Group lessons can also work for the first year or two of instrument instruction if students are well matched in ability and age because most of the students will be struggling with the same challenges. And group lessons work well with more advanced adults who may be at different levels but who each bring something different to the table—a new piece of repertoire, an interesting question, or a different perspective.

But with students beyond the first year or two, group lessons are rarely successful, especially on a solo instrument. Intermediate students deal with the individual mechanics of interacting with their instrument, and they all struggle with different issues at different times. Some may be good readers but poor listeners; others may have quick fingers but poor reading skills; and some may have good pitch, or rhythm, or expressive abilities, but may be deficient in other areas. These differences are crucial at the intermediate level, and trying to teach all of these basic skills to students who grasp them in vastly different ways is indeed like herding cats. With rare exceptions, intermediates do better in private lessons. And in fact, one disadvantage of some group programs is that they sometimes try to hold on to students who are more than ready for private lessons.

Types of Group Lessons

Group lessons are limited only by your imagination. Formal group programs may offer teacher training, dedicated curriculum materials, and certification. Or you can develop your own curricula to meet the needs of students you already have or students you want to attract. The lessons might include only your primary instrument or an ensemble of instruments. You may even work with another teacher.

Formal and Franchised Programs

A number of well-developed group teaching programs already exist. Perhaps the most famous is the Suzuki program, which started with violin instruction for young children but has branched out to include guitar, cello, piano, and other instruments. More recently, the low prices of electronic keyboards have made group piano lessons a booming business, at least for beginners.

Sometimes formal programs include not only teacher training and a set curriculum, but also licensing and franchise fees, as well as marketing and advertising materials. Many of these programs are worthwhile, and a few, such as Kindermusik, have brand-name recognition with parents. The teacher training is certainly valuable to teachers who have no experience working with groups. In some programs, teachers learn group management, classroom pacing, and troubleshooting, along with how to use keyboards, computers, games, and diversionary tactics to keep several children happily working independently while one gets attention.

But at the same time, some programs are highly profit oriented (profit, that is, for the course developer). You may even be sworn to secrecy (via your contract with the proprietor) about the contents of the program. You may be subject to a strict noncompete clause, or you may be asked not to teach using any other materials. Some of these restrictions may be anathema to a teacher whose true goal is to be the right teacher with the right materials for each student.

Teacher-Designed Group Curricula

Of course, there's nothing to stop you from designing your own group lessons. In many cases, some of the teaching materials available on the market lend themselves well to being used in group settings.

One caveat, however: beginning teachers may find that they've bitten off more than they can chew trying to design and implement a group program. Classroom teachers have very big toolboxes of tricks and techniques to keep a class moving and under control. If you don't have this background, I recommend some teacher training.

One good place to start experimenting with groups is by offering occasional studio classes in which you cluster a group of private students together and have them perform for each other, then discuss each student's performance and the piece that was played, including its musical structure, the various interpretations possible, and information about the composer's style. This can give you a bit of experience with classroom dynamics, as well as a sense of whether you enjoy the group teaching experience. These studio classes aren't a substitute for private lessons, but if they work well for you, it might be an indication that you might be able to expand your offerings to include group lessons for beginners.

It's possible to fall into group teaching by accident. For example, you could find yourself teaching a cluster of homeschoolers of the same age and it occurs to you that you could put together a duet or a trio. Or perhaps your intermediate guitar shows up at his lesson one day with his best friend, the trombone player, in tow.

Performance and Jam Classes

Performance and jam classes give students the invaluable experience of making music with and for each other. In performance ensemble classes, students can work on perfecting a chamber piece—or a rock band song—with a recital as the end goal. They can learn how to rehearse and work with each other, and, as with members of a sports team, they may take more responsibility for practice and showing up because they are accountable to the group.

Performance classes can also involve soloists taking a turn playing for each other, which forces them to polish their pieces to performance standards. These lessons can be a valuable supplement to private lessons, for several reasons:

- They are a performance opportunity, and students tend to practice a little harder with a performance looming.

- They give students an opportunity to show off a little. A particularly talented or hardworking student may inspire younger or less advanced students.

- It is illuminating for students to hear their peers, and it is educational for students to hear other music that they might want to attempt.

- Performance classes help students face and deal with stage fright.

- Performance classes also develop critical listening abilities. Students can practice reading along with a score as another student plays (you can even play "stop the music" and check to see that students reading the score are following along correctly). This helps students develop both aural and reading skills.

Jam classes are basically group improvisations in which students learn to play the different roles in a group: holding the rhythm, improvising leads, comping chords, or perhaps participating in calls and responses, trading fours or eights, and learning how to play off of each other.

Performance and jam classes also offer a comfortable environment in which everyone is there to learn and there's no penalty for messing up. More skilled students can get ideas not only from a teacher, but also from each other, and they can see how other players solve the same problems or approach the same improvisation. It's also a chance to get over performance nerves, develop camaraderie among the students you teach, and have fun with music.

Take Note

A performance class moves to a whole new level by scheduling a "real" performance at the end of it. Possible venues include local coffee houses, a lounge in the off-season or on a slow night, or civic events such as community festivals. Encourage students to invite guests. And you might also invite friends and fellow musicians to lend reliable back-up support.

Partner and Parent-Child Lessons

Whether partner and parent-child lessons work has a lot to do with dynamics beyond a teacher's control. One very big advantage to parent-child lessons is the example it sets for the child. It tells the child that music lessons are not just some school thing that kids have to do, but that they are a privilege that adults enjoy, and that music is about lifelong learning. Seeing the example of a parent practicing at home (and maybe struggling with the same new ideas that the child is tackling) is invaluable to the young student. And, given that most parents understand the basics of counting and the music alphabet a bit faster than their children, even adult beginners can help their children at home.

Parent-child lessons can be a lot of fun on an instrument such as guitar (or bass and guitar, if you can teach both), where the parent and child can support each other playing rhythm and lead in a sort of mini-band. Join in yourself as a second instrumentalist; invite a friend who plays keyboard and maybe the kid down the street who plays sax, and your boring old guitar lesson turns into a grooving blues jam. What kid won't look back on *those* guitar lesson with Dad as a wonderful musical memory?

Partner lessons combine two students of similar ages and (hopefully) abilities. Often these will be friends who giggle a lot and talk about forming a band. But this is precisely the energy that keeps a young student interested in music. However, if one student pulls ahead, or if the other student is holding her back, you may need to advocate for private lessons to be added to the mix. Partner lessons work especially well for guitar.

Mixed Instruments and Ensemble Work

Coaching ensembles is another way to work groups into your schedule. This can be a challenging task, especially if you don't play all the instruments in the ensemble.

If you're a piano teacher, teaching students the valuable skill of accompanying instrumentalists and singers gives them a lifelong skill that is actually marketable (not to mention fun), because there is a constant need for church musicians and accompanists. As a pianist coaching, say, a piano trio, you may not be able to help the violin player with her bowing, but you can certainly make comments about phrasing, dynamics, cues, tempo changes, rhythm problems, intonation, and on-time entrances.

Similarly, a violin teacher coaching a clarinet quintet will need to be able to speak not only to the string players, but to the clarinet player, too. Again, musical issues such as phrasing and dynamics transcend the particularities of individual instruments. At the same time, be careful not to step on other teachers' toes when working with their students.

One way to get the cooperation and support of other teachers is to recruit them to participate in your scheme: tell them what you're up to and what you want from them (a kid who can play the violin part for a Beethoven trio, a sax player who can do Brubeck's "Take Five"). You might even take turns coaching the ensemble.

One-Time Workshops and Seminars

Another potentially lucrative income stream is to hold one-time workshops and seminars. You can host a one-, two-, or three-day program at your studio during which you cover a particular subject in detail for students who come to you for just that one workshop. An ideal number of students might be six to eight, if it's a hands-on topic with lots of technique and playing involved, and up to 10 or more if it's largely lecture based. (In larger groups of 10, you could have an assistant instructor and break the class into subgroups for playing time.)

Small group workshops that you run yourself can be quite lucrative; it's not unusual for teachers to charge $100 to $150 for a day, per student, and more if a second teacher is brought in or if meals are served.

Take Note

Marketing a group workshop requires a fairly long time frame because you're asking people to commit several days to the seminar. Start at least four months in advance. Develop brochures and distribute them to your current students. Then post them on bulletin boards around town. Set up a website, using keywords such as "guitar workshop," "learn Neil Young songs," or "guitar lessons in Music County." Send out an e-mail notice to your students and music colleagues. They can easily forward it to *their* students and colleagues, too. Be sure your local music store knows, get on the community events calendar in the local paper, and send out a press release. See Chapter 9 for more marketing ideas.

Some possible topics for studio workshops might include these:

◆ Performing. Participants get a song ready for a performance.

◆ Jamming. Participants learn the techniques of group improvisation.

◆ Learning about the work of a particular band or songwriter.

◆ Developing certain skills— for example, jazz chords, guitar strumming, or song arrangement for solo guitar or piano.

◆ Writing and arranging of original songs.

◆ Public address system and recording equipment basics.

Group workshops can be an interesting supplement to your teaching income, and they may even bring some regular students (not to mention friends) into your orbit.

If you live in a rural area, however, be aware that you might quickly run through the number of potential students able and willing to spend a couple hundred dollars on a weekend music class.

Making Group Lessons Work

So where can you teach group lessons? You may be able to handle a small class in your home studio. In addition, opportunities for group teaching already exist in your community. Music classes may be part of an already-existing curriculum offered at a community college, a day care center, or a continuing education center. In this case, you would likely become a part-time staff or faculty member, and the organization would pay you per class or per course. At home, of course, you're free to set your own price and collect payments directly from students.

Finding the Right Location

To find places where group programs and enrichment classes are already offered, check out music schools, elementary or high schools, summer camps, day care facilities, community colleges, community arts programs, and community centers. You'll find information about programs on calendars, websites, and brochures, and in advertisements and events listings in local papers.

Facts and Stats

According to the National Center for Education Statistics, there are more than 1,000 public community colleges in the United States. Numbers vary by state, ranging from only one each in Alaska, Rhode Island, South Dakota, and Vermont, to 107 in California. Other states with large numbers of community colleges are Texas (67), North Carolina (58), Georgia (54), Minnesota (51), Illinois (49), and New York (47). Most of these colleges offer noncredit group classes in music taught by adjunct faculty members (that is, independent teachers).

Once you know what types of programs are offered, you can recommend yourself as a teacher or you can suggest a complementary program. Start with a call to the administrator's office to learn the deadline for proposing classes for the next semester (at colleges, this may be as much as six months in advance, because they need to print calendars and do publicity for your class). Then e-mail the director, including your suggested program and a brief bio. Follow up with a phone call to ask for an appointment. You might fit right in with the program. For instance, an after-school program might welcome a new way to keep kids busy for an hour before parents pick them up. As with giving regular after-school music lessons, note that private schools are often more open to arrangements with private music teachers than are public schools, which tend to have larger bureaucracies. Also, in some states, there may be legal reasons why private teachers can't use public facilities for independently offered seminars and programs.

Group programs at a facility other than your studio require extra preparation. One concern is instruments and materials. Of course, it's much easier to get a group program going if everyone already has instruments. Group keyboard classes require an investment in keyboards, and then the issues of storage and security arise. But ensembles of mixed strings or winds, a group guitar class, and a percussion class are more easily accommodated. The room just needs to be large enough for the musicians. Note that you'll need armless chairs so instrument-playing students can move their arms freely. Also consider any ancillary equipment such as amplifiers, music stands, instrument stands, and microphones.

Take Note

Many group programs are held in facilities after normal working hours. Double-check which doors will be open for you and who will lock up when you leave. Find out where the light switches are for the hallways and rooms you'll use. Acquire emergency numbers for the director or security staff.

Using Your Home Studio

If your home studio is big enough, you might be able hold group classes. You will need more places for people to park. If the lesson involves children (instead of adults), you'll also need a place for multiple parents to wait during the lesson.

Realize, too, that neighbors may be willing to tolerate a succession of single students coming in and out during the afternoons, but they may be less happy living next door to a rock band or the equivalent. Local zoning may also play a role. Although it may be acceptable to teach one student at a time in your home, your local municipality may draw the line at teaching groups.

Group Size and Composition

Once you've found a home base for your group program, you need to establish group size. If you are using a formal group teaching curriculum, the authors of the method may have some suggestions. Beyond that, it very much depends on age, level, the method you are using, and the type of class. A basic group guitar class, for example, might be most effective with between five and eight students. Some group piano teachers limit class size to four; others handle a dozen or more. A rhythm and movement class for young children might run to 10 students without devolving into total chaos. (You could give a musically inclined parent a discount to help out if the group gets too unwieldy.) A lecture class might be able to accommodate 20 or more students, assuming that you have the space.

With most group music classes, homogeneity is key, not only in terms of levels, which are discussed next, but also in terms of musical interests, which are often related to age. Try to offer classes that are as specifically described as possible: "a beginning guitar class for high school kids," or "introduction to chamber music for adults," or "a Beatles workshop for intermediate guitarists." Homogeneity in age is especially important in groups of children, who learn radically different at different ages. But it's also an issue to consider when teaching adults: a 20-something student learns differently from the way a senior citizen learns.

Balancing the Skill Levels

If you are offering several different classes, break them into general levels, perhaps beginners, beginners II, and intermediate. Possible exceptions are vocal and cabaret-style classes in which people take turns singing. An advanced singer may not especially enjoy listening to a beginner—but the beginner isn't likely to hold back the class.

If you're teaching at home, of course, you'll field questions from interested students directly. If you're teaching at an outside program, perhaps at a community center or a community college, it's a good idea to invite phone calls from prospective students to talk about the class levels and your expectations for each. Otherwise, when you get your class together, you may find that the student who described himself as advanced isn't much more than a beginner, and the student who said she was a beginner belongs in your intermediate class. Plus, you might have a nice older lady who can't seem to find her fingers, and a young guy who seems to "get" everything lickety-split. Welcome to the world of teaching music!

Out of Tune

The main reason group lessons get a bad rap is that they leave some students behind, while boring quicker learners. If it's not possible to group students by ability, have some supplemental work for quicker learners to pursue independently. For example, an agile guitar student could be given a more complex rhythm or picking pattern while the slower learners simply strum once per measure.

The trick in group teaching is to teach to the middle level of the class while keeping an eye on the periphery. The student twiddling his thumbs (or, more likely, noodling around on his instrument) because he is bored and the student with the blank stare of incomprehension are both problems you need to deal with.

Not everyone can learn in a group setting, and the one thing you cannot permit to happen is for one person's slower learning to hijack the entire class. Of course, you can't let another student's show-off faster learning hijack the class, either. Sometimes switching the student to a class more suited to his or her level can solve the issue.

Here are some more strategies for balancing the levels:

- Use stronger students as examples and assistants. Helping to teach something solidifies the skill. In fact, there's no better test of whether a student has truly learned something than asking him to teach it to someone else.

- Inspire slower students by having more accomplished students demonstrate (but not in a show-off sort of way). The slower students see that the skill really is achievable and is not something that only the instructor can do.

- Use performance. Each student benefits from playing for others, no matter what the level. Meanwhile, the other students learn critical listening skills and get to evaluate different musical options, styles, and choices.

- Teach finer points. Faster learners can always learn more about finesse, expression, phrasing, and execution, even on seemingly simple pieces.

- Put supplemental and supporting material on your website, both for students who want to move ahead and for students who need reinforcement.

- Invite e-mailed questions so that problems don't linger all week between lessons.

If nothing seems to work, it may be time to suggest private lessons for the student who just can't seem to fit in. Or have the student come in for an additional 15 minutes of one-on-one review before the class gets started.

Tips for Effective Group Teaching

Whether your group is a chamber quartet or a rock band, a kiddie keyboard class or a Suzuki class, a few tips can help you keep the class running smoothly.

- Learn names. If you're bad with names, ask students to sit in the same place every week so you can address them by name. It makes a difference.

- Start lessons with questions from the last class and a quick review. Encourage students to ask questions. If one student has a question, someone else probably wants or needs to know the same thing, too.

- Arrange the seats so that you are close to students and can hear who is playing what. With most instruments (except, perhaps keyboards), a semicircle is ideal.

- Look at people while you teach. Let your eye rove from student to student to see if what you're saying is getting through.

- Divide the class into lecture and playing time, to vary the pace, keep things interesting, give new information and skills a chance to sink in, and give people a break from the physical strain of playing an instrument.

- Make sure you have adequate supplies: white board, music paper, extra picks and strings (for guitars), a metronome, and so on.

- Cater your musical selection to the age and preferences of the group. Undoubtedly, you know what the evergreen material is on your instrument. But a group of seniors may want to play old standards, while Boomers will respond to classic rock. And be sure to ask; people's musical choices can be surprising.

Finally, have fun! Remember, if you're not enjoying being in the class, there's no way your students are having any fun. And that is the whole point of sharing music.

The Least You Need to Know

- Group music lessons can involve every level and type of student, from preschoolers to advanced classical players.

- Teachers may provide group lessons at a home studio or in affiliation with an existing program or curriculum.

- Successful groups should be made up of students of roughly equivalent interests and levels.

- Group lessons need to be carefully planned, with a balance of lecturing and playing.

Part 2

The Business of Running a Successful Studio

Running an independent music teaching studio requires more than the ability to teach or the ability to play an instrument. You also need to know how to run a business. How much do you charge for lessons? What business and legal issues are involved in running a home studio? Do you know whether your home insurance covers you? What kinds of records do you need to keep for your accountant?

You'll also need to know the ins and outs of scheduling and managing your time. I cover the essential topic of studio policies, and you'll learn how to make decisions regarding business policies for your studio and to communicate them effectively to parents and students. And last but certainly not least, where will you find students? I take you through the ins and outs of marketing, advertising, networking, and doing public relations to get your studio started with a full roster.

Chapter 5

How Much to Charge

In This Chapter

- Lesson fees based on community norms, your training, and your experience
- Whether to charge by the lesson or by fixed tuition
- Make-up lessons and summer schedules, and how they affect your pricing
- Pricing for group lessons
- How and when to raise prices

How much to charge is one of the most important and difficult decisions a new teacher has to make. Charge too little, and you will always be playing catch-up. Charge too much, and students will find their way to more reasonably priced teachers.

Pricing for music lessons is community based. While some music teacher associations run occasional surveys of rates, such surveys are of limited use. Between high-priced urban centers and low-income rural areas, the rate for a half-hour lesson may vary by a factor of 10. It makes no sense to be looking at New York City rates if you live on a ranch in Utah. In fact, it makes no sense to be looking at New York City rates even if you live in upstate New York!

Basic Pricing Principles

Three factors go into pricing:

◆ Community norms

◆ Your credentials and experience relative to those of others in your community

◆ Your income needs

To figure your rate, you need to consider each of these and then balance them against each other. The first step is to research the going rate in your community. Then you need to figure out where on the spectrum you want to charge, without either under-pricing or overpricing yourself.

Determining the Going Rate

What you want to charge and what you need to charge are only part of the equation. You can, after all, charge whatever you like, but people have to be willing to pay your rate.

Take Note

If you don't want to call direct competitors to find out their rate, approach teachers of other instruments, the local music store, and the community music school, if there is one.

The going rate is what the average qualified teacher in your community charges. It is not the rate charged by the master concert pianist who takes a few artist-level students, nor is it the rate charged by Johnny the high school drummer who will do anything to earn gas money for his car. Neither is it the rate charged by lovely Mrs. Oldtimer who lives on a nice retirement income and hasn't raised her rates in 20 years.

Underpricing Versus Overpricing

Overpricing is probably the easiest way to make sure no one comes to your studio for lessons. However, if you have something special to offer—you are a master teacher with major concertizing experience, you teach four different instruments, or your students routinely win national competitions and get into prime music schools—you may be able to set up a master teacher studio that attracts only the most serious students. As a new teacher, however, you will be much more successful positioning yourself in the middle of the spectrum. If your ambition is to become a master teacher of budding superstars, you will have to work up to that level over time.

On the opposite end of the spectrum, underpricing is a time-tested way of undercutting the competition to get people to pay for what you have to offer. But it's not a viable long-term strategy for an ongoing service, for several reasons.

First, a teacher who prices far below community norms may be viewed as the "bargain basement" teacher who is undercutting other teachers. When Mrs. Established who teaches down the road can't take the new family of three who moved into town in the middle of the school year, she's not going to refer them to someone who is undercutting the professional rate. She may even think that your low rate brands you as inexperienced, substandard, or someone who simply doesn't know the business. In many communities, there are plenty of students to go around, so it's not productive to undercut other teachers. No one can teach all the students in town, or even all the good students. Yes, you may occasionally lose a student to another teacher, but more often, other teachers are a source of referrals and support. Far better to earn your students with your skills and reputation than with low prices.

Second, if you are a qualified teacher, you should be paid what other qualified teachers are paid. It's that simple. The reason there is such a thing as a "going rate" for any service in a community is that the socioeconomic and educational factors have created a situation in which most people are willing and able to pay that rate for a particular service. Charging far beneath that rate will brand you as not quite top drawer.

Third, once you start at a lower-than-usual rate, you will always be playing catch-up. A music teacher has only his or her time to sell. There are few ways, short of starting a music school or acting as an agent for other teachers, for music teachers to make money other than by teaching. In addition, the possible working hours are limited because of children's school schedules. So most serious music teachers soon realize that to pay the bills themselves, they have to charge a rate that compensates them fairly, not only for the time they spend teaching, but also for the time they spend preparing for lessons and running their studios. The reality of everyday life is that the cost of living rises every year. To keep up with inflation, you'll need to raise prices on a reasonably regular basis—usually every year or two. If you start far below your community's going rate, you'll also need to raise prices to catch up, and you might meet resistance among parents who chose you simply because your price was low.

Of course, it is true that if you are new in a community, you have to find some way to make inroads. In that case, a trial period of discounted lessons, free demonstration lessons, or an inexpensively priced summer music "camp" are all ways to get people in the door without charging too little. We explore these strategies in Chapter 9.

Figuring *Your* Bottom Line

Your income as a self-employed person is based on a fairly simple formula:

Billable hours worked per year × Dollars per hour – Expenses = Annual income

Let's look at each of these in turn.

Billable Hours Worked Per Year

Private music teachers don't work eight-hour days, five days a week. That's not the nature of the job. The vast majority of students are schoolchildren and teens who are in school until 3:00, 3:30, or later in the afternoon. Summer further complicates the picture because many families expect to take the summer off, leaving a music teacher with diminished income for two or more months. Most teachers see their incomes drop by as much as 50 percent in the summer. You also need to factor in school holidays and vacations.

Your particulars may differ, but a good starting point is to figure a 36-week teaching year, spread out over the 10-month school year. (This accounts for some school holidays and vacation periods.) Add to that about 50 to 65 percent of your weekly student load for eight weeks in the summer.

> **Facts and Stats**
>
> Surveys of "full-time" music teachers find that most teach in the neighborhood of 1,000 hours a year, rarely more than 1,200. When calculating your annual income, be realistic about how many teaching hours a week you think you are able to work. And to save your sanity and your budget, factor in a little for attrition.

Now let's assume you teach 25 hours a week for 36 weeks. Simple multiplication tells you that your school year adds up to 900 teaching hours, plus the summer. To account for the summer, for the sake of illustration, let's figure 15 hours per week for 8 weeks, which gives you 120 more hours. The grand total is 1,020 teaching hours for the work year. Let's round down to 1,000, which should take care of student attrition, snow days, your sick days, or other unforeseen scheduling interruptions.

If 1,000 hours doesn't sound like a lot compared to, say, an office worker, consider that these are billable hours, not working hours. As a music teacher, you will actually work many more hours than you can actually bill for. Parents will see the money they pay you as covering the time you spend teaching their child. What they don't see is the time you have to spend preparing lessons, reviewing and purchasing materials, doing bookkeeping and other chores, maintaining your instruments, learning new repertoire, planning recitals, and continuing your own musical and pedagogic education. If, in addition to teaching music, you also gig, you need to schedule your own practice time above and beyond your teaching hours.

It is also important to note that teaching music is an intense one-on-one job. There are no gossip breaks at the water cooler, no quick jumps onto your Facebook page on the Internet, no chats with the co-worker in the next cubicle. Several oft-cited recent surveys have reported that American office workers waste as least 20 percent of their work-day time doing personal chores, playing computer games, chatting with co-workers, or just daydreaming. This is not true for music teachers. Every minute in a lesson is a working minute, during which you are paying close attention to what the student is doing.

Calculating Dollars Per Hour

The second part of the pricing equation is dollars per hour. It can be a little tricky to calculate the going rate *per hour* because most professional music teachers charge tuition rather than a per-lesson or per-hour fee. Everyone works the math a little differently, so it can be hard to figure out exact equivalencies. *Note:* We get to the subject of tuition versus individual lesson fees in just a bit.

You don't have to sweat the details: You just need a general sense of what others are charging. Let's say a teacher offers 34 half-hour lessons a year for $1,000, and another offers 32 lessons plus a make-up plus three group lessons for $1,200. Don't get bogged down in the details. We're looking for approximate numbers here. For the first example, the teacher is charging $1,000 ÷ 34; that works out to almost $30 per lesson. In the second case, the teacher is providing 35 time slots (32 plus 3 group lessons), so that's $1,200 ÷ 35; she's charging about $34 for a half-hour lesson. Say another teacher is charging by the semester, offering 16 half-hour lessons for $450. She's getting $28 per lesson. Now you have a starting range of what music lessons cost in your community: $28 to $34 per half-hour.

You call a few more teachers, and in addition to asking their rates, you ask how long they've been teaching and what their musical education has been. A pattern begins to emerge: in your neck of the woods, the cheapest teacher is getting $40 an hour, the most expensive is getting $70, and most seem to be sitting at around $45 to $55. Not many of them have college degrees in music, but most have 10 or more years of teaching experience. Where do you fit in?

It can feel a little like throwing darts in the dark to set your rates at first. Here are some considerations:

- Do you have a degree? A Bachelor's? A Master's? Having a degree in music should put you, at the very least, smack in the middle of the going rate, even if you're a brand new teacher.

- Do you have any specific music education training?

- Do you have other related training, such as education classes, student teaching, or experience teaching performance arts at a summer camp?

- If you have prior music teaching experience, how much?

- What other work and life experience do you have? It may not be fair, but a 40-year-old can get away with charging a bit more than a 22-year-old.

- If you have prior music teaching experience, what achievements can you point to? Students who went on to study music? Students who became performers?

- What other skills do you have? What other programs can you offer your students?

As much as possible, try to set your rates in line with those of other teachers in your community with a similar balance of skills. Then listen closely to parent reactions when you quote your rates: the easiest time to make adjustments is when you have only a few students.

Expenses

The third part of the equation is teaching expenses. Chapter 6 details expenses and how to account for them. Here we simply want to consider any ongoing expenses that are directly related to your teaching music—that is, expenses that you wouldn't incur if it weren't for your studio. These might include the following:

- Teaching materials (staff paper, notebooks, student awards, games, and so on)

- Business insurance

- Studio rental (f you must rent space)

- Gas and transportation (if you are a traveling teacher)

- Housekeeping (if you will have your studio cleaned)

In addition, factor in an "overhead" percentage to cover benefits and expenses usually paid for by employers, including self-employment taxes, an employer's typical share of medical insurance (around 80 percent), and an employer's typical share of contributions to retirement benefits (around 50 percent). Generally, employee benefits cost an employer 20 to 30 percent of a worker's paycheck. But in this case, *you* are the employer, and you are responsible for those expenses. Your teaching rate has to take that into account.

You'll no doubt have to estimate some of your expenses. But go ahead and add them up, to the best of your ability.

Now flip back to that equation we gave you a few pages ago. Plug in your numbers—your billable hours, your newly calculated hourly rate, and your expenses. Hopefully, the result will be enough to pay your bills!

How to Charge Tuition

How you charge your tuition is an important decision, and determining your hourly rate is only the first step. Beyond that, you need to decide whether to charge by the lesson, by the month, or by the semester.

Figuring Fees for Half-Hour and Hour Lessons

Say you've done the math, and you hope to teach 20 hours a week. The going rate for an experienced teacher with a degree in your community is $25 for a half-hour lesson. You have a major in elementary education with a minor in music, some classroom teacher training experience, but very little experience teaching music—and that little comes from working at a summer camp. You decide that your degree and training are solid, but your experience puts you at the lower end of the going rate. You decide your fee for a half-hour lesson will be $20.

Take Note _____

Although it's a nice idea, giving discounts to families with multiple students actually puts you at risk because if one quits, often they all quit. And of course, if the family moves, you lose all the students. Also, it takes the same amount of time to prepare lessons, regardless of whether the students are in the same family. This is a judgment call. In a community in which people are struggling to pay for lessons, discounts are certainly appreciated. In a better-off community, it may not be necessary to give $10 discounts to the children of lawyers and CEOs.

How much will you charge for a 45-minute lesson? Some teachers simply do the easiest math. If a half-hour lesson is $20, a 45-minute lesson is $30, and a full hour is $40.

Sometimes the math doesn't work out quite that evenly. What if you are teaching half-hour lessons for $25? Will you charge the awkward (but proportional) amount of $37.50 for 45 minutes, and $50 for an hour's lesson? Many teachers round down in such cases for the longer lessons. For example, they charge $25 for 30 minutes, $35 for 45 minutes, and $45 for an hour. One of the reasons is that you don't annoy everyone (including yourself) by charging a silly amount like $37.50. Another reason is that it takes less preparation (and energy) to teach one student for an hour than it does to teach two students for a half-hour each—especially because half-hour students are often younger and more fidgety, and require more intense hand-holding during the lesson.

There's no right answer about whether to charge an exact proportion, or to round the numbers up or down. Either way, as time goes on and you raise your rates, you're bound to get some awkward numbers, especially if you give discounts for referrals or siblings. You'll just have to make these adjustments as you go.

Charging by the Lesson

Now that you've set your hourly fee, how are you going to collect it? Every week? Every month? Every semester?

Charging by the lesson is the most obvious way to set a price, and it is the easiest for parents to understand. They pay you $20; the child gets a 30-minute lesson. Simple.

But a simple solution is not always the optimal one. In fact, most professional teachers don't run their studios collecting a single check every time little Suzie comes in the door. First of all, for a busy teacher, collecting a check from every student for every lesson may mean having to account for, deposit, and manage 200 or more different checks a month. This makes accounting and bookkeeping unwieldy, especially when little Suzie's mom routinely forgets to send payment, and you have to remember to call and remind her, but oops, that's when you find out that they're missing next week because Suzie has a basketball game.

And that brings us to the second reason to avoid per-lesson charging: it is difficult to hold students who pay by the lesson accountable for lessons they miss. Charging by the lesson means that if Suzie does not walk in the door, there's no check that week. Parents who know they pay for a lesson whether or not they show up for it are much more likely to arrange the family schedule (and maybe even miss a basketball game) to get to lessons reliably.

Charging by the Month

Charging by the month solves part of the problem. Some teachers charge by the month according to however many lessons are in that month. For example, suppose the first of November falls on a Monday. There would be five Mondays in November, and the student would pay for five lessons. In December, perhaps there are only two lesson Mondays because of the Christmas holiday; therefore, in December, the student would pay for only two lessons. This method has the advantage that the students pay for exactly the number of lessons they schedule each month, so it's clear and easy to explain to parents. Also, by paying in advance, there is less chance that the student will arbitrarily miss a lesson, particularly if your studio policy limits the number of make-ups you are obliged to give.

Out of Tune

Resist the temptation to negotiate your prices. People talk, and it creates bad will. If one of your favorite students is having financial difficulties, you can instead start a partial scholarship, complete with practice and achievement requirements necessary to keep it. Also, some communities have funds that help with music and arts education scholarships. Your music teachers association may have one as well.

There are two disadvantages to charging by the month according to the number of lessons for each student in each month. For both parents and students, the amount paid every month will be different, which wreaks havoc with personal budgets and bookkeeping. The second disadvantage is that this method opens the subject of lesson schedules to constant renegotiation. For example, if little Suzie misses that first Monday, there's no way her parents are going to want to write a check for it when they show up the following week, no matter what your studio policy says. Or the parents may tell you they want to pay for only four lessons instead of five because "we want to go away next weekend," or because "the third Monday's no good for us because Aunt Sheila is in town," or because "he has a birthday party/orthodontist appointment/sleep-over/soccer match." If you have a lot of time available for rescheduling (and are willing to reschedule constantly), this approach may work for you. But most teachers with full studios don't have that flexibility and soon abandon any kind of per-lesson pricing in favor of charging regular tuition.

Charging a Fixed Tuition

Charging a fixed annual tuition (payable either in one lump sum or in installments over the course of a year) has become an increasingly popular policy for professional music teachers. This method has several advantages.

First, it reinforces the fact that taking music lessons is a long-term commitment and that learning an instrument can be accomplished only with regular study and lesson attendance.

Second, it reflects the reality that a music teacher does not sell one lesson at a time. The service a teacher provides is a series of lessons, just like a college class. Contrast this with other appointment-based services, such as a doctor's appointment or a restaurant reservation. If a patron at a restaurant cancels a dinner reservation, or if a patient at a doctor's office cancels an appointment, chances are good that the restaurant or the doctor can fill that slot with another customer or patient. (Of course, it's also true that many doctors do have a required cancellation notice period to give them enough time to rebook those slots.) This is not to say that cancelled appointments are not a hassle for doctors and restaurant managers—but it is at least possible to fill the slot.

The same is not true for a music teacher. Students book lesson times, and when a teacher's schedule is full, she has to turn away further inquiries. If students who have those appointments then start canceling them, the teacher cannot "sell" the unused time slot to other students because people don't come for single music lessons. Occasionally, and with enough notice, the teacher may be able to use one student's missed lesson time to give a make-up lesson for another student, but that is the exception, not the rule. Usually, the time is lost.

Finally, charging tuition reflects the reality that music teachers are not working only when they teach; they are working during nonteaching time by planning lessons, purchasing books and materials, reviewing new method books, and picking out recital repertoire. Charging an annual tuition also covers studio expenses (instrument maintenance, recital hall rentals, replacement of overly used library materials) that are incurred whether a student shows up for his Monday lesson or not.

Factoring in Make-Up Lessons

Students miss lessons for all kinds of reasons you can think of, and some you probably wouldn't. Here's a partial list taken from real life: going to a play date, taking the dog to the vet, hosting an out-of-town aunt, staying home because "it might snow today," attending a birthday party, attending a Halloween party (but not on Halloween), rock-climbing with a friend, going to an orthodontist appointment, going to the sister's orthodontist, getting lost on the way to the lesson when Grandma drove, getting a speeding ticket, forgetting, and (my favorite) "I couldn't find him to bring him to the lesson that day."

And at least four times out of five, the parents will want to know when they can make up the missed lesson.

Teachers have very different ideas about make-ups, so the first thing you'll need to do is decide where you stand on this issue.

Some teachers make up all lessons missed, feeling that students should pay only for lessons they actually get. The problem with this is that your flexibility is too often abused. With a small studio, giving make-ups for all missed lessons might be feasible, although it certainly interferes with personal time and schedules. With a large studio, it simply isn't possible. Some teachers start by trying to be reasonable and make up everything. That might work until they get 20 rescheduling requests in a single week and realize that being reasonable about make-ups has to be a two-way street.

But a policy of no make-ups seems overly harsh to most teachers, who realize that some misses are inevitable. Indeed, we want students to stay home when they are sick. And a strict policy doesn't endear a teacher to parents; when faced with such a strict policy, parents feel coerced into coming, with no recourse for illness or other legitimate reasons to miss a lesson.

What works for some teachers is offering a tuition plan that covers, say, 34 lessons in a school year with 2 make-ups. In other words, your agreement is for 34 scheduled lessons, 2 of which may be rescheduled for any reason. That way, there is some flexibility for unavoidable misses, and you've built the make-ups into the tuition. And two make-ups per year seems adequate for most students under most circumstances. Your studio policy should spell this out clearly, including the information that you will not promise make-ups for more than two missed lessons.

When setting your tuition fees for the year, you have a choice. If you really want to give away the make-up lessons for free, base your annual tuition on 34 lessons multiplied by how much you want to make per lesson. So if you want to make $30 per lesson, your annual tuition will be 30 times $34, or $1,020, and that will buy 34 lessons. Students will be entitled to up to 2 make-ups if they miss any of those 34 lessons. The make-ups are entirely free.

Some teachers, however, feel that they should be compensated for the full 36 weeks (the 34 weeks they have to be available for the regularly scheduled lessons, plus the 2 weeks they have to be available to give the make-ups). In this case, you could set your fee by multiplying 36 lessons by the amount you want to make per lesson. (In the case above, 36 lessons times $30 per lesson is $1,080 per year.)

Basically, what this means is that in the first case, the student is paying $30 per lesson and getting two free make-ups for which the first teacher isn't compensated. In the second case, the student is actually paying a little more. The second teacher has determined that she wants to earn $1,080 for the 36 weeks she must be available for the student, in order to offer the 34 promised lessons, plus give 2 make-ups at the end of the year. $1,080 divided by the 34 scheduled lessons equals about $31.75 per lesson, as compared to the first teacher's $30 per lesson. That small extra amount per lesson compensates the second teacher for the time she has to be available for make-ups. In other words, a slightly higher lesson fee "buys" the student in the second teacher's studio the right to miss two lessons for any reason and have them made up at the end of the year. The first teacher is simply giving the make-ups away for free.

There's no need to go into detail about how you arrived at your price with the parent, and whether you're pricing based on 34 lessons for the year or 36. Here's one way to present your pricing. This example assumes you are using the most popular pricing method: annual tuition, payable in equal monthly installments (discussed in the next section).

Simply say, "Lessons cost $1,080 for the year. That includes 34 half-hour lessons. In addition, I will make up up to two lessons that you have to miss for any reason. We charge by the month, so that works out to nine payments of $120 each month, from September to May. Usually you'll get four lessons per month, but it depends on the calendar. Because of holidays and school vacations, some months might have more or less than four lessons. But by the end of the school year, you will have been scheduled for 34 lessons. I don't charge by the lesson, because your tuition also includes recitals, two make-ups, and studio expenses, but for comparison purposes to other teachers, you can figure that it works out to about $32 a lesson."

Having the two free make-ups makes parents feel better about their obligation to come to lessons, and having them built into your fee will make you feel compensated for your time. It's a little bit of goodwill that goes a long way. And if you price your lessons to reflect the make-ups, it doesn't even cost you anything.

Tuition by the Month, Semester, or Year

The problem with charging an annual tuition is that very few parents are able or willing to write a check for $1,000 or more in September to cover lessons through June. They might worry about what will happen if Sammy breaks his arm, gets onto the swim team, or decides he doesn't like trumpet.

Charging by the month is probably the most common choice music teachers make. Payments are the same every month, which makes remembering to pay easier and helps with monthly budgets.

The only downside is that people are conditioned to think of a month as four weeks, so they expect four lessons. Parents need to understand (and sometimes it takes repeated reminders) that the monthly payments are merely a staggered payment plan—there may be five lessons in January, but only two in December.

Another alternative, which sits halfway between the mammoth annual fee and the monthly checks, is to pay by the semester. This is a nice compromise that avoids the problems of the annual fee (too much up front, too much commitment) or the monthly fee (subject to misinterpretation and often forgotten). But in reality, semester billing is mostly workable for higher-income communities: those checks can still be pretty large, especially if more than one child is taking lessons.

Out of Tune

Note that as nice as it is to have the student's commitment—and check—up front, the teacher takes on some risk in charging by the semester or year. If a student quits, the family is apt to want a refund. No matter what your policy states, it's hard to justify charging for half a year's lessons that the student doesn't take. At the very least, refusing to refund money will earn you a bad reputation among parents in your community. The alternative is unappealing, too—having to write a big refund check. So before accepting a big semester check, be sure there is a firm commitment on both sides.

A final thought about tuition schedules: try to calculate your payment schedule so that you stay ahead of the student. This means that the student is always paid up a little in advance of how many lessons you've given. For example, you might plan your school year to cover 34 scheduled lessons, and two make-ups at the end of the year. In your thinking and your budgeting, you may have set your fees with the assumption that these 36 weeks will stretch over the course of 10 months, September through June, because of school holidays. But you might schedule your payments so that they run from September through May. That way, at the end of the year, you owe the students lessons, not the other way around. If they quit suddenly, at least they won't owe you money (which can be difficult to collect). The only downside to this is that you have to budget for diminished income in June, when you will have to teach some lessons that were paid for in advance.

Fees for Group Lessons

Group lessons are an entirely different matter. In a group, the participants are responsible not only to the teacher, but to each other. So group lessons are almost always paid for in advance, perhaps in one or two installments. Some programs have a trial period of a week or two, during which a child may decide she doesn't want lessons and withdraw with no penalty. After only a week or two, it may be possible for another child to take that spot in the class. But after that, the commitment is for the term of lessons, usually for a school semester.

Fees for group lessons are generally less per student than a private lesson of comparable time would be. The hourly fee to the instructor, however, is usually more, to reflect the fact that planning group lessons and equipping a group studio takes more time and money. Teaching group lessons takes more energy than teaching one on one, as well as more administrative time (for scheduling and billing) and more parent-contact time. A common formula is to charge a student in an hour-long small-group (three to five students) lesson what you would normally charge for a half-hour private lesson.

With more than six students, the rate per student might drop even farther, perhaps to $10 to $15 per hour (if your normal half-hour rate is $20 to $25). If, however, the increased enrollment requires an assistant instructor (perhaps to coach a group of mixed instruments), or if you bring in some adult players to support the student band, you might need to raise the rates a bit. With larger groups, because of the number of students involved, there is some flexibility in pricing, which makes it possible to add a few bells and whistles to the program you are teaching.

Take Note

Asking about competitive and comparable group activities in your community is a good first step in figuring out a fair price for group music lessons. If no one else is doing group music lessons, cast the net a little wider. What does a ballet class cost? An ice skating class? Swimming lessons? The answers are bound to vary widely, but they will give you a starting point.

Other Fees

Music teachers incur expenses beyond the teacher's lesson time. The most common "extra" is the cost of hosting a recital or music parties and jams in your home. Some teachers charge extra for these activities, and some figure the expense when calculating tuition rates. Other common additional fees, which you'll probably want to recoup from the parents, include the cost of attending out-of-studio events, such as participating in state music association adjudications and contests, and going on field trips to concerts.

It's best to list the activities that you are likely to offer in your studio policy (you'll see this in Chapter 7) so that parents have a heads-up about expected additional expenses. If you *require* participation in a recital or in competitions or adjudication programs that charge fees, this needs to be made completely clear at the outset. Some teachers simplify the process—in theory—by signing up their students in bulk, paying registration fees in advance, and then trying to collect from parents. Other teachers require the student families to sign up themselves, which eliminates the problem of forgotten reimbursements but may lead to the problem of forgotten sign-ups.

Some teachers additionally charge registration fees or deposits to hold slots for the next tuition period. Usually, teachers collect these fees at the start of each school year. The registration fee may be used as a contribution to the teacher's sheet music library and teaching supplies fund. Deposits are down payments against tuition; most teachers apply the deposit against the first month's tuition in the fall. Charging a registration fee or a nonrefundable deposit helps avoid the otherwise entirely predictable problem of cancellations from parents who had sworn they were coming back and insisted on you holding the prime after-school spot for them. In music lessons, as in every other facet of life, people take their commitments more seriously when a monetary commitment is involved.

Raising Rates

As a group, music teachers tend to be careless about raising rates. For most of us, it's an unpleasant topic we'd rather avoid. The result is that our paychecks don't keep up with inflation, and we find ourselves falling behind the market rate so far that to get back on track, we'd have to initiate a huge price jump. That, of course, is when most parents start balking. To avoid these kinds of problems, make evaluating your rate a yearly activity. This doesn't mean you necessarily have to raise your rate every year. You should, however, continue to be aware of what the going rate is in your community for teachers with similar levels of training and experience.

Cost of Living and Other Factors

Two factors go into the issue of raising your rates: your own increasing skills and experience, and the general cost of living.

The cost of living is fairly easy to look up. However, don't just rely on the U.S. government numbers, because different areas of the country can experience wildly different fluctuations. Your chamber of commerce likely has statistics for your particular community or region.

Beyond the cost of living, consider whether what you are offering today differs from what you were offering when you set your current rates. Perhaps you started your teaching studio with fees at the lower end of the spectrum. Now you have more experience and perhaps added credentials: some teacher training, workshops with master pedagogues, maybe some additional performance experience. You may have become one of your community's premier teachers, with a full studio, accomplished students, and a good reputation. Giving yourself periodic raises above the inflation index reflects the added experience you now share with your students.

How Much and How Often?

The straightforward answer to the question is this: "as much and as often as you need to in order to keep up with inflation and pay yourself a wage that reflects your increased experience and skills."

Raising rates might be as simple as increasing tuition for half-hour lessons by $5 or $10 a month. Or you might decide to raise rates on only some lessons. Say you've been teaching mostly half-hour students, and you charge based on a $25 half-hour. And let's say you've been charging $35 for 45 minute lessons. If you have a lot of half-hour students moving up to a 45-minute lesson, you could raise the 45-minute rate to $37.50, which will be exactly proportional to what the students were paying when they had half-hour lessons. For you, this represents a raise, because your 30-minute students are taking longer lessons. Also, your 45-minute students from the previous year will be paying the slightly higher new rate as well. The $2.50 raise per week is hardly likely to raise eyebrows among your old students. The next year, you can raise the rate on half-hour lessons.

There's one caveat to all of this: in a bad economy, use your judgment. Music teachers are extremely lucky in bad economies because, unless you live in a one-industry town, you are unlikely to lose all your students at once, as opposed to corporate employees who might be making a huge annual salary but who can be laid off at a moment's notice when their companies are bought or relocated to a country on the other side of the world. If your finances are in okay shape and you don't seem to be losing students, it might be wise to count your blessings and hang tight in a slow economy.

If you don't feel that you can raise your rates, you can change your scheduling. For example, if your tuition had included 36 private lessons per school year you might change what that tuition covers to include, say, 34 lessons. This solution may meet the parents' needs not to lay out any more money, while meeting your need to earn a bit more per hour.

When and How to Announce a Rate Increase

The best time to announce that you are raising your rates is at the end of the school year, when you are sending out flyers for re-enrollment for the fall. The re-enrollment forms should have the new rates on them: be sure that you point this out to parents, because some of them will miss it.

There is no need to make excuses for raising your rates. Everyone knows that fees go up over time. The only reason you would need to offer an explanation is if you were raising your rates by a large amount. In that case, you might explain the reasons. Perhaps you haven't raised prices in five years. Perhaps you've been below the market rate for a while but feel that your experience and qualifications are in line with those of other teachers in your community, so your rates should be, too. Or perhaps you have recently improved your credentials—you've finished a Master's degree in music education, made a critically acclaimed CD, gotten your kids into Juilliard, or received certification from a prestigious society of music educators.

Do make sure that parents confirm that they understand the new rates, and send an e-mail reminder before the start of the term, when you confirm the fall schedules.

The Least You Need to Know

- ◆ Base your lesson rate on the going rate, your experience, and your expenses.
- ◆ Charging tuition by the month, semester, or year helps control bookkeeping and avoids problems caused by students missing lessons and forgetting checks.

◆ Factoring some make-up lessons into your fee can help avoid problems, resentments, and misunderstandings for both teacher and students.

◆ For group lessons, students pay less per hour, but teachers earn more per hour than for private lessons.

◆ Evaluate lesson rates once each year in terms of the community's going rate, the cost of living, and your own increasing skills and experience.

Chapter 6

Business and Legal Issues and Expenses

In This Chapter

- The basics of accounting for a music teaching business
- Business expenses
- Managing your sheet music teaching library
- What music teachers need to know about copyright law and fair use
- Effective and efficient billing

Fortunately, business and legal issues are a minor part of the private music teacher's job. Most of us would rather teach and play music than mess around with legal forms, bookkeeping software, and spreadsheets. But we can't avoid them entirely. Good recordkeeping for tax purposes is essential. Home business insurance is another issue you'll need to look into. In this chapter, we look at some of the regular, predictable expenses you'll need to track, as well as a few less common—but equally important—tax, legal, and business issues you might encounter.

The Tax Man Cometh

As a home business owner, you constantly incur business-related expenses, sometimes whether you realize it or not. If you are just starting out, put "visit the accountant" on your list of things to do, because you need someone to walk you through what is and is not deductible. There also may be tax repercussions for some purchase decisions, and you may need advice on expense recordkeeping as well. Although many experienced teachers successfully use computer software, such as TurboTax, to do their own taxes, others appreciate having an experienced accountant who can advise them on "red flag" audit issues and at least get them started on the right path.

You'll also need help on retirement planning. Your accountant can advise you on what kinds of tax advantages retirement savings plans, such as IRAs, Roth IRAs, and SEPs (simplified employee pension plans), are best for your situation.

The Importance of Keeping Track

For a music teacher, the most important accounting challenge is keeping up-to-date records. Checks sometimes seem to come in fistfuls (not that anyone would complain about that). Expenses range from major instrument purchases to scores of small cash amounts for music books, picks, and guitar strings—these are easy to overlook, but they add up over time.

Some teachers use software such as QuickBooks or Quicken, which are accounting and budget-tracking programs that sort payments and expenses into neat categories, produce invoices, and keep track of expenses and income, all in their correct categories. (Of course, this presumes that you actually enter the information into the computer; if you leave records and payments sitting in a pile on your desk, there isn't much that *any* computer program can do for you.)

Other teachers keep their accounting short and simple, using basic spreadsheets such as Excel or even a handwritten (gasp!) ledger. At the very least, you need to record all student payments, perhaps checking them off against each student's name. On the expenses side of the ledger book, you need to sort and tally expense receipts. You should also keep a tax diary that lists any studio-related travel (to the music store, the recital venues, the concert halls) and expenses (mileage, parking, tolls, and so on). This can help prove that you were where you said you were, buying what you said you bought, and doing what you said you were doing, in case of an audit. A student calendar and attendance sheet should also be part of your records.

Take Note _____

Barter is an increasingly popular way to trade services without cash changing hands. An electrician parent of a student may fix your wiring while you teach his kid; someone who owns a lawn service might cut your grass. You can even barter with a teenage student directly: you teach her for an hour, and she watches your kids for the rest of the afternoon while you teach others. Be sure that both parties feel their work is fairly valued, and talk to your accountant about any bartering that must be declared as income on your taxes.

If you do your own accounting, you should know that many accountants encourage clients not only to keep cash register receipts from stores, but actually to have some sort of proof of what specifically was purchased. A cash register receipt from a music store may be acceptable to the IRS, but sometimes purchases aren't so clear-cut. Say, for example, you must purchase distilled water for your instrument's climate control system. Most accountants would prefer that you have a receipt that actually says "distilled water" on it instead of a simple register tape with a list of numbers that could refer to anything. For small, easily explainable amounts, the occasional register tape is probably okay, but do write down exactly what you bought. For larger purchases or anything unusual, you should collect whatever proof is possible to collect (itemized receipts, for instance) of what you bought, and make note of what its business use is.

Filing Your Taxes

As a self-employed business owner, you are responsible for filing your taxes with the IRS, including a Schedule C, which itemizes your business expenses.

You are also responsible for the entire burden of your Social Security and Medicare tax payments. This means that you pay more than traditionally employed people pay because their employers pony up for a portion of these taxes.

In addition to yearly tax returns, self-employed people must fill out quarterly estimated tax returns and make estimated tax prepayments. Don't ignore this, because if you don't prepay enough of your annual tax according to the schedule, you'll get hit with penalties. The IRS has strict rules about when these reports must be filed and how much you need to pay. You can either base your payments on current earnings or pay a percentage of your previous year's tax. Doing the latter is safer because if you miscalculate, you won't have to pay penalties. Estimated taxes can be quite complicated, especially if your income and expenses fluctuate a great deal. In this case, you should consult an accountant.

Out of Tune _____

Estimated taxes are due in June, September, January, and the usual "tax day" in April. If you owe money at tax time, having to write checks for your tax bill, your estimated taxes, your IRAs, and your accountant fees can put a huge hole in your budget just two months before the summer income dip begins. To avoid this financial black hole, be sure your estimated tax payments are adequate, and try to fund your IRA throughout the year instead of waiting until tax time.

In addition to state and federal taxes, you may be subject to local taxes, which can include local income taxes, taxes on business property, taxes on any inventory you have for sale to students, and sales tax on anything you sell at a profit. Local laws vary widely, which is one good reason to use an accountant in your community.

The Costs of Doing Business

Once the major studio expenses have been accounted for—instruments, PA equipment, and recording equipment—the typical music teacher's expenses tend to be minimal but ongoing. Books and sheet music can eat up a large part of your budget, along with recordings. However, all of these costs are deductible.

Studio and Office

Space in your home that is exclusively used for business purposes is tax deductible, which means that you can deduct a portion of your rent or mortgage payment, heat, electricity, and any other expenses, usually based on square footage. Home office deductions have at different points in time been "red flags" for audits, so be sure to discuss this issue with an accountant. Your home office space includes your studio teaching space, as well as the space used for your desk and computer. Deductible home office expenses can also include the cost of purchasing and maintaining your computer, business telephone, printer, photocopy machine, and any electronic recording or listening equipment you use in your studio. However, if business equipment is also used by your family for other purposes (such as a computer being used for the kids' homework), it may only be partially deductible, although any specialized music teaching software will obviously be deductible. Sorting these issues out is a good reason to consult with an accountant.

You might also be able to deduct a portion of housekeeping expenses if you have your studio cleaned or pay someone to plow any parking spots that are used exclusively by students.

Instruments, Repair, and Maintenance

Instrument repair and maintenance is an ongoing responsibility. Depending on your instrument, maintenance may cost very little or may cost a few hundred dollars a year. Don't forget climate-control expenses such as humidifiers, dehumidifiers, or even air-conditioning for high-end wooden instruments such as pianos and string instruments, including violin-family string instruments and guitars.

The purchase of new instruments used in your business is also deductible, as are any ancillary instruments such as drums, percussion instruments, auto-harps, or keyboards.

Special Events

The expenses associated with any music-related events you host for your students, whether in your studio or elsewhere, are deducible. These include taking your students out to play at an open mike, renting a coffeehouse to use as a performance space, renting a recital hall or a meeting room, holding a music party at your home, renting PA equipment to perform at a community function, or serving meals for group workshops you may offer.

A partial list of other expenses might include the cost of going to concerts, competitions, adjudications, and student performances, as well as the cost of recording student recitals and performances. (We talked in Chapter 5 about whether you absorb any or all of these expenses or whether you collect these kinds of fees from your student families.)

Insurance

Most small home businesses such as a music teaching studio are insured via a rider to the homeowner's policy. The cost of the business rider is tax deductible as a business expense. Your business rider should provide coverage for the following issues:

◆ Damage caused by students or their families to the parts of your home used for business, during the course of business

◆ Liability coverage, in case a student or family member is injured while in your home for a lesson

◆ Theft and accidental damage coverage for your business property, including electronic equipment, office equipment, and instruments

◆ Accidents, damage, or theft to any outbuildings that are used for business purposes (for instance, if your studio is in a separate building on your property)

Be sure you understand the fine print of your policy. Make a specific written list of your concerns and issues to give to your insurance agent, to be certain that you really are covered for the Steinway and the Stradivarius.

Legal Fees

Legal fees are not an ongoing or particularly significant concern for most music teachers. The legal issues music teachers confront are few and far between, and quite honestly, not many music teachers are willing to go to court to collect an overdue lesson fee. However, here are a few scenarios in which you might need to consult a lawyer.

◆ Help in dealing with issues pertaining to your right to conduct your business in your home. This might include conflicts with neighbors or with your local zoning authority.

◆ Help in writing a studio policy, particularly if you want it to be enforceable by law, or if you have had complaints from parents.

◆ Questions and assistance regarding copyright clearance, which can affect public performances, CD recordings, and the use of printed sheet music.

◆ Help in writing or reviewing contracts if you work with other teachers, are hired by other teachers, or hire other teachers yourself.

◆ Representation in a lawsuit arising from a student or student family because of an accident or injury that occurred on your property.

If you have a lawyer you use for real estate transactions, estate planning and wills, or other matters, it might be worth a call to discuss your new business. That way, if the need arises, your lawyer is already in the loop about what you are doing.

Managing Your Music Library

Music teachers use teaching materials from a wide range of sources, including all the books and materials they ever used when they were learning or performing. Your music library contains all your personal music, your notes, your books about music and composers, your CDs, old records (if you still have them), and even collections of playbills from performances you've given or attended. It also contains all your teaching materials: method books, repertoire books, etudes, "fake books," music theory books, manuscript notepaper, and orchestra and chamber music scores.

It's a business expense, of course, but it is more than that: your music library is a repository that is used both in your own development as a musician and in your work as a music teacher.

Lending Music to Students

Sometimes it is necessary to lend music to students. Most teachers keep on hand a large selection of books and teaching materials with different repertoire selections. But often you'll have only one copy of something on hand, and if you're working on, say, jazz chords and your student loves a particular song that you have in your library, you might want to lend him the book instead of making him wait to order one.

Similarly, a student might benefit from doing a review exercise, reading a chapter, or working on a theory drill, and you might not feel that he needs the entire book, so you lend him yours. Lending books is a dangerous habit if you care about your library. Often books don't get returned, and those that do are sometimes the worse for wear.

Some teachers have a statement in their policy about loaned materials having to be returned in good condition or the student will be asked to pay for them. But quite honestly, with books and students going in and out the door, many teachers simply lose track. Usually, it's only a matter of small amounts of money, but those small amounts add up. And once in a while, you lose a book that isn't replaceable because it's out of print.

Take Note

Buy a stack of big gaudy book stickers that say "This book belongs to … " and put the sticker on the front cover (not the inside) of any sheet music you lend. Write your name and/or your studio's name in big magic marker letters and add "PLEASE RETURN!" People don't keep borrowed books out of meanness; usually they just forget. Make it easy for them to remember.

The best advice is to take the time to note all books and pieces of sheet music that leave your studio, and be sure to let parents know about loaned materials as well. Keep a designated notebook in your teaching area so that you can record the music being loaned, the borrowing student's name, and the date right when the transaction occurs. Don't wait until after the lesson; you'll forget. When a piece of music comes back in, just cross out that line item in the notebook.

Selling Music to Students

Some teachers sell music to students. Selling sheet music to students can be another (very small) income stream if you set up your business as a small retail shop and sell supplies such as CDs, guitar strings, and sheet music. Most teachers find that any profits from the sales aren't worth the headache of the paperwork and tax implications.

Teachers do, however, usually receive a discount when they purchase music from retail stores and from online music publishers and distributors. The standard discount is 10 percent, but many publishers and distributors have seasonal sales and incentive programs for teachers. Most teachers simply pass the discounts on to their students. A few charge students the retail cost of the book, plus taxes and shipping, and thus make a few pennies off the discount, which they figure contributes to the time spent hunting down music. Note, however, that if you are selling sheet music at a profit to students, this income is taxable. Talk to your accountant.

The Copyright Law and Fair Use

Unfortunately, music is not always published in a way that teachers can use. Often only one or two songs in an entire book may be of use to a teacher on a regular basis. In such cases, teachers may want to photocopy songs for student use.

The U.S. Copyright Act of 1976 and its "fair use" provisions are complicated, so it's no wonder music teachers either don't always understand it or agree on how to follow it. Basically, the fair use provision says that it is legal to use certain amounts of copyrighted material for certain purposes. Unfortunately, the law is terribly vague about what those amounts and purposes are. Some photocopying for educational use, is acceptable under the law; limited photocopying for educational use is one of the few specifics the law includes.

You would be in violation of copyright law if you photocopied large numbers of songs from different sources, bound them all together, and sold them to students for a profit. However, photocopying a single song from a collection is not an ethical violation. If you want Johnny to play "Here Comes the Sun," it's unreasonable to ask his mom to buy the entire Beatles book. However, if "Here Comes the Sun" is available in the same arrangement as a single folio, then it's unethical (and illegal) to be making multiple copies of it at home and giving it out to students.

It's unlikely that the copyright police are going to come banging at your door anytime soon, but there's another important reason to obey the law. You'll be setting an example. In the current Internet environment, people completely ignore the idea of intellectual property. Everything is free for the taking. (And in fact, there are plenty of free music sites on the Internet for some of the classics, although the editing tends to be abysmal. Use at your own musical risk.) Music teachers know that the composers who write our educational materials need, deserve, and have a legal right to payment for their work. By having students purchase music when it is available, teachers are passing on a respect for intellectual property and supporting the composers and editors whose work they use.

Take Note _____

The U.S. Copyright Act includes a provision for fair use, meaning that you can copy part of a work given certain conditions, which include the following:

◆ The purpose and character of the use. For example, is it commercial or educational?

◆ The nature of the work. Is it a simple list, straight facts, a long poem, or an opera?

◆ The amount and substantiality of the portion used. How much of the work are you copying, and how important is the copied material to the work?

◆ The effect on the potential market for or value of the work. Will your use of the work hurt the monetary value of the work to the rightful owner?

The National Association for Music Education (MENC) has an extensive section on its website about how these provisions, and copyright law in general, apply to musicians and educators. Follow the Resources link at www.menc.org.

Another reason not to photocopy is a practical one—the pages fall apart. For any music that is going to end up in a student's repertoire, a photocopied copy is simply not good enough.

Billing

Teachers handle billing in a variety of ways, from simply asking parents to remember to bring checks when due (not always effective), to sending formal invoices and enforcing late-payment fees. You'll want to get into a routine regarding billing; don't leave it to chance. Most parents don't mind a monthly reminder, whether verbal or by invoice or e-mail.

Getting Paid on Time

Several effective ways that help you ensure that you are paid on time are:

◆ Collect post-dated checks for the entire year when the student signs on for lessons. Then deposit them on the first of each month.

◆ Send monthly e-mail reminders and/or invoices. This works in communities where *most* people have and use the Internet.

◆ Send invoices by postal mail, or hand-deliver them. Giving out invoices by hand works only if you actually see the parents. Some parents transport their kids; some have nannies or babysitters do the job. Do not deliver invoices to anyone other than the person responsible for paying the bill unless you are instructed or cleared to do so by the parent.

As soon as you receive a check, check it off in your accounting ledger. With enough students, and enough checks, you'll soon find it hard to remember from one month to the next who has paid and who hasn't. And most important, record the receipt of any cash payments at once. Have a place—a box or envelope—right near your teaching space in your studio where you put cash and checks. Don't put them on the piano or stick them in your pocket. Then at the end of the day, or every couple days, you can check your accounting ledger against the "stack" of checks and cash to make sure everything is in order.

For parents who are routinely late, a pleasant and friendly separate e-mail reminder may be in order—especially if they missed a payment.

Wise Words

I write a monthly newsletter that goes to students the last week of the month, and I put a reminder on there that lesson fees are due the first week of the month. The biggest problem is when spring break or a major holiday occurs during the first week of the month. The second week comes, and parents forget that they haven't paid. By charging the same tuition every month and not sending bills for different amounts, my paperwork has been greatly simplified.

—Karen Monroe, music teacher, Chehalis, Washington

Collecting for Incidental Expenses

Billing also needs to include collecting money for any incidental and additional expenses, such as sheet music you purchase for the student and fees for various out-of-studio events. If you are tacking these on to students' monthly bills, be sure you send a note specifying the amount; otherwise, some parents will show up with their checks already written for the usual amount.

To keep up with the sheet music, be sure to tell parents when you give Jenny a new book, and ask them to bring $13.50 next time to cover the cost. Of course, it's possible that next week Jenny might miss her lesson, be brought by the babysitter, or be dropped off by Dad and picked up by Mom, neither of whom has a checkbook. If chasing down $13.50 checks isn't your idea of what you should be doing as a music teacher, try these strategies (which work for other incidental payments, as well):

- ◆ When you give a new book to a student, jot down the name of the book and the price in the student's assignment book; then check it off when the student's parent pays for it.

- ◆ Include a handwritten invoice with every book. Keep track of invoices sent and paid on a spreadsheet.

- ◆ If you invoice monthly, add the cost of the book to the next month's invoice. Be sure to tell the parents in person as well, since half of them won't read your e-mail invoice.

Checks, Cash, Credit Cards, Internet Payments

These days, fees for music lessons seem to be just over that magic line of what people are willing to pay for with cash versus a check or credit card. A few parents pay in cash; when they do, it's not uncommon to be asked for a "cash discount," the assumption being that you won't report the amounts to the IRS. Remember that all income—whether it comes to you as cash, check, or credit card payment—is taxable and must be reported. If word gets around that you are offering discounts for cash, you could find yourself in tax trouble. Beyond that, it's perfectly fine to accept cash payments, as long as you keep records of them. It's a good idea to give out receipts for cash payments: one copy for you and one for the student.

Personal checks are by far the most common mode of payment for music teachers. Checks can be photocopied, or you can record the numbers in a payment log or student record book. Or simply keep the record of your bank deposits in your business account. Ask your accountant for recordkeeping suggestions.

In addition, some more tech-savvy parents use electronic bill-paying services to have checks sent to you periodically. They might even want to pay by wire transfer or PayPal. Before accepting any such payments, be sure you understand whether there are any fees involved. For instance, PayPal is free for personal transactions, but it charges a percentage for accepting money for the sale of goods and services. Some teachers take credit cards, which also involves fees. The convenience may make up for the fee, or it may not. You'll have to be the judge.

Out of Tune

Many parents resent being asked to pay extra fees to cover the cost of electronic or credit card transactions, especially if you are the one who initiates the suggestion. If you plan to require that payments be made via PayPal or credit card, and if there are fees in the service you use, you might want to build the fees into your tuition when you calculate your rates.

Late Fees and Bounced Checks

Some teachers are either willing or able to let "forgotten" payments slide a week or two, but doing so puts you at a disadvantage. First of all, it complicates your bookkeeping and puts an edge on your relationship with the student family. Also, if the student who is behind on payments suddenly stops taking lessons, you may be left with money owed to you that is all the more difficult to collect.

Not all teachers are comfortable with late fees, but if you write them into your studio policy, it's a tool you can wield if necessary. Perhaps because of the deeply personal nature of the music teacher relationship, many teachers simply don't think it feels right to go after a student family with late fees. If you can't feel good about a strategy, you shouldn't use it—but remember that it is an option. Many chronic late-payers can simply be gently embarrassed into better behavior by being told, "Look, I don't charge a late fee because I really value my relationships with my student families and I don't want to be that kind of teacher. But I need for you to try to remember to pay on time. It's just not fair for me to have to keep asking."

Similarly, you need a policy for bounced checks. Always have a small cushion in your business bank account. That way, you won't get into the domino-effect problem of bouncing checks because one of your student checks bounced. (You might also talk to your bank about overdraft protection.) The bounced check fee you charge a student should cover the time, hassle, and fees occasioned by a bounced check.

As a last resort, you might need to seek legal or bill-collection assistance for overdue bills. Again, the vast majority of teachers will look for other ways to resolve the issue of unpaid bills without resorting to courts or bill collectors. For one thing, this is a highly preventable problem. There is absolutely no reason to let unpaid tuition build to the point that it is worthwhile to call in a bill collector. Plus, being involved in an ugly conflict like this can damage a reputation, especially in a small community. Also, bill collectors take a portion of the money due. As a practical matter, it is far better to avoid the problem entirely by not continuing to teach a student whose tuition is not up-to-date.

The Least You Need to Know

- As a home business owner, your tax situation may be more complicated than you are used to; professional advice from an accountant can help.

- Every penny you spend on music education–related items is a tax deduction, but you have to keep accurate and detailed records.

- The fair use provision of the U.S. Copyright Act permits music teachers to photocopy some learning materials, but it prohibits copying of complete works or reselling them at a profit.

- Collect payment by check, cash, credit card, electronic transfer, or PayPal, but be sure you are aware of any fees, and keep good records of all payments.

7

Studio Policies

In This Chapter

- ◆ The purpose of a studio policy
- ◆ Writing a studio policy that sets the right tone for your studio and your relationship with students and parents
- ◆ The responsibilities of teachers, students, and parents
- ◆ Using a studio policy and communicating with parents to prevent misunderstandings

A studio policy is, quite simply, a document you write that sets forth the relationship you expect among your students, the parents, and you.

You may write a studio policy as a formal, legally binding contract, or you may present it as a simple understanding among friends. You may write a single page that sketches the basics of payment, schedules, and student absences, or you may write a tome covering every eventuality that ever has happened or might possibly happen in the future. You might wield your policy every time a student walks in late or forgets his books, or you might never refer to it. The important thing is that you have a policy that covers the mutual responsibility among teachers, students, and parents.

The Purpose of a Studio Policy

A studio policy is a business document that establishes an agreement about how the relationship among student, parent, and teacher is going to work. It is also an educational document that explains that the prerequisites for learning music include regular attendance and practice. It sets out mutual expectations and responsibilities. A studio policy sets the tone of the relationship so that lessons get off to a good start, with everyone knowing what is expected. You also can refer to it if things start going off track.

Why Do I Need a Studio Policy?

If you have only a handful of students, don't depend on your teaching income, have all the time in the world to reschedule lessons, and don't much care whether you get paid, you may not need a studio policy. For the rest of us, it's one of the most important studio-management tools ever invented.

A teacher-student-parent relationship is a long-term commitment, and over time, children's lives, activities, and priorities change. A student who starts out coming to every lesson may start missing lessons because of basketball or chronic illness. A parent who used to pay on time might start getting careless and forgetting to bring a check. A studio policy sets forth your policies on the issues you are most concerned about. The policy communicates your expectations to the parent. And having parents sign a copy of the policy indicates their understanding and implies their commitment to abide by the policy.

Out of Tune

Don't be too formal and legalistic in your studio policy. You may cover every single thing in your studio policy that could ever possibly happen, but if the policy sounds too picky and punitive, you will alienate your clients.

Whether you consider yourself a "by the book" type of teacher or prefer to be a bit more flexible, having a studio policy simply means that if there is a misunderstanding or a disagreement about such issues as payment due dates, student make-up lessons, or late fees, you have a written record of your agreement with the parent. It is a tremendously effective tool. Even if you never use it, it acts as a safety net for your business. When experienced private music teachers are asked for advice by beginning teachers, the studio policy is invariably one of the top two or three points they mention.

The majority of your studio families will be lovely people who are happy to work with you and follow reasonable procedures that have been explained to them. But there are always a few who demand extra make-ups, miss more lessons than everyone else, and constantly ask about rescheduling. Not surprisingly, these also tend to be the very families whose children never quite find time to practice and who miss recitals in favor of a baseball game. Studio policies can be of enormous help to teachers who are reluctant to engage in protracted arguments or business negotiations with parents.

Most important, a studio policy sets the tone of the relationship. A studio policy puts forth the idea that music lessons are a long-term commitment that requires mutual responsibilities, and that your studio is an educational business, with both educational and business policies that must be respected.

Wise Words

I wish I had known to have a studio policy and enforce it when I first started to teach. When I started demanding that people treat me as a professional, I had a much higher caliber of students. In your mind, add 'NDM' to the end of your name—standing for 'not a doormat.' When I started presenting myself as a professional teacher, and not just the lady at church or in the neighborhood who teaches piano, my studio got better, my teaching got better, and I am now a much happier piano teacher.
—D'Net Layton, music teacher, Mesa, Arizona

Because a studio policy summarizes your business expectations, it is worth consider-ing it in detail. You can change and update it as time goes on, but most experienced teachers report that it is better to have a strong studio policy to begin with than to make changes as you go along. Changes will, of course, need to be made as your studio grows and your family situation changes. But people adhere best to a simply stated policy that is consistent from one year to the next. As much as possible, start out on the right foot.

Responsibilities: Student to Teacher

Music lessons generally involve a triangle of responsibility: the student, the teacher, and the parent. Of the three, the student's job is the most important. Interestingly, not many studio policies involve the student, but including the student is a great way to use the policy as an educational tool and start the relationship on the right foot.

Children can certainly take on responsibility, as long as they understand what is expected. The sooner students feel accountable for practice and attitude, which is their part of the triangle, the better their progress will be.

Devote a whole page of the studio policy to the student. The typeface can be big and friendly; you might even decorate the page with clip-art pictures of notes and smiley faces and other kid-friendly graphics. (Of course, you wouldn't give such a page to a teenager; if you have students of varying ages, you should have a couple different variations of the student "contract.") This page describes the student's responsibility. Students can even sign the page, after having it explained, so that they understand that by taking music lessons, they are agreeing to do certain jobs.

The "student responsibility" part of the policy might include some combination of the following, depending on the teacher's approach and the age of the student:

- I agree to practice at least (four/five/six) days a week for (10 minutes/20 minutes/30 minutes).

- I promise to look at my homework book so I don't forget anything.

- I agree to practice how my teacher tells me to, including counting out loud, using the metronome, naming notes, or tapping rhythms.

- I promise to write down how many minutes I practice every day in my homework book.

- I will ask my mom or dad to sign my homework book every week.

- I agree to do all the written homework.

- I will remember my books for my music lessons.

- I promise to ask my teacher if I don't understand something.

Many young children take their responsibilities seriously if the jobs are carefully explained. You may need to go over the student jobs each week, pulling out the "contract" and asking the student if he or she did each job. This establishes a sense of habit and routine, which are so key to musical progress.

Responsibilities: Teacher to Student

The studio policy also sets forth what you provide as a teacher. At a minimum, the policy should cover the number of lessons you will be giving and the schedule. If you have any scheduling oddities (such as that you always take two weeks off in February, or you never teach the week of Thanksgiving), that information should be included as well. The policy should also include a statement about your responsibility to make up lessons you miss.

If you provide additional services such as recitals or group performance classes, those should also be covered. If you are willing to help with instrument evaluation and purchase, or if you purchase supplies such as sheet music, metronomes, tuners, or other equipment for resale to students, note that as well.

Responsibilities: The Parent

The business responsibilities of the parent include bringing the child to lessons on time, attending lessons regularly, informing teachers of anticipated absences, paying for lessons, and being sure that the child has an adequate instrument to practice on. (These business issues are discussed later in this chapter.)

Beyond business, however, the parent has a responsibility to support the student's learning by encouraging a regular practice schedule and helping to monitor whether the student is meeting his or her obligations. But it is difficult to legislate this via a studio policy; it is more a matter of communication and ongoing parent education. This is the educational part of the studio policy.

Parents have very different relationships with their children, as well as different abilities to help. Some parents would like to help but know nothing about music (and declare themselves unable to learn). Others may play an instrument and can help at home. But sometimes children don't accept help from a parent, insisting that they can "do it themselves." And sometimes, unfortunately, what is intended as "help" from a possibly overbearing parent has exactly the opposite effect.

As a teacher, you can do little to affect what goes on when the child and parent leave the lesson. However, most parents find some guidelines useful to help them become partners in their child's learning. Some teachers include such suggestions as part of their policy, or perhaps as an addendum to the policy. Consider including a page of suggestions on the following topics as an addendum to your policy:

- Practice expectations for each age and level
- What to listen for when a child practices
- The importance of a regular schedule and a regular practice time

◆ The difference between noodling around and concentrated practice—and the benefits of each

◆ How to encourage a child (ask for performances, ask to hear lesson songs, ask to hear a favorite song or old songs)

Contents of a Studio Policy

Teachers differ widely on the tone of their policies. A policy is not a substitute for a mutually respectful personal relationship. In general, keeping it as simple as possible is probably the best way to start.

No matter how long or short, formal or informal, your studio policy needs to cover some fundamentals. You can put the elements in any order you like, but be sure to include the following subjects:

◆ Fees and payment schedule, late fees, and payment options

◆ Refunds and make-up policies

◆ Early termination

◆ Weather

◆ Student illness

◆ Teacher absence

◆ The yearly calendar

◆ Summer lessons

◆ Purchase of books and materials

◆ Communication

◆ Other considerations

◆ Studio policies for group lessons

Fees and Payment Schedule, Late Fees, Payment Options

How much do lessons cost? Your policy should include your pricing schedule for the various lesson lengths you offer. If you charge by the month, give your monthly charge; if you charge by the semester, give the semester fees. You needn't go into your whole rationale for your rates, but do give parents an understandable breakdown.

Sample Studio Policy Language: Tuition

The monthly tuition is calculated by dividing the yearly tuition into nine equal payments, to make bookkeeping easier for all of us. Monthly tuition is due at the first lesson of the month and is always the same amount, regardless of whether there are two, three, four, or five lessons in that month. You will be scheduled for your 34 lessons during the course of the school year, and you may receive up to 2 make-ups for missed lessons at the end of the school year. For students who start in the middle of the month or school year, prices and the number of make-ups are prorated.

Refunds and Make-Up Policies

Refunds and make-ups are two different things. Refunds are a return of money paid—in this case, a refund would go from the teacher to the student family. Make-ups are rescheduled lessons that take place because a student missed scheduled lessons.

Sample Studio Policy Language: Refunds

Refunds cannot be given for missed lessons, even if you give notice that you will be absent. The entire monthly tuition is due in full on the first lesson of every month regardless of any lessons you expect to miss.

Many teachers have found that the problem with make-ups is that parents don't understand the issue from the teacher's point of view. Therefore, some teachers take the opportunity in their studio policy to explain the issue briefly.

Sample Studio Policy Language: Explaining the Make-Up Policy

Please understand that while you may have a perfectly good reason to miss a lesson—anything from school events to family emergencies—I cannot absorb all of the changes in all of my students' plans, nor is it fair for me to have to decide what is a "good" reason and what is not. The time slot that you have chosen for lessons is yours, and no one else's. It has been reserved for your use throughout the school year, whether you show up for your lesson or not. Very simply, I cannot provide the service of teaching music if students do not show up for and pay for their weekly scheduled lessons.

The studio policy should spell out the make-up policy in detail and, in the initial meeting with the parent (described in Chapter 10), make sure it is understood. Most parents just assume they will get make-ups for any lessons they miss, so part of your job is to educate them. Whether you give no make-ups or unlimited make-ups, you have to come up with a make-up policy you can explain and feel good about.

Sample Studio Policy Language: Make-Up Policy

Please call or e-mail to tell me if you must miss a lesson. Sometimes it is possible to reschedule, and I am happy to fit you in if I can. However, please understand that due to the limited number of lesson times available in my full studio, I cannot make up every lesson that every student misses.

I offer every student up to two free make-ups at the end of the year. Please understand that this means that I will be giving as many as 50 hours of make-up lessons for which I charge no extra tuition. Therefore, no student will be offered more than two make-ups. To ensure that you get all your lessons, I suggest that you save your two make-ups for unavoidable absences due to illness or weather.

Early Termination

Early termination means that the student decides to stop lessons before the end of the agreed-upon term. Some teachers have policies that ask for a month's notice if the student decides to terminate lessons midyear. Some policies additionally note that a student who terminates lessons before the end of the school year loses any make-up lessons to which he may have been entitled.

Sample Studio Policy Language: Early Termination

If a student decides to terminate lessons during the school year, I ask for one month's notice. Make-ups will not be given to students who stop lessons before the end of the school year.

Despite what's in your studio policy, the fact is that students do quit, and sometimes they quit suddenly. Sometimes the reasons are unavoidable—there's a family health emergency, the family is moving, a parent loses a job. And sometimes the reasons are more discretionary—the student is bored or wants to be in the Christmas play.

Whatever the reasons, early termination can create a problem for teachers. Students sign up for music lessons in droves at the beginning of the school year and after New Year's. They do not typically start in mid-May or early December. So if you have a full studio and have been turning students away, it can cause real economic hardship if a handful of students decide that they would rather play softball.

If you have a long relationship and good communication with a student family, chances are, they will adhere to a policy that asks for notice. But the practical truth of the matter is that once a student has decided to quit lessons, they're pretty much done. You have a choice. If you've put a required termination notice in your policy, you can try to hold them to it, insisting that they take (or at least pay for) those last four lessons. Among other things, it gives you a chance to tie up loose ends and end the lessons on a positive note. Or you can just accept that every student ultimately terminates lessons and be glad that they didn't all do it on the same day.

Occasionally, a parent who plans to continue lessons in the following school year will suddenly decide to terminate lessons in the spring. This is certainly understandable; by April or May, people are cranky from the winter, spring sports are starting, the school year is winding down, and music lessons are just one more thing on an always-too-full to-do list.

But for the teacher, this is unworkable. If parents have agreed to take lessons for the school year, it's not fair for them to bail out a couple months early, when it's unlikely that the teacher can fill their slot. Usually, a teacher can explain that this doesn't work for a whole range of reasons, not the least of which is that if the child takes off from May to September, by September, the backward slide will likely be precipitous. You can also point to your studio policy if it requires a month's notice, or if it says that students who terminate early will forfeit any make-ups. Finally, you can also refuse to accept back any students in the fall who terminated early the previous year.

Note: If you have figured your payment schedule so that you are always at least a few lessons ahead (we talked about this in Chapter 5), and if your studio policy states that your fees are clearly nonrefundable, at least you will have been paid for all lessons given, and you may even have been paid for some farther in advance.

Fortunately, these incidents are few and far between. If you've built a "flake-out" factor into your budget, you should be able to ride these situations out.

Weather

Lessons must sometimes be cancelled because of weather, and your studio policy needs to have a section dealing with this issue. Clearly, it's not fair to charge students for a lesson they can't possibly get to during a blizzard.

Closing when schools close doesn't always solve the problem; schools close because of morning conditions, and most music lessons take place in the latter part of the afternoon, by which time roads may be perfectly clear. Sometimes schools even close because of a bad weather *report*. So you'll have to be the judge of when it's reasonable to expect people to come and when it isn't. Clearly, you don't want to be subjecting student families to danger on icy roads.

Sample Policy Language: Weather

Please call if you must cancel due to bad weather! I do not automatically close when schools close. If the weather causes you or me to cancel, I will try to reschedule your lesson, or I might need to use the year-end make-ups to make up those lessons.

One way to handle weather-related make-ups is this: if more than 50 percent of your students are able to come to lessons, the ones who miss can use one of their end-of-year make-ups for the lost lesson. If it is completely unreasonable to think that anyone could go anywhere in the middle of a 20-inch blizzard, then you make up the lost lessons as extras in a couple of group performance lessons or a foul-weather music party.

Student Illness

Many teachers differentiate between absences caused by conflicts of scheduling and absences caused by illness. Student illnesses are, first of all, something completely beyond the student's control, so some teachers feel that they fall into a different category than missing lessons to go to the homecoming pep rally.

Second, students can't learn well when they have headaches and sniffles and scratchy throats. Insisting on lessons can be counterproductive.

And third, children's illnesses can be highly contagious. It's neither good business nor good education to encourage sick children to come to a music lesson where they can easily spread their illness to other students, not to mention to you—*and* your family members. Most parents will appreciate your putting the welfare of all the children first by encouraging sick children to stay home.

But what happens during flu season, when you get a rash of cancellations? Even if you want to make up all the missed lessons, you may not be able to. A teacher who has extra room in her lesson schedule might give priority in making up lessons to a student who had to miss because of illness, or might, if the time is available, tack on a few minutes to a subsequent lesson to make up for the lost time.

Sample Studio Language: Student Illness

Please help us keep our studio healthy! Sick children should not come to lessons. A sick child can't concentrate well, and I'd like to avoid exposing other students (and my family and me) to contagious illnesses. In addition, I will try to make up lessons missed due to illness when possible. If that isn't possible, please remember that you have two make-ups at the end of the year that can also be used to make up lessons missed due to illness.

If you have a hole in your schedule, you might additionally use it for a monthly group lesson that can act as a make-up for any students who missed lessons due to illness that month. Be sure to limit enrollment, and have some fun activities planned so the child is not simply getting two lessons in a week, but is rather getting a special "extra" lesson.

Teacher Absence

Most studio policies state that the teacher will make up any lessons that the teacher misses as a result of scheduling conflicts or illness. Some policies also state that if it isn't possible to make up these lessons at a mutually convenient time, the teacher will offer refunds.

Sample Studio Policy Language: Teacher Cancellation

If I have to cancel lessons because of illness or other conflicts, I owe you a make-up and will offer it at a mutually agreeable time or at the end of the year.

Some teachers know that they won't be able to make every lesson every week due to other commitments such as a concert schedule that requires traveling. In that case, you might have a policy that includes payment for a certain number of lessons to be offered over a certain number of weeks. For example, one teacher offers a yearly program in which tuition covers 44 lessons over the course of the 52-week year. Some of the remaining eight weeks could be reserved for teacher vacations and absences, and some for student vacations and absences.

The Yearly Calendar

Many teachers run their studios in conjunction with the school year calendar. But even if you run in concert with your local school, you need to make some decisions and adjustments.

- Your students may not come from only one school district, and different districts have different calendars, vacations, and stop-start dates. It sounds sensible to close down during spring break, when "everyone" goes away, but it may turn out that your students from three different schools take three different weeks off for spring break. This is especially true if you have students from both public and private schools.

- What are you going to do about Halloween, the Wednesday before Thanksgiving (and the Friday afterward), all those Monday holidays, and Christmas break? Teachers willing to teach during some holiday and vacation periods sometimes use these times for make-ups, especially if the teacher has missed lessons or the weather has caused lesson cancellations.

- Teaching on Monday holidays often results in a truncated teaching day because some of your students go away, some stay, and some want to change times, throwing your holiday into chaos. But simply shutting down for all the Monday holidays means that Monday students either get fewer lessons (in which case, their tuition should reflect that) or go later into June to make up all the missed lessons. One solution is to teach on some of the Monday holidays, but not the "biggies" (Labor Day, Memorial Day). Another solution is to give Monday students an extra make-up for use if they go away on one of the Monday holidays.

Once you've decided how to handle these issues, make up a studio calendar that shows lesson days, perhaps in color. Distribute a yearly studio calendar along with the studio policy.

Summer Lessons

We talk about whether to require summer lessons in Chapter 8. Your studio policy should simply state your preference.

Many teachers require students to take at least some summer lessons in order to be able to register for the fall and get a preferred time slot. Teachers with a waiting list who require summer study sometimes even dismiss students who don't take the required number of lessons. Requiring summer lessons works for some teachers and not for others. One thing, though, is certain: if you don't require summer lessons, your income is going to take a precipitous drop once school lets out, so you will have to calculate your year's tuition and budget your year's expenses accordingly.

> Sample Studio Policy: Summer Lessons
>
> To help your child retain what he or she has worked so hard to learn, I encourage/ require at least [four] summer lessons. Summer lessons can be taken at your convenience. Please schedule and pay for lessons at the beginning of each month. I require 24 hours' notice for cancellation or for rescheduling requests.

If you *require* summer lessons, you might add something such as this:

> Students who take summer lessons have scheduling priority for fall. Students who do not take the required summer course of study will be put on the waiting list, should they want to resume lessons in the fall.

Whatever your decision, make sure you state it clearly in the policy. And if you are going to strictly enforce your rules, even if a family *always* goes away for the entire summer, be sure to discuss this when presenting your studio policy to the family.

Purchase of Books and Materials

A studio policy should also cover how books and materials will be purchased. Teachers are divided right down the middle about this issue. Some give students a list of required materials and expect them (or, more likely, their parents) to order and acquire them. Others buy all their student materials and then ask for reimbursement from the student.

The bottom line is that students need to have the right books and materials on hand for lessons and practice. The problem with asking parents to take care of this is 1) they often don't realize how long it can take to track down and order the right books and 2) they sometimes find the book lists confusing, as so many of the methods have similar names, such as *Mastering the Classics* versus *Classical Masters*.

If you live in a rural area, the problem is compounded because music stores are few and far between, and the only option may be Internet orders. Ordering from Internet music sites can be extremely confusing even for music teachers, and if parents aren't quite sure of which books they are supposed to be getting, there may be delays while one set of the wrong books is returned and the right books are ordered.

Sample Studio Policy Language: Sheet Music

I will purchase appropriate sheet music and study books for each student. The cost of the books will be noted in your child's assignment book and added to the following month's tuition. Depending on the student's level, progress, and interests, you can expect books to cost between $[xx] and $[yy] a year. Highly motivated and advanced students may need a bigger budget.

Communication

How will you communicate with parents? There's no doubt that accepting phone calls during a lesson is disruptive, but many teachers accept calls from students who call to say they aren't coming or to say they're going to be late. Caller ID is helpful in this regard. You can screen calls and pick up only calls from that day's students. It is also helpful to parents to put in your studio policy that you are willing to discuss any issues with them during certain hours of each day.

If you have strong preferences about how you wish to be contacted, make sure these are spelled out in your studio policy. For example, teachers who schedule one student right after the other may not want to have lessons cancelled via e-mail, because they won't see e-mails until after their lessons. The same kind of issue applies to teachers who travel to student homes: It doesn't do any good to call the teacher's home number if the teacher is already en route to a student's house, so traveling teachers might specify a cancellation notice policy (perhaps 24 hours for anything but emergencies) and request to be notified via cell phone, not a land line.

Other Considerations

You can put whatever you want into your policy. Other issues that some teachers cover include who gets to watch a lesson (covered in Chapter 10), cell phone usage for students and parents, the right of the teacher to end a lesson if the student is misbehaving, eating and drinking in the studio or the teacher's home, bringing students early (don't) or picking them up late (don't), showing up late for lessons, and literally anything else you can think of.

Some new teachers go overboard, trying to cover every problem they can imagine and everything they've ever heard of anyone else encountering. But it's better to start with the crucial basics: the more you include, the more people's eyes will glaze over. And really, if no one ever spills M&Ms into your couch cushions, you may not need to include the bit about no food in the studio. A general statement about common courtesy and reserving the right to terminate any activities that interfere with a student's learning ought to cover cell phones, bawling babies, and students having to hang around during someone else's lesson because their moms are late picking them up. When it comes to rules and regulations, less is probably more.

Studio Policies for Group Lessons

Studio policies for group lessons are necessarily different from those for private lessons. Studio groups, once formed, depend on each member of the group to be present—just like a sports team (an analogy most parents will understand). There is a commitment of teacher time and studio resources to that group.

Most studio policies require payment for an entire semester up front, and, after perhaps a short trial period of a week or two, do not permit students to drop out. The commitment has to be for the rest of the semester, especially in a class with limited enrollment.

For the same reason, most teachers don't offer make-ups for group lessons. As with most group activities children are involved in, if you miss the lesson, you miss it, but the lesson goes on without you. The only exception might be snow days or other unavoidable cancellations on the part of the teacher or the facility that hosts the lessons.

The Least You Need to Know

◆ Studio policies are a chance for you to set the tone of your business relationship with a student family and prevent misunderstanding about business issues.

◆ At minimum, a studio policy should include information on fees, payments, make-ups, refunds, snow days, teacher absences, and summer lessons.

◆ Studio policies can also be customized to include any additional issues you feel you need to cover.

◆ Studio policies set the tone for a good relationship but can't create one; for that, you need good communication.

Chapter 8

Scheduling and Time Management

In This Chapter

- ◆ The school year calendar
- ◆ Extra hours for teaching and related work
- ◆ Scheduling private students and groups
- ◆ Summer lesson policies
- ◆ Balancing work and family time

Teaching music privately is a scheduling conundrum. On the one hand, private teachers can work when they choose, within the limits of student availability. They may have large chunks of the morning and early afternoon hours free—but it's not exactly free time, with lesson planning, recital planning, their own practice, student performances, group lessons, performance attendance, activities to keep up with musical events in the community, recording projects, accompanying jobs, cancellations and make-ups, and occasionally performances themselves.

As for teaching hours, once 3 P.M. rolls around, it's crunch time, with students coming in back-to-back-to-back. Sometimes it's difficult to keep it all organized, especially when you add personal life and family life to the equation.

The Music Teacher's Schedule

Music lessons take place when everyone else isn't working or studying. This means that just as your kids come home from school, your workday is starting. Just as your spouse is ready to call it quits for the evening, you are in full throttle with teenaged and adult students. And weekends? What weekends?

Teachers who live alone, who don't have kids, or whose kids are grown are at a distinct advantage when it comes to scheduling lessons. Those with young children will have inevitable scheduling conflicts.

A Typical Workweek

The music teacher's most in-demand times are during the immediate after-school hours, from about 3:00 P.M. until about 6 P.M. You'll find that those right-after-school to just-before-dinner spots are the most coveted, and as your studio fills, you'll have to find some way to deal with the fact that everyone wants Tuesday at 3:30 and no one wants Friday at 5.

How late you teach after 6 P.M. or so depends on you, your family situation, and the ages of your students. You might break for dinner (especially if you have a family) and then teach again till 8 or 9 P.M., or you might teach through till 6:30 or 7 P.M. and then call it a day. Some teachers work late on one or two evenings and end the other workdays a bit earlier. Most professionals who make a living teaching music teach between 20 and 25 hours a week, with a few teaching 25 to 30 hours. That works out to four or five, sometimes six, teaching hours a day, five days a week.

Some music teachers start their days early. If you are a morning person and you have interested students, you might be able to get a lesson or two in before students have to go to work or school. This is certainly not the norm, but it works for some teachers.

More commonly, a music teacher may have a few daytime students spread out during the work and school days. These students may be adults with unconventional work schedules, retired adults, homeschooled students, or preschool children.

Try to clump daytime students together. Having a student from 9 until 9:30 A.M., a one-hour break, another student until 11, a break until 12:30, and then another student until 1:15 P.M. (and so on) fragments your entire day.

Take Note

Try to reserve a couple large blocks of time a week—three or four hours on Monday and Thursday mornings, for instance—as time for you to get personal business done. Cars need to be repaired, lawns need to be mowed, banking and groceries need to be done, and appointments need to be made with doctors, hairdressers, and piano tuners. Having a regular "business time" will help ensure these jobs don't get shunted aside.

Weekend Teaching

Weekend teaching is another option for teachers who want to schedule more students. It also may be a good choice (perhaps the only choice) for teachers working in communities that have implemented or are experimenting with expanded school days. If school days run until 4:30 or later, weekends may be the only time left for piano lessons, especially for those who teach younger students.

There are advantages and disadvantages to weekend teaching. Schoolchildren, of course, are off on weekends. But that doesn't mean they are available. You may have to deal with constant requests for rescheduling and make-ups because of athletics and weekend plans. Before you accept weekend students, quiz the families on their typical weekend activities. Some students will come religiously every Saturday morning, while others will as predictably call to cancel.

Lining Up the Lessons

Most teachers offer lessons of varying lengths, usually ranging from half-hour lessons to hour lessons (and occasionally longer). If you teach lessons of different durations (half-hour lessons, 45-minute lessons, hour lessons, or longer lessons), it can be a bit of a challenge to line them up so you don't have lots of 15-minute gaps in between. Some teachers want to work straight through the available teaching time (mostly because the after-school hours are so limited), so they schedule students back-to-back.

Others like having the occasional 15-minute break between students to throw together a salad for dinner, check on a child's homework, do bookkeeping, or simply clear their heads. Plus, people seem better able to remember that they are supposed to get to a music lesson at 4:00 than at 3:45 or 4:15. Perhaps because we are so accustomed to so many other activities starting on the hour or half hour, it also seems to make it easier for students to swap lesson times if they have a conflict and if they can find another family willing to trade lesson times.

> **Take Note**
>
> Keep a calendar by the phone where you can note any changes to your regular schedule. Next to the calendar, keep a copy of your normal studio schedule. That way, when people call wanting lessons or needing to change their times, you know what your regular schedule is at a glance, and you also can check to see if you've made any changes on any given date.

These 15-minute periods can also be used for "make-up lesson" time if you owe students time, perhaps due to a snow day or a teacher absence. If the student is ready to move up to longer lessons, adding two 15-minute segments to two half-hour lessons is an excellent way not only to make up the missed time, but to sell the student and the family on the idea of longer lessons. Most students who are ready to move up to longer lessons will make marked improvement with the extra time.

Group Lesson Schedules

Group lesson schedules are perhaps the most difficult to arrange because each group requires finding a mutually compatible time for three, four, or more students. Group lessons usually run longer than private lessons—typically an hour. Because group lessons involve different activities and games, hour-long lessons are appropriate even for very young children.

Therefore, scheduling groups is mostly a matter of availability. Because it can be so difficult to find a time when three or four compatible students are all available, teachers who give both private and group lessons should schedule the groups first.

Groups should be put together as early as possible during your scheduling process. For groups starting in September, try to collect enrollments in July. For lessons in January, you should have enrollments by early December. (Most of your January students will be continuing, so second-semester scheduling is not quite as difficult.) On the enrollment form, you should have the following information: the student's age and grade, previous musical study or level, and every possible day and time the student can come for lessons. Based on this information, you can come up with a preliminary schedule. Once the schedule is in place and the parents have confirmed it, ask for deposits in order to hold student spaces.

If groups are supplemental to private lessons (perhaps as a performance class), it is possible to mix students of different ages and abilities. Older, more advanced students can act as "assistant teachers," and, of course, younger students gain inspiration by seeing what lies ahead. If you offer occasional group lessons, try using a sign-up sheet, where each parent is given a choice of two times (or three, if possible). Give parents plenty of time, and remind them the week before (with a written note!) of the group lesson time. An extra e-mail wouldn't hurt, either.

Scheduling Individual Students

Beginning teachers are spared the massive headache of annual scheduling, mostly because they have so few students that incoming students can choose whatever time slot they like. Teachers with full studios, however, have an annual Rubik's cube to solve, as it were. Unfortunately, there are only a few prime slots in any given week, and most parents of elementary school students all want the same times. Parents joining your studio for the first time understand that they have to take whatever times are available, but after that, it may seem that everyone is angling for the same few places.

Scheduling is an annual problem that begins in late spring, when some parents start asking about fall schedules, and when many teachers start sending out re-enrollment forms so they have an idea of how many new students they can accept over the summer.

To start the process, you'll need a master calendar showing all the days and time slots of the week. You can use a simple computer spreadsheet. Map out your preferred teaching times. Also, block out any times when it is impossible for you to teach.

Wise Words _____

I put out a scheduling form that has a smiley, straight face, and frowny face for every 15 minutes on the days I teach. Families color in the face that represents *all* the times they can come. Smileys represent "This time is best." Straight faces represent "It will work, but it's not my first choice," and frownys represent "This time won't work with my schedule at all." Then I take everyone's forms and put together my fall schedule.

—Jennifer Foxx, music teacher, Goodyear, Arizona

Then the job of assigning student time slots begins. Here are a few different strategies that teachers commonly use:

◆ Nonrefundable deposits are due by a certain date; spaces are given on a first-come, first-served basis on and after that date. The advantage is that everyone understands first come, first served. The disadvantage is that it's not necessarily workable when a lot of people are willing to put down their money to be first in line. You could have parents camped out on your doorstep to get that coveted after-school slot. And you will certainly have requests in April to hold slots for September.

◆ Nonrefundable deposits are due by a certain date, and current students are given priority to keep their current time slots. If they want to switch, it's first come, first served. This plan can work, but it doesn't take into account that students' schedules may have to change because school schedules and after-school activities change from grade to grade. Also, as they get older, they may need longer lessons, which pushes other students' lessons back. Finally, always giving returning students their same time slots means that the older students who have been with you for a long time will have priority on earlier times that you may need for very young children, who don't do well with late afternoon lesson times.

◆ Trying to please all the people all the time is the most work but may work the best over time. The teacher collects deposits and a list of time preferences, then tries to organize a schedule that fits everyone's preferences. Preference is given based on the nature of the conflict. For example, you may give preference to a student who is trying to avoid a conflict with volunteer work at the soup kitchen over a student whose family wants to avoid rush-hour traffic.

Working Within the School Year

Most children's lives are governed by the school year calendar, which means that most families' lives are governed by the school calendar, too. Music teachers typically schedule anywhere from 32 to 36 lessons over the course of the school year, which runs roughly from Labor Day until some time in June. (Be aware that most private schools get out earlier.) Teachers may or may not then offer additional lessons in the summer. A few teachers offer a tuition package that covers year-round lessons. This works well for adult students, who don't follow the school calendar and who treat July lessons the same as January lessons.

School Holidays and Vacations

If all of your students come from the same school district, then you can base your calendar on the school calendar and take off all the weeks and holidays that students have off. Of course, this means that you'll lose a lot of teaching hours by doing so. Many teachers use some of the holiday times for make-ups, or take off some holidays and not others.

If you teach children from a variety of schools (especially public and private schools), you may as well schedule lessons through all the vacation periods—you can't very well take three weeks off during March to account for three different school systems' spring break schedules. And you (probably) can't afford to work part-time, either. If families go on vacations, they'll have to use one of their end-of-year make-up lessons to cover the lost time.

School Activities and Other Scheduling Issues

After-school activities—particularly sports—are the bane of the music teacher's existence. It wouldn't be so bad if sports were every Monday and Thursday, leaving Johnny free to take piano on Tuesday, Wednesday, or Friday. But no. Practices are Monday and Wednesday one week, Tuesday and Thursday the next, and games are on a schedule made by someone who, it seems, was determined to make life as inconvenient for as many people as possible. And the coaches yank kids off the team for missing practices, let alone games. And then there are playoffs. And championships.

And it's not just sports. In addition to every team sport imaginable, consider this list of conflicts taken from real life: swimming, skiing, karate, Tae Kwon Do, Chinese sword dancing (yes, really), African drumming, Boy Scouts and Girl Scouts, gardening club, science club, the regional school play (rehearsals and performances every single day for an entire month), the school play, ballet classes, driver's ed, cooking class, after-school tutoring … the list is endless.

And every single one of these things, it seems, is more important than the regularly scheduled music lesson.

Well, perhaps they are important. Being well-rounded is a good thing, too. But the bottom line is that learning to play an instrument takes years of lessons and concerted, regular practice. That's just the way it is. The problem goes beyond conflicts with lessons or the inconvenience to a music teacher; it also extends to lack of time for overcommitted kids to practice. If parents are going to spend thousands of dollars on music lesson and instruments, they need to find a way to deal with these conflicts.

Out of Tune _____

If you are the type of teacher who is more accommodating than organized, your willingness to reschedule students can lead to confusion. If Johnny's mom calls to ask if he can come 15 minutes later, and Jenny's dad wants to come 15 minutes earlier, you're looking at opening the door to two students at the same time. Write everything down—immediately.

And all of this talk of conflicts brings us back around to the issue of missed lessons and make-ups. But here's something to consider: While many of these after-school activities are purely recreational (even if uniforms and referees are involved), some of your students may indeed be both serious piano students and committed and talented athletes. Indeed, the character to work hard at one endeavor frequently translates to another. If you do have any open slots during your weekly schedule, you can use them, at your discretion, for make-ups for these students. Even having one or two open slots can make a big difference in being able to offer make-ups to students who really are trying to do two things well.

Rescheduling and Communications

You will also need to figure out how you prefer to be contacted by students or their parents regarding cancellations and requests for rescheduling.

E-mail is one way to stay in touch, but people still have wildly divergent ways of using it. Some are online practically all day long, so communicating via e-mail is almost like communicating in real time. Others check once a day, once a week, or almost never. If you do accept e-mail correspondence, it's up to you to check messages frequently. A good use of e-mail might be when two students arrange a lesson swap and one of them e-mails to notify you about it.

But e-mails that require extensive back and forth may not be practical. For example, it may not be as efficient to let parents try to reschedule lessons via e-mail because the conversation usually involves a lot of discussion. ("No, this lesson time doesn't work—no, that lesson time doesn't work. Yes, it does—wait, no, he has soccer that day.") In the time between the e-mails with Student A, Student B may call and want one of the times under discussion with Student A.

Be aware that many people use e-mail as a way to avoid personal contact. For this very reason, many music teachers discourage it, and asked to be notified about cancellations in person.

With teenagers, you will also want to determine who is responsible for cancelling lessons. Teenagers are usually more than happy to cancel a lesson, and if told that they have used up all their make-ups, they're likely to shrug and say, "That's okay." After all, they aren't (usually) the ones paying for those unused lessons. If you have a student calling to ask if he or she can miss a lesson, and the student has used all of the allotted make-ups, be sure there is no misunderstanding between you and the parents about your make-up policy for those lessons.

Hot Summer Blues

Some teachers require summer lessons and some don't. Whether to offer or require summer lessons depends on your financial requirements, your educational philosophy, and your schedule.

Most private music teachers experience a sudden income drop in June. Even teachers who try to insist on summer lessons often find themselves confronted with families who send their kids to summer camp or who go on long family vacations. While the teacher's need to make a living is certainly legitimate, most parents will balk at paying for lessons they don't want.

Some teachers require students to take a certain number of summer lessons in order to preregister for the fall and get a good scheduling slot. Students who don't take summer lessons are welcome to rejoin the studio in the fall if there is room, but they will almost certainly be left with a less desirable time slot.

Wise Words

In my policy, I have it written in that when a family signs on for the year, that includes a five-lesson summer session. This session is not optional for basic elementary and standard intermediate course students; therefore, if they decide to take the summer off, they are, in essence, forfeiting the five lessons because the final tuition payment is still expected for this session in order to hold their spot in the fall. This usually takes care of any rash decisions to take the summer off.

—Gretchen B. Taylor, music teacher, Carlinville, Illinois

Other teachers simply try to encourage students to take lessons when possible. If you have a good relationship with your students, your advice and recommendations will be worth something to them. This may be the best course of action if many of your students have summer plans that make it impossible for them to have summer lessons.

Remember, the economic part of the summer lessons issue can be solved by factoring in the summer lesson drop-off when you price your tuition and decide how many students to take during the school year. If you do, looking at a half-empty August calendar should fill you with relief at a nice vacation, rather than financial dread.

Advantages of Summer Study

A more important consideration, at least from a pedagogical point of view, is the educational benefit of summer lessons. Every music teacher knows the advantage of summer study. Without summer lessons, the first week back from vacation is a study in frustration as small fingers fight to find where the right hand goes and where the left hand goes, yet again. From June to September is a very, very long time in a young child's life, and without reinforcement, skills that seemed solid three months ago recede to the most distant reaches of a child's memory. The material can be relearned, of course, and will almost always be relearned more quickly than the first time, but in the meantime, students experience frustration at having to review old material. Getting back into the habit of practice (assuming there was a habit of practice) is also a chore for students whose summers were full of sun and fun. The reimmersion process is no picnic for the teacher, either.

Facts and Stats

An article published by the *Review of Educational Research* examined 39 studies and concluded that achievement test scores decline over summer vacation. Combined results from 13 selected studies indicated that the loss caused by a two-month vacation was one month of learning. Anecdotal evidence among music teachers, however, is that the loss may be even greater, particularly among younger students, because of the practice habits involved and the fact that music is both a physical and intellectual activity.

Even intermediate students who have had three or four years of lessons are guaranteed to slide backward if left to practice on their own, without lessons to correct whatever mistakes they are inadvertently learning. To be able to work independently for a month or more, students really have to be not only at an advanced level, but also mature enough to act as their own practice coaches.

Summer Attrition

Another issue that affects students who don't take piano over the summer is attrition. Quite simply, many students who take the first opportunity to stop regularly scheduled lessons and practice never quite get back to it. For the teacher, that means the inevitable August phone call: "Johnny started eighth grade and is worried about all the homework," "Lydia is going to a new school and wants to try out for cheerleading." Summer lessons can help prevent attrition because they keep the momentum going (especially if you do something a little different and fun in the summers)—assuming, that is, that you want to keep the student.

If you've collected a deposit, you'll have to decide whether to give it back. If you'd labeled it nonrefundable, you're within your rights to keep it. You'll have to judge whether that is the best course of action in a small town where people talk. You might base your decision on how late in the summer you learn that the student is quitting, and whether you've actually turned students away who could have taken that spot. In any event, one thing is true of summers: the schedule you think you have all nice and tidy in July will be turned on its head by attrition and requests for changes of schedule in late August.

Special Summer Programs

On the other side of the equation are the parents who, after a week or so of summer, are desperate for something for their kids to do. Offering special summer programs—a music camp, a summer recital, or a piano party—can provide a break from the regular structure, yet keep students motivated.

Summer schedules can be as flexible or inflexible as you want them to be. One nice compromise between rigidity and chaos is to ask students to schedule and pay for summer lessons at the beginning of each summer month. You might also limit the days you teach, to get a bit of a break for yourself.

In addition to regular lessons, you might offer some summer specials:

- ◆ **Music camp**—You could offer a week-long program during which kids come every day for two hours, perform for each other, and play music games.

- ◆ **Summer recital**—Hold a special summer recital for students who take summer lessons.

- **Summer pop fest**—Abandon technique books and etudes, and let students experiment with music they want to play.

- **Band camp**—Do you have the skills to coach a rock ensemble? Guitar teachers are perfectly suited to hosting a rock 'n' roll camp, provided they have a studio where the neighbors won't object.

- **Recording CDs**—Do you have recording equipment? Build your summer session around perfecting a few pieces to record on a student's own CD.

Managing Personal Time and Work Time

Probably the biggest scheduling challenge for the music teacher is balancing the teaching schedule with personal time. All self-employed people have to deal with the problem of work time bleeding into personal time. With private music teaching, the problem is exacerbated because the odd hours of a teaching schedule directly conflict with traditional family time.

Family Time

If you live alone or with one other adult, the family time conflict may not be much of a problem. You may eat dinner a little later than most couples, or you may teach on Saturday mornings. But a music teaching schedule that ends at, say, 7 or 7:30 P.M. every evening is not necessarily intrusive into the home life of an adult couple.

It can, however, be problematic if you have young children who need continual supervision, or elementary school children who need to be transported to or from their own after-school activities. One thing is for sure—and you undoubtedly know this if you are already a parent—you cannot teach piano and be the adult-on-duty with young children at the same time.

Assuming you don't have regular child care, here are a few other ideas:

- Family support. Perhaps your mom lives in the neighborhood and is willing to watch the kids a couple afternoons a week.

- A spouse. Does your spouse's work schedule permit him or her to help during teaching times?

- After-school day care.

- ◆ Barter. A neighbor might take your child on an afternoon play date, and you give her child a piano lesson in exchange. Or a teenage student may be available for a baby-sitting exchange.

- ◆ Away-from-home teaching. Teach outside the home at a music school or a music store. Sometimes creative solutions are available. For example, if you teach at a community center, you could enroll your child in age-appropriate programs at the center while you teach.

You may also want to schedule one or two nonteaching days while your children are in preschool or elementary school, if you can afford the reduced income. Your children are young for only a short while; your teaching career can last the rest of your life.

Teacher Vacations

Vacations are not generally a problem for music teachers. To the contrary, most students don't mind a break once in a while, and most parents are understanding, as long as you make up any missed time. Indeed, some music teachers close down for a month, and perhaps even the entire summer. It is the rare student indeed who objects to this! Of course, teachers who take the entire summer off have the same problems as teachers whose students take the summer off: September is bound to be spent reviewing everything that has been forgotten. But one of the beauties of being a private music teacher is that you can make these kinds of choices.

Likewise, shorter vacations are no problem. Many music teachers schedule their vacations around the school year schedule, taking a week or two at Christmas, and then either a midwinter or a spring break, as well as time during the summer.

Health and Meals

Music teaching is a sedentary activity, except, perhaps, for rock 'n' roll drummers. Vary your position as much as possible when teaching. Sit for half a lesson, then stand. Then stand and sit through the next lesson. And stretch in between students.

By far the biggest problem is mealtimes: the prime teaching hours are from about 3 until 5:30 or 6 P.M., and many teachers teach older teens and adults well into the evening.

Take Note _____

Making time to exercise is one thing that shouldn't be a problem because most music teachers have significant morning and midday hours free, when exercise classes are empty. But reserve a dedicated exercise time for each day, and don't give it up to accommodate last-minute make-up lessons. Most people find that, just like with students' practice, workouts are more successful if you adhere to a schedule.

Study after study underscores that eating too late in the evening is not healthy, and the alternative—eating a larger meal before the student rush—will not work for most families, or even for most couples, particularly if the other partner has a job with a traditional schedule.

So the choices are these: break for dinner or eat late. Of the two, breaking for dinner is probably healthier, and definitely what you'll want to do if you have children. So you'll need a meal strategy and plenty of help from family members.

◆ Buy a slow cooker. You do the chopping and cutting in the morning; it does the cooking throughout the day.

◆ Cook a couple meals on the weekend that will keep as leftovers for Monday and Tuesday.

◆ Make a cookbook of your family's favorite 15-minute meals. Get your family to help take ownership of both meal planning and meal preparation.

◆ Have a takeout night. Yes, it's expensive, but it's a treat, and a reward for the supportive family.

Setting Limits

Some music teachers thrive on a chaotic schedule, with students coming and going at all hours. Some start by enjoying all this activity but then burn out. Giving too many make-up lessons is one way to burn out and start to resent people making too many demands on your time.

If you have a studio of advanced students, you may get requests to attend recitals and competitions. At first, you will be thrilled that your students are doing so well that they want to participate in these events and they want you to come and see them. But if you have 20 performing students, you simply may not be able to hear them all play—and that's okay.

Other requests may come in. Kate needs help recording an audition tape (which will easily take an hour or more, depending on the requirements). Jimmy would like some help figuring out the chords for a song he really wants to play. Jane wants you to help her and her friend Ted prepare a duet for competition.

Ironically, just as your studio is getting more successful you will have to start saying "no" a lot more. And you may feel that you are rejecting the very things that made you successful in the first place—going the extra mile, showing up, supporting your students. But everyone has limits, and the bottom line is, you won't have anything left to give to your students if you burn yourself out. You need time for yourself.

The Least You Need to Know

♦ Music teaching hours are limited because children and adults are available for lessons only when they aren't in school or working.

♦ To schedule students, ask for firm commitments early and collect as much information on student availability as possible so you can juggle the schedule, hopefully to everyone's satisfaction.

♦ Teaching homeschoolers, preschoolers, retired adults, and adults with unconventional work schedules can expand your teaching day.

♦ Teaching a creative program of summer lessons can keep your students motivated and keep your income stable.

♦ Setting limits and reserving time for meals, health, and family is one way to help prevent burnout.

Chapter 9

Marketing Yourself to Find Students

In This Chapter

◆ Use your personal, business, and musical networks to find students

◆ Advertising strategies to attract potential students

◆ Create winning marketing materials

◆ Use public relations and local resources to reach your community

You've decided to teach, and you've hung out the proverbial shingle. You have a piano (or a guitar or a violin), a library of teaching materials, and enough enthusiasm to fire up a team of cheerleaders. Now you just have to find some students. But where do you start?

The short answer is "everywhere." You'll find potential students at the library, in line at the grocery store, in a town meeting, at church, at the PTA, and at parties.

But although students are, in fact, everywhere, most teachers learn that it takes some time and effort to bring them to your doorstep. Rome wasn't built in a day, and neither are music studios. Fortunately, a music teacher doesn't have to jump in full-time all at once. Because so many students take lessons after school, after work, or on weekends, it's possible to keep your day job and teach "on the side" while you market yourself to new students. Then as you find more students, you can make the decision to teach full-time.

Marketing Materials

Marketing materials speak for you when you can't speak for yourself. Whether it's the business card hanging on the music store bulletin board, a fancy brochure that sits at the local piano shop, or the elaborate website that shows YouTube videos from your last recital, your marketing materials extend your reach beyond your immediate network.

Making a Mission Statement

When major corporations start new ventures, they frequently pay consultants lots of money and spend lots of senior management time coming up with what's called a mission statement—a succinct summary of what they are doing and what they hope to accomplish. Your mission statement is your opportunity to define what you offer as a music teacher. For example:

◆ "Mrs. Recreation offers individualized learning programs for students of piano and guitar. My goal is to help you learn music for lifelong enjoyment."

◆ "Mr. Prestige offers a classical music education for students intending to pursue advanced study at major conservatories."

Both Mrs. Recreation and Mr. Prestige can use their mission statements in their brochures and advertisements. In each case, it's clear what the teacher is offering. Who would you go to if you were hoping to get into Juilliard? Who would you call if you wanted to start a rock band?

Business Cards

The basic business card must contain essential information. At a minimum, include your name, phone number, website address (if you have one), and teaching specialties.

The size of a business card limits the amount of information you can include. Obviously, you can't put your whole resumé on a card, but you can list any quick tidbits that highlight your competence as an artist, teacher, or both. For example:

"Professional studio musician," "Juilliard-trained violinist," "Member, Sun City Chamber Orchestra," and "Master's degree in Music Education," are all phrases that might convince a potential student that you're the teacher to call first.

You can make business cards in several ways:

♦ Make print-at-home cards on thick-stock paper that is presized and cut for business cards (available at office supply stores). Most word-processing programs include a template for printing these.

♦ Quick-print shops (and Internet-based print businesses) also produce business cards. You can walk into a shop or carry out the whole transaction online. They save you the hassle of uploading and learning another computer program, and may offer more options and more professional results.

♦ Finally, old-fashioned embossed cards with raised lettering might be going the way of the dinosaur, but they make a nice impression. If you are sure you will be staying at your current address, they might be worth the splurge.

Brochures

A studio brochure gives you a chance to write up what you think are the most important aspects of your studio and teaching philosophy. A brochure can be a simple 8½-by-11-inch sheet of paper folded into thirds, or you can purchase heavier trifold brochure paper at an office supply store. The templates look more professional than something you might come up with using your word-processing program on your own.

The contents of the brochure should include the following:

♦ A section about you—your background, training, college degrees, performing experience, and teaching experience

♦ A section explaining what you teach (piano, violin, lower brass, and so on), what type of music you teach (classical music, jazz, pop, ear training, music theory, improvisation), and what kinds of students you are willing to teach (preschoolers, elementary-aged beginners, advanced, adults)

♦ A section about your teaching philosophy

♦ Contact information, including website, e-mail, and phone number

The brochure is a chance to show your personality and your approach to music. What you emphasize and highlight tells a lot about you. You might focus on learning to make music in a fun, supportive environment. You might stress your skills in teaching technical proficiency and performance preparation for advanced students. Or you might highlight group jams and recreational get-togethers. Your brochure is your chance to reach out to the type of students you want to attract.

You may be able to leave brochures at music stores, piano shops, and libraries, and with school music teachers.

Studio Website

Increasingly, a personal studio website is a must for music teachers, even those with full studios. When people get your business card or your brochure, they often look for a website to find out more information, and if they can't find it, they'll Google you (which can lead down all sorts of interesting roads, including those of people who have your name but aren't you). Parents expect that a reputable business will have a website, and many parents will research you online before making the first call.

A studio website can be as simple to set up as signing up with a host, buying a domain name (such as www.yourname.com), choosing a template, and starting to write. If you haven't done this before, you might want help, especially if you'd like to upload photos, videos, and recordings. (Or barter with one of your high school students—they'll get you up and running in an hour!)

Take Note _____

Use free blog software offered by the major blog platforms to host a simple website. Most blog software includes static pages (where you can post your biography and studio information) and dynamic pages, which you can easily update to post information about student recitals or to share news with students. You can ask (or require) students to sign up for an RSS feed, which means that they will receive an e-mail each time you post a blog entry. Best of all, blog software is easy to use.

Think of your studio website as yet one more chance to expand on the information you give to students. Basic elements should include the following:

◆ Your musical biography, including teaching affiliations and certifications.

◆ Links to any performances or recordings you have made. (Links can be video links, such as to YouTube, or links to sites that archive recordings to upload.)

- Links to recordings or videos of student performances or recitals.

- Statements about your teaching philosophy.

- A list of instruments and subjects or styles you teach.

- Your basic teaching hours.

- Information about special programs you offer: recordings, ensemble opportunities, summer camps, or recitals.

- Contact information.

It is not necessary to include your rates on your website unless you really want this information to be visible to the whole world. Most teachers feel that rates and studio policies are best discussed in person. In addition, many teachers include only e-mail addresses, not phone numbers, on their website, thinking that the Internet is simply too public a place to be putting a phone number. Other teachers think that it's in their best interest to make it as easy as possible for prospective students to contact them. You'll have to make your own choice on this subject.

Starting the Search for Students

How you go about finding students depends on your community and who you are in that community. Are you a new college graduate? Or are you an established professional with a lot of contacts? Maybe you've been playing organ at your church for 10 years, or you're known for playing in a local band or orchestra. Or perhaps you're new in town and don't know a single person.

For most music teachers, word of mouth is the primary way of getting new students. If you are well established in a community, it may be fairly easy to put the word out that you are now taking music students. If you're new in town, you will have to work a little harder.

No matter who you are and how long you've been in the community, start with who you know. Personal networks are the place to start generating word of mouth. People can't ask you to teach music unless they know what you do. The bottom line: tell everyone you meet what you do.

Personal Networks

Your personal network consists of everyone you know, starting with your family and extending to relatives and friends and, beyond that, to their relatives and friends.

It also includes your children's network of friends and your sibling's children's network of friends. The parent you stand next to at your cousin's daughter's birthday party is a potential client or a potential referral. So is your real estate agent, the receptionist at your doctor's office, and even the doctor. Make it a habit to tell everyone you meet what you do, and always have business cards on hand to pass out.

Sometimes the easiest way to start being a music teacher is to act like one. Play a rousing and showy "Happy Birthday" at a kid's birthday party, then spend 15 minutes teaching a few second-graders to play "Heart and Soul." Take your keyboard to your nephew's birthday party and be the piano player for "Musical Chairs." Take your guitar to a cookout and play songs around the campfire. Music is about sharing—so start sharing yours.

Professional Music Networks

Networking within the local music community is another effective way to get the word out about your new business. The local music community is larger than you might think, and it can be the source of enough referrals that, once you get started, you never have a shortage of students.

Your music community includes other private music teachers (some of whom may have full studios and may be looking for other teachers to whom they can refer inquiries). Other teachers are not your competition; they are your community. As soon as you start interacting and exchanging information with them, you'll begin reaping the benefits of mutual support.

Out of Tune

Negative gossip travels faster than Van Cliburn's fingers, and always reflects badly on the person sharing it. Never repeat negative information about another music teacher's experience, training, or methods. Instead, highlight your skills and what you offer that is unique. Your potential students can draw their own conclusions.

Your community also includes music store owners, school music teachers, church musicians, performing musicians, piano tuners, instrument repair technicians, recording studio owners, and people who book musicians into local clubs and restaurants. All of these people are involved in some way with music, so it's just smart business to get to know them.

Start by making the rounds of local arts- and music-related businesses. If you are visiting the local sheet music or instrument store, arrive looking like a competent professional, not like an unemployed would-be rock star. And be prepared to buy something, even if it's only a handful of guitar picks. Have a business card and brochure on hand.

Take Note

Music stores are ongoing sources of referrals. Be sure that you cultivate them. Take the time to thank store owners every time a prospective student calls you. When appropriate, return the favor by recommending the store or shopping there yourself. A music store may not have the right guitar for your new left-handed classical guitar student, but that student can still buy a capo, strings, and strap there; get the guitar set up there; and check out their selection of sheet music. Be sure to let the store owners know when you're sending them business, and give them feedback if you hear good reports about their service.

If a store owner is busy, you might have to wait, or be content merely to introduce yourself. It may take several visits before business owners start putting your name together with your face, and a few visits more before they remember you are the new music teacher in town. Be patient: shopkeepers are busy, but they are one of the biggest sources of music lesson referrals in a community.

As you're looking around and introducing yourself, you'll also want to take note of what the music store supplies. Local independent music stores fill an important niche in the music community, but they are under constant competitive pressure from larger chains that can offer better prices. As a music teacher, you will often be asked by parents about where to buy an instrument, and you need to be able to recommend a business that charges fair prices, offers good-quality merchandise, and can service and maintain instruments.

School music teachers are another important source of referrals. Most school music teachers teach group instrumental lessons, along with their classroom, band, or orchestra duties. Some may teach privately on their primary instrument, but many refer queries about private instruction to private teachers. However, you can't just drop in on a school music teacher who has his or her hands full with 40 sixth-graders trying to play "Stars and Stripes Forever." Instead, send a letter (or e-mail) introducing yourself. You might also offer your services as an accompanist or as a resource, especially if you have a special or unusual skill. If you do have a program you can offer—perhaps a class on drumming, or a music history/listening program—be sure you describe it, then follow up with a phone call or an e-mail. People rarely refer people they don't know, or at least know by reputation, so getting yourself in front of the kids (and the music teacher) may be your best avenue to some referrals.

If you don't have a classroom program, don't worry. This is a long-term game. Your introductory letter will put your name in front of the teacher, and maybe that's all you can do for now. Later the teacher may see your name in an advertisement, or hear it from a parent, and then one of your students might play in the talent show, and another may accompany the school chorus. Over time your efforts, word of mouth, and your students will have a cumulative effect, and more referrals will come in.

While you're at it, don't ignore private schools. Private schools often have large budgets for arts programs, and many offer on-site lessons taught by private teachers who come in for an afternoon (or more).

Business Networks

Your business networks are also a potential source of students. As you move into a new community, chances are, you will be dealing with a real estate agent or property rental agent, a new banker, a new lawyer, a new insurance agent, new health-care providers, and a wide variety of other service providers.

Tell everyone what you do. Real estate agents, for example, may know that the family that just moved into town has three kids looking for a new piano teacher. A chat with your local banker may reveal that the piano teacher she served with at the Chamber of Commerce is retiring and looking for teachers to whom she can recommend her soon-to-be-teacherless students.

Advertising

Local advertising can be an effective way to get the word out about your new business. It's an especially good choice for teachers in a new community who may not have established their networks of friends, acquaintances, and business contacts.

The trick to good advertising is to put your message where people interested in your service will look for it. Very few people see an ad for piano teachers and think, "Oh, maybe I should start taking piano lessons." Instead, they decide they want piano lessons and then go looking for a teacher. Where do they look? That's where you want your ad to be. This means understanding your community and where people get their information. There is no sense in advertising in the local paper if that's not where people are going to look for you.

This important question is easily answered by polling people you meet in the course of your daily life. Simply tell them you're opening a music studio, and ask them where they would go if they were looking for a music teacher.

> **Wise Words**
>
> Half the money I spend on advertising is wasted; the trouble is, I don't know which half.
>
> —Attributed to John Wanamaker, merchant and founder, Wanamaker's Department Store

Yellow Pages

In spite of the Internet, the *Yellow Pages* remain a preferred source of local information in many communities. However, although the *Yellow Pages* is one of the first advertising strategies that pops to mind, few music teachers find them cost-effective. Rates tend to be somewhat higher than other forms of advertising, and in most communities, parents don't actively look up "music teachers" in the phone book.

A quick look at your local *Yellow Pages* should tell you if this is a viable option for you. Check under "Music Teachers" and see how many others advertise. If a lot of music teachers are listed, this may be an effective advertising strategy in your community. But if only a few music stores and larger schools are listed, you can be sure that private teachers have not found this a good use of their advertising dollars.

Local Advertising Papers

Local advertising papers (your community's version of the *Pennysaver*, for instance) are often a cost-effective place to advertise. Another advantage: unlike the *Yellow Pages*, you can advertise seasonally or just when you need to. Check to see if your local ad paper has a section for the arts or education, and whether other music teachers are advertising. Choose a paper whose circulation is limited to your immediate locale; people rarely want to travel far for music lessons, so there's no sense in paying to reach out to students who live an hour away.

You'll have a choice whether to place a display ad (a larger, boxed ad), which can range from a couple of square inches to a whole page, or a classified ad, which is less expensive and includes only a few lines of text. When starting out, a good strategy is to place a moderately sized display ad once every month or so, and reinforce it with weekly classified ads.

> **Take Note** _____
>
> Even if you have a full studio, publish a display ad once a year or so. Even if you aren't taking students, you could advertise your recital, thank students and families for another successful year, announce any scholarships or prizes students have won, or publicize their performances in local community events. This helps keep your name recognition strong in your community even when you aren't trolling for students.

Local Newspapers

Advertising in local newspapers works the same way as advertising in the local ad paper, although it may be more expensive. This option makes sense only if people in your community actually go to the local newspaper to look for music teachers, so check to see whether other music teachers are advertising there.

As with free ad papers, in most communities, teachers are better off advertising in the smallest, most local paper available. Choose the weekly county paper instead of the bigger daily. This is especially true if you live in a large city.

Local free papers are the giveaways available in bins at the supermarket and drug store. Some of them focus on specific niches such as the arts; others cover everything under the sun. They all take advertising, and many of them even allow advertisers to write advertorials about their services.

Internet Advertising

Internet advertising goes beyond having your own personal website. Internet advertising can be free or paid. Its effectiveness depends on where you are located, what resources are available for community-based Internet ads, and how popular they are.

Online Bulletin Boards

General boards such as Craigslist work for some teachers in some communities, but they don't work for everyone. This is another time when it depends on how people in your community get their information. It seems that online boards work better in more densely populated areas, where more people are using them. Some local news websites have free advertising for local businesses.

Because even "local" boards cover such broad regions (an entire metropolitan area, for instance), responders often turn out to live too far away. (You can mitigate this problem by specifying your general locale in the ad, to filter out people who live clear across the county.)

Basically, these bulletin boards allow posters to advertise services. Most teachers give an e-mail address instead of a phone number, to avoid broadcasting their phone number on the Internet, and then deal with queries as they come in.

When advertising online, beware of common scams perpetrated against music teachers. (Similar sorts of scams are prevalent in other home-based businesses as well.) A common scenario is for the responder to send an e-mail telling you that his or her child will be coming to your locale for a several-week or several-month visit, and that the parent wants the child to continue his or her music studies. The scammer asks for daily lessons with you, implies that cost is no object, and asks how to send you money for prepayment. (The "daily lessons" seems to be a standard part of this particular scam, and it should set off warning bells because virtually no music student ever takes daily lessons.) The upshot of this scam is that the check is sent and the music teacher deposits it. Then the scammer cancels the lessons and implies that there is a huge emergency that requires the teacher to send an immediate refund. If the teacher complies, he or she then finds out that the scammer's check has bounced.

Out of Tune

Virtually any music teacher who advertises on the Internet is guaranteed to get scam e-mails in response to Internet ads. Be wary of any requests that seem in any way out of the ordinary; for example, never give out personal or financial information (such as bank account numbers, which a scammer may request in order to deposit tuition into your account). Insist on an in-person meeting before accepting students.

Online Teacher Search Websites

A number of Internet websites offer web-based advertising for music teachers. The general layout of these sites is for teachers to fill out a form containing basic information (instruments, levels taught, location, special training). Prospective students visit the site and search by zip code to find teachers nearby.

Most of these sites charge a fee, although some may have an entry tier of service through which teachers can advertise limited information for free. If you're interested, www.MusicStaff.com is a site that offers such a two-tier system. Paying teachers get priority listings, but it is also possible to have a bare-bones listing for free. The problem is that most student families look locally for teachers rather than searching the Internet, so investing in these sites may not be an effective use of advertising dollars. But it doesn't hurt to try the free option.

E-Lists and Social Networking

If your studio includes performances of any kind (open mikes, student jams, student recitals, performances at local community events, real paying gigs), you need to develop an e-list of interested potential audience members.

Potential audience members aren't only listeners—they are also potential students. Current students also find their teachers' performances impressive and inspiring. By performing, you are "walking your talk." Hopefully, your performances showcase the lifelong joy that is to be found in performing and sharing music. This is a case of actions speaking louder than words.

Anyone who has ever shown the slightest interest in your music should be on your e-mailing list. This includes all your professional music colleagues, current students, former students, musicians you've played with, friends, family members, and anyone who has ever showed up at one of your shows and signed up to be on your e-list.

Obviously, you don't want to saturate your friends' e-mail boxes with spammy self-promotional e-mails. But assuming you play out only periodically, you can safely send notices giving time, date, and basic program information. Be sure there is a clear way to unsubscribe, and honor all such requests promptly.

Similarly, if you use social networking sites such as Facebook, MySpace, LinkedIn, or Twitter, be sure to post information on your concerts, gigs, and student recitals.

Out of Tune

Social networking websites such as MySpace and Facebook are huge, and chances are good that some of your students are already on them. Participating puts your name out to a wide network of people. If you are making the transition from university life to professional life, be aware that what may have been fun in college might not be appropriate for a professional teacher, especially if your students ask to link to you.

Community Resources

Each community has its own rhythm of life and local business. Where do people find out the latest news? How do they network? Do you live in an artsy community in which public bulletin boards announce all the latest shows, or are you in a tidy suburb where door-to-door or thumb-tacked flyers are frowned on?

Notice Boards

Libraries, colleges and universities, coffee shops, town halls, music stores, bookstores, restaurants, and community and senior centers—this is only a partial list of places that often have bulletin boards on which locals can post business cards or flyers about their studios, gigs, and shows. Ask first, or follow any posted rules about what can go where or how much space you can take.

The best way to post on a notice board is to create an 8½-by-11-inch flyer that contains the basic facts about your studio. Include any information that sets you apart from the crowd. Have you played with a big-name pop star? Have you been teaching for 20 years? Can you handle a variety of styles? Do you have a degree from a top-ranked school? Do you have a website? Save the bottom couple of inches of the page. This is where you will post info people can tear off and take home. Using scissors, cut strips along the bottom of the flyer that people can tear off. Each strip should contain your name, what you teach, and your phone number.

Community Organizations

Performing arts organizations put on regular shows and sell advertising in programs. While you certainly won't make your money back advertising in the program for a Lincoln Center concert in New York City, you might do well with an ad in your local summer stock production.

Local schools sometimes offer advertising in programs for school plays and productions. Advertising in your local school's program guide shows support of the local school. Plus, you could hardly hope to reach a more targeted audience; most of the readers will be families of local school-aged children. You might run a straightforward ad for your studio, or you might congratulate your students who are participating in the production. Either way, you build name recognition and goodwill.

Performances in the Community

Any performance you give automatically generates name recognition for you. It also confers legitimacy: people hear that you can play. During breaks, or when introducing yourself (or being introduced by bandmates or ensemble partners), be sure to identify yourself or be identified as someone who "teaches music right down the road, in Pianoville."

Participating in church music is also a quick and effective way to become part of a receptive community. Churches are often looking for pianists, organists, and sometimes guitar players to sub at the last minute, so show up at a church function and let the minister or music directors know you would be available on short notice. If you are a churchgoer, this would be a good time to choose a church and start making friends. Some churches have elaborate music programs. Youth music programs are a great place to start. Fellow members of the congregation are likely to think of you when they are shopping for a music teacher.

Public Relations

Public relations is the art of getting your message out to the public via media such as radio, TV, newspapers, and the Internet. It is often called "advertising you don't have to pay for." Creating a professional public relations campaign does, however, take time and skill, and money, if you hire someone else to do it. Most music teachers don't have the budgets to hire professional public relations consultants, but they can still use some simple techniques to encourage media coverage.

Local Listings

Most newspapers, ad papers, and community papers contain local listings of events of interest to the public. Such listings are good places to list any events that are open to the public: free demo lessons, an open house, an open mike you are hosting at a local café, your annual student recital, and any performances you give or participate in. Newspapers usually list submission guidelines at the bottom of this section of the paper. Follow their format exactly: if it says you are limited to the title of the event and 10 words describing it, don't send an essay! Always include contact information where you can be reached with follow-up questions.

Press Releases

Some activities in your studio may be of interest to your local paper, although it depends on the size of your community and the scope of your paper. Examples of media-worthy stories might include a notice about the formal opening of your studio, a feature article about you and your new CD or Internet teaching site, an article about a performance for charity that your students are giving, or a story about an achievement of one of your students who won an award or recorded a CD. You might pitch an article to the paper offering to be interviewed for a story about finding a music teacher.

 Take Note _____

The Five *W*s of a press release answer the news reporters' five basic questions—*who, what, when, where, why.* A snappy title or a catchy lead sentence are acceptable, but after that, get straight to the point and answer the questions.

In smaller communities, you may be able to network your way to the local reporter who would handle your story. In larger communities and at larger papers, a more formal approach may be necessary.

If you can't network directly with a reporter, the appropriate approach is via a press release (sent via e-mail—you can usually find the address in the paper or on the paper's website). Press releases are short announcements (no more than 300 words) that basically pitch a story to a reporter. The first paragraph summarizes the event.

Take Note _____

Make a reporter's job easier, and you are more likely to get media coverage. Always include the date and convenient contact information (your name, phone number, and e-mail) at the top of press releases. Remember that a journalist on deadline doesn't want to get an answering machine, so give your cell number and be ready to take the call personally.

The second and third paragraphs should then give the reporter a reason to want to interview you and write the story. What is interesting about your event? Is there a unique angle? Perhaps you are raising money for a music scholarship charity. Perhaps you have just written a book about student recitals and your students are giving a recital. Perhaps you have a collection of instruments from around the world and your students will be playing some of them at a local nursing home.

The last paragraph should give background about you, including information about your experience as a music educator and a performer, your training, and any particular areas of expertise.

Be sure to proofread your story, spell-check it, and have someone else read it through as well. Writing is every bit as much of a professional job as teaching music, and you want to put your best foot forward. At small papers, press releases are often reprinted verbatim, so be sure yours represents your most professional side.

Interviews with Local Reporters

If a local reporter does call, make yourself available. Straighten up your home or studio for the event, and dress appropriately because the reporter will most likely be carrying a camera.

It's always a good idea to outline talking points so that your answers are articulate and to the point. Think what you would ask a new music teacher if you were the reporter. Be prepared to answer questions about how and why you started your studio and what is special about it. Make note of any points you would like the reporter to cover, and come back to them whenever it seems appropriate.

Promotions and Discounts

Music teachers disagree about the long-term value of promotional offers, but special deals are a way to get people in the door when business is slow or when you're just starting out. Examples include free or discounted lessons, a short inexpensive summer "introduction to music" program, a two-for-one offer for the first month, rebates for students who refer others, or discounts for families with multiple students.

Free Trial Lessons

Trial lessons (see Chapter 10) are introductory lessons during which the teacher and student have a chance to get to know each other. Some teachers combine a family interview and studio policy explanation, an evaluation of the student, and a short lesson. Other teachers give a full-blown lesson, almost as if they were auditioning for the student. Whether or not to charge for these initial meetings is up to the individual teacher. Generally, teachers don't charge for initial interviews, but many teachers do charge for trial lessons if they are full-length sessions.

There is no doubt that advertising "free introductory lesson and evaluation" will bring people in the door. However, many teachers feel that the type of student who is lured into a studio by the promise of something for nothing may not be the type of long-term student they are looking for.

Summer Promotions

Summer is a good time to experiment with special offers. By August, kids are bored and looking for something to do, and parents are thinking about school-year schedules and activities. A group "introduction to music" program or a set of three or four discounted private lessons can be a way to introduce yourself to potential new students.

Be aware that if you offer discounted lessons to new students, old student families who hear about it may ask you if they can get the same rates. So be sure that you specify that your offer is limited to a particular number of lessons and a specified period of time. It's up to you whether to honor any requests for discounts from your current student families.

Discounts and Rebates

Referrals are the lifeblood of a music studio, and they need to be acknowledged. If your studio is full and humming along nicely, you may not need to solicit referrals. But if you are trying to expand, don't be shy about asking for them. Most people are pleased to be able to recommend a teacher they like.

Some teachers offer rebates to families that refer students to them. There are many ways to handle this: you could offer 10 percent off a semester's tuition, or you could give out discount coupons, or offer a free make-up lesson or free summer lesson. Whether or not you give rebates, be sure to express your thanks.

Some teachers additionally give discounts for siblings. Music teachers are of two minds regarding discounts. Teachers opposed to giving family discounts feel that every student takes the same time and preparation. They also note that families pose a greater economic risk because they take vacations at the same time, and if one child misses a lesson, the other usually does, as well. And very often, entire families stop lessons at the same time, leaving a large hole in your schedule. But teachers who give family discounts believe that the goodwill is worth it and that discounts can make a difference to families with several children all participating in expensive after-school programs. A 10 percent discount for the second child is often a workable solution.

Wise Words _____

Students in my studio participate in an incentive program in which they earn an ice cream party. When the day of their ice cream party comes, they are allowed to bring a friend to their lesson. At the lesson, the student and friend eat ice cream loaded with candy and play simple piano games that even a child with no music experience can learn, and the student performs for the friend. My original purpose of the ice cream party was for motivation and a chance for my student to 'show off' to a friend. The added bonus has been new students.

—Rebecca Brown, music teacher, Murray, Utah

However you price your lessons or offer rebates, remember that your reputation and word of mouth are the premier elements in your long-term success. Goodwill goes a long way to establishing a strong and healthy business. Always acknowledge those who bring students in your door. Before long, you may not need to look for students because they will be looking for you.

The Least You Need to Know

- ◆ Personal networking and word of mouth are a music teacher's best sources of students, so tell everyone what you do.

- ◆ Advertising locally is a good way to get started, but be sure that you advertise in the places residents look for information. Ask other teachers, and check out where they advertise.

- ◆ A website, business cards, and a studio brochure are three marketing materials that all teachers should have.

- ◆ Telling everyone you know what you do, getting word out through local resources and media, and creating goodwill with student families will help ensure that people remember your name when they are looking for a music teacher.

Part 3

The Teacher-Student Relationship

Students are calling, you've set your price and written your studio policy—now what do you do? Student-teacher relations begin with your very first phone contact with a prospective student's family. And they continue as you meet the student for the first time, evaluate the student, and discuss policies with the parent. With luck, mutual communication, and encouragement, your relationship with a student family can continue for many years.

In this part of the book, I discuss the whole reason for your career—your students, whether they are preschoolers, elementary students, middle school students, high school students, special needs students, or adults. I talk about solving common studio problems so that the relationships you start can continue on track—and what to do when things go wrong.

10

Interviewing Prospective Students

In This Chapter

- ◆ Handling preliminary phone calls from interested parents
- ◆ Conducting introductory interviews or trial lessons with prospective students
- ◆ Presenting your studio policy
- ◆ Evaluating transfer students
- ◆ Implementing a trial period

You've put out flyers, set your rates, and written a studio policy. You've purchased and organized a library of teaching materials. You've advertised and told everyone you know that you are open for business. Now the calls are starting to come in.

At first, you will probably be willing to take just about any student who walks through the door. That's not a bad decision: as a new teacher, you don't yet know which types of students you will best click with, and the only way to find out is to gain some experience. You might think that you want only serious students who are ready to play sonatas, and be surprised to learn that you love teaching kindergarteners. Or you might think that you'd be good with the elementary school crowd, only to find that you connect with adults who are finding their way to music for the first time. You might find that you enjoy the diversity of teaching a lot of different levels and styles, or that you gravitate to classical, or to jazz.

Getting to Know You

Most beginning teachers' studios are a bit random because you start out with whoever happens to respond to your advertisements. As the years go by, the students you work with best will stick around, and the others will either quit or migrate elsewhere. The ones who stay with you will refer others like themselves. You may gain a reputation as being patient with the youngest students, or cool with the teenagers, or reassuring with adults. And your studio will develop a character that reflects your personality as a teacher.

At the beginning, though, it's all new—perhaps all up in the air. And that means your first encounters with prospective students are important because they will set the tone for how you work with them and how you run your studio.

Students might find their way to you through an ad, a website, a printed brochure, a recommendation from a friend, or a business card you left at the music shop downtown. In some tech-savvy communities, or if your major marketing efforts are web based, you might initially be contacted via e-mail. Whatever form the referral or initial contact takes, most prospective students will want to have a conversation with you, and most teachers prefer at least a short phone call to gather certain information before the first lesson or meeting.

The Introductory Phone Call

Because most initial inquiries come through the telephone, you need to ensure that your first telephone impression is a professional one. If your spouse has the habit of answering the phone with a brusque "Yeah!" or if you let young children answer the phone, you'll have to implement some new rules about phone etiquette. Similarly, your answering machine message should avoid the "Hi, you've reached Ed and June, Maya, Kristin, Johnny, and their three pet bunnies" tone. Instead, either formalize the telephone rules in your home, install a business line, or use your personal cell phone for work-related calls. If you take this route, be sensible about what you're doing when you take a call. Conducting a business call while grocery shopping, supervising a group of 3-year-olds, or driving doesn't make sense. Instead, return the call when you are otherwise unoccupied and able to concentrate on the conversation.

You must, however, return calls promptly—within half a day, whenever possible. People who are looking for a music teacher may have a list of several candidates, and when they sit down to find a piano teacher, they are often on a focused family-scheduling mission. If they can't reach you, they may keep going down their list.

Prospective student families and teachers need to exchange a few basic pieces of information in the initial phone call. At the beginning, it's a good idea to keep a list so you don't forget anything. As the teacher, you will want to know the following:

- ◆ The student's name, age, and grade in school

- ◆ Any previous study on this instrument, and if so, how much and at what level

- ◆ If the student has had previous study, why he or she is changing teachers

- ◆ Any previous musical study on other instruments or in early childhood music programs

- ◆ Whether the student reads music

- ◆ The family's scheduling flexibility, priorities, and limitations

The student (or, more usually, the parent of the prospective student) may ask about your training and experience, although questions about your qualifications are not as common as you might expect. Somewhat surprisingly, if prospective students have gotten your name somewhere and chosen to contact you, they have already satisfied themselves that you are qualified. Nonetheless, be prepared to give a quick summary of your experience.

More commonly, parents are concerned with more practical issues. What is your availability? Do they come to your house, or do you go to them? (If the former, where are you located?) And how much do you charge?

Some teachers feel a little put off if the first question is about rates because they think that prospective parents should be more concerned about other, more important issues (such as the teacher's qualifications or teaching philosophy). But rates are an essential issue for both students and teachers, so it's best just to deal with the issue when it comes up and move on. If your rates are in line with those of other teachers in your community, there isn't any need to justify or discuss them. Indeed, if a caller tries to negotiate the rate or argue about it, that's probably a sign that this person needs to find a teacher more in line with his or her expectations. Don't be tempted to negotiate rates. Presumably, you've set your rates where they are for a reason. Stick with them.

Beyond these basics, the introductory phone call is a chance to collect as much information as possible about the student. Whose idea was it for him to take bassoon or trombone or bass guitar, anyway? And does he have an instrument to practice on? Be open to any information the parent may be directly or indirectly communicating regarding learning disabilities or special talents. And don't forget to ask the parent how they got your name; this information can be helpful as you fine-tune your marketing campaign.

The initial phone call is also a chance to summarize your studio policy. Explain briefly how you bill and how you handle missed lessons and make-ups; whether you offer recitals, group lessons, or other programs; and what your general teaching schedule is. But don't overwhelm callers with too much detail; this is a summary, not an oral contract.

Assuming that both parties have had their initial questions answered to mutual satisfaction, the next step is a face-to-face meeting.

Pleased to Meet You

After the initial phone call, most teachers schedule an introductory meeting, which usually includes some time to discuss schedules and studio policies with the parent, as well as some time for a brief lesson and evaluation with the student.

Wise Words

Don't set up a meeting in your studio with a new client if you are alone in your home studio area. Or have your phone/cell phone beside you and make sure that someone knows you are meeting with a potential client. Of course, if the person arrives dragging three kids behind them, there is probably very little for you to worry about. But if you are a female teacher and you are meeting an adult male, take steps to ensure personal safety at all times. Have a friend call 10 minutes into the interview with instructions that if you give the "emergency word," she is to call 911 immediately. (Or, if you don't answer the phone, she is to call 911 immediately.) It is much better to be *overly* safe.

—Shelagh McKibbon, music teacher, Brockville, Ontario

Sometimes parents ask if they can have a trial lesson (which amounts to the same thing as an introductory meeting). Or they will tell you that they are "shopping around" and are planning to have trial lessons with several teachers. Some teachers take umbrage at the idea that the student is shopping around, feeling that, if anything, the student should be auditioning for the teacher, and not the other way around. However, this reaction is more about ego than it is about real life. The fact is that no matter what you call it—a first lesson, an introductory lesson, or an evaluation—any first meeting is a trial session for both parties. Either the student or the teacher is free to decide whether to continue.

One way to reframe the issue is to agree, saying that, in fact, you prefer an introductory meeting to get to know each other, work together a little, and be sure that the match is right. You might also mention that you can't reserve a time slot until both parties are sure they want to go ahead. Depending on how much time you allocate for these sessions, and how much actual teaching you plan to do during that first meeting, you may decide to charge for your time, or you may offer it as a free initial consultation.

Take Note

Resist the urge to accept a student over the phone and start teaching the minute he walks in the door! Even if the parents are certain they want Junior to take lessons with you, insist on a 15-minute introductory period during which you chat with parent and student before you start teaching. You'll want to cover your studio policy and any questions, but more important, you'll want to make the student feel at ease. Talk to older students about their music preferences. Ask younger ones about their favorite songs. Make children feel that you see them as people as well as students.

The fact of the matter is that, in most cases, you won't know how "good" a student (or the family) is going to be after one lesson, or even after a month or so. However, insisting on an introductory meeting formalizes your studio procedures and sends a message that signing up for lessons with you is not a casual recreational activity.

Talking to the Student

The initial meeting will probably break down into two parts: The "grown-up" talk, where you discuss policy issues with the parent, and the "student" part, where you discuss the student's responsibilities with the student. Of course, the student part of the equation will vary drastically, depending on whether the student is a shy 6-year-old, a garrulous teen, or an accomplished transfer student.

Wise Words _____

> Always take the child aside, away from the parent, and ask him why he or she wants to take lessons. You may find out that he or she really does not want to! Never take a student who is taking lessons under duress. One can accomplish learning only when the student desires to learn.
>
> —Kevin Coan, music teacher, Vernon, Connecticut

This is the time to make friends with the student and go over the student's responsibilities and what will be expected. The important thing is to balance communicating the hard work of music with the joy of music—and putting it into language a young child can understand. How you do this will depend on your personality and approach, but some basic improvisations, clap-backs, and call-and-answer games can highlight the fun part of the equation. Don't underestimate the importance of this. Children practice what they enjoy, and they learn by playing. But they also rise to the occasion and meet expectations when clearly given. Your job is to balance both.

Forms to Fill Out

Some teachers have extremely thorough application and information forms that they ask parents to fill out. But complicated forms, where students (or parents) are asked to give reams of information about themselves, are the exception, not the rule. They can be off-putting, and the majority of teachers don't need all that much detail on a form to find out what they need to know to work well with a student.

You will, however, want complete contact information. Be aware that many of your students have complicated family lives, with divorced parents (custodial and non-custodial) and stepparents and babysitters. So your contact form has to have room for every adult contact's home phone, work phone, cell phone, and e-mail address. You may have to reach students in an emergency, for instance, to cancel lessons at the last minute, and you need as many points of contact as possible, as well as an indication of which method of communication is preferred. Note that many parents do not check e-mail regularly, some are frequently out of town, and others don't communicate with each other (let alone with you).

Going Over Your Policy

Whether it's a first lesson or a simple meeting, e-mail your studio policy to parents ahead of time so they have a chance to read it and note any questions or concerns. Parents often forget to bring their copy to the meeting, so have another one on hand.

Hopefully, the parent will have read the policy, but don't count on it. Many parents don't want to spend the time on nitty-gritty studio policy issues, or they just wave them away with "whatever you do is fine by us." But it's important to say, "Let's just go over the basics because this is hopefully a long-term relationship, and I've found that this really does prevent misunderstandings down the road." You'll want to go over the main points and make sure parents understand the payment options you offer, your make-up and refund policy, and your summer lessons policy. They also need to be able to ask questions.

Also go over any other requirements you have (for example, mandatory recital participation, mandatory entry into adjudication programs or competitions, and group lessons or classes you may give), as well as other opportunities you offer—for example, the annual performance at a local nursing home or the Christmas music party.

Determining Lesson Length

The introductory meeting is also the time to determine the appropriate initial lesson length for a student. Teachers usually develop a system of recommendations regarding lesson length, and it's different among age groups and instruments. For example, a guitar teacher may recommend half-hour lessons for all beginners, whether adults or children, because after half an hour, the pressure of the strings on a beginner's fingers starts to hurt. A piano teacher has no such problems, so her lesson length recommendations may be different: perhaps half-hour lessons for young beginners, 45-minute lessons for older beginners and intermediates, and hour lessons for motivated advanced students or adult beginners who feel they need a little extra time.

If you have a general game plan of increasing lesson times as students reach certain levels and milestones, you might also mention this to the parents. For example, you might teach half-hour lessons only for 6- and 7-year-old beginners, and hope to move them up to 45-minute lessons after a year or two, depending on maturity and progress.

Take Note _____

Don't be fixated on the half-hour lesson! In Mozart's time, children whose families could afford music tutors might have had lessons several times a week and were often supervised during their practice as well. While today's weekly half-hour is convenient, reasonably economical, and common, many music teachers feel that it is not optimal. Young children might do better with twice-weekly 15- or 20-minute lessons, and some teachers are experimenting with much longer, 75-minute lessons for brighter and more committed students. Tweaking lesson length may be a way to work with children with shorter—or longer—attention spans.

Whom You Allow into a Lesson

Do parents watch lessons or not? This needs to be discussed in the introductory meeting. The short answer: it depends. The long answer: it depends on the parent, on the student, and on the teacher.

As a general rule, most teachers welcome parents of young children into the studio. (In fact, some insist on it, and in Suzuki classes, parents are expected to take notes so they can be practice coaches at home.) Parents who pay attention during lessons are more likely to support the child's practice routine at home. Hearing the teacher's instructions to "count out loud," or "play the piece three times with no mistakes," or "use the metronome for this song" can give parents ideas about what they should listen for during the child's practice time.

Elementary school children don't usually object to their parents being present at lessons, but some parents can inadvertently interfere. For example, a teacher may allow a wiggly 7-year-old a bit of unfocused noodling time, only to be interrupted by a parent ordering the child to "focus and pay attention." Or a parent eager to help might stand near the child and say "That's an A, Johnny, play the A!" just as the teacher is trying to coax the child to figure out that the note is an A all by himself.

At the same time, having parents in the lesson can be helpful because the parent is witness to the child's learning patterns with the teacher and to any problems that might be showing up repeatedly. It also acts as a reality check to have Mom or Dad sit in the lesson and see what's going on rather than hear second-hand from a child about what the teacher did or didn't say or do. In some cases, the child may be playing power games with divorced parents, telling Dad that he hates piano lessons while Mom is insisting on them. If Dad sits in on a lesson and sees the child actively enjoying his lesson, and maybe even saying "Cool! I love this piece," and "I'm going to go home and practice this right away," Dad might realize that "I hate piano" has, in fact, nothing to do with piano and everything to do with Mom and Dad.

The old "children should be seen and not heard" quotation needs to be turned on its head in music lessons: the parents should be seen and not heard, at least during the main part of the lesson. It's not at all productive for a parent to start wildly cheering a student's sloppy and haphazard performance of the most recent piece assigned if the teacher is getting ready to present a long list of improvements that need to be made. One good way to think of and explain it is that the teacher and the student are enclosed in a learning bubble, and the parent is outside of it. The parent can watch but shouldn't do anything to puncture that learning bubble. Assure parents that there will be time to answer questions at the end of the lesson.

Take Note

Your studio arrangement can make parents feel welcome, but it should discourage them from actively participating in the lesson. Something as simple as furniture arrangement can be highly effective. If you want to minimize parental involvement, have a welcoming seating area on the other side of the room, not directly facing the lesson area (it can even be behind you). Make it comfortable and well lit, and have a stack of magazines parents can turn their attention to if they get bored.

Teenagers, of course, won't want their parents in the lessons (or maybe even in the same county). Some teens drive themselves to lessons or walk. Those who are delivered by parents often order the parents to stay in the car or the waiting room; some parents do errands.

Whatever your policy regarding parents observing lessons, discuss it during the introductory meeting. And remember that this an age in which educators are trained not to touch students, for fear of being accused of doing something inappropriate. It is not a good idea to have a closed-door policy. Parents should be welcome to stick their heads in and check out what is going on at any time in the lesson, without even knocking, and they should frequently be reminded that it is perfectly okay for them to enter the lesson area.

Guests in Lessons

You may also want to make a point about bringing guests to lessons. This is especially important if during the introductory meeting the parent has younger siblings in tow.

As a practical matter, parents can't clone themselves, and many of them simply have no choice but to drag other family members along to lessons. If you have a waiting area, this is no problem (unless you want the parent to come into the lesson, in which case you're stuck with the sibling, too). Just be sure your waiting area is fairly child-proof, with nothing breakable at toddler or small-child level.

Out of Tune

Insist that parents supervise siblings or tag-along friends at all times. Having young children playing unsupervised on your property is an invitation to disaster. Accidents can happen when children play on your retaining wall or slide around the icy puddle by the front door; gardens can be trampled; and things that you never even thought of as breakable can be broken. You are a music teacher, not a day care service.

If you have an open studio space, having younger siblings and babies in the lesson is an almost guaranteed distraction. You may have to be up front about saying that the parents will have to wait in the car, on an outside deck, or in the yard while the lesson is going on. This may not be acceptable to the parent; some parents believe they should be able to bring their young children anywhere and everywhere, and it's better to find out right away if this is what you are dealing with. You might have to suggest they find a teacher with a more suitable teaching space for them.

Students sometimes also show up with a friend. Of course, you have the right to tell the friends to stay in a waiting room or to wait with the parent of your student outside in the car. But there are some reasons to allow a friend into a lesson occasionally. Sometimes they are simply there because of the expediency of a play date after the lesson. Sometimes the friends are checking you out or considering the whole idea of music lessons. Perhaps the friend plays an instrument, and if you happen to have spare instruments in your studio, as many teachers do, you can whip up a duet for the kids to do. (At the very least, you'll probably have a drum or two.) Finally, performing for a friend gives your student a chance to show off a bit.

Simply be gracious to the guest and ask her to sit quietly. You might offer a picture book for her to look at. If your student starts clowning around or trying to get the friend's attention, put a quick and stern stop to it. Generally, a simple "Your friend is welcome here, but if you can't concentrate because of it, I'm going to have to ask her to leave." Beyond that, be especially gentle when teaching a child who has a peer watching, and effusive with any praise that is due.

Instruments and Equipment

What kinds of instruments must the students have to practice on? This can be a tricky subject, because not everyone has the finances to buy expensive instruments just because Janie decided she wanted trumpet or guitar or piano lessons. After all, many children's interests are fickle.

At the same time, it is absolutely impossible to learn to play guitar on a "cheese grater" (a cheap guitar with such high action that to push down a string almost shreds a finger) or to learn piano on a 61-note $50 electric piano with no touch control and unweighted keys. Have a list of reputable instrument dealers, technicians, and (for pianists) tuners, and be sure they know who you're sending to them and what you are recommending.

Rental instruments are one solution. Although over a long period of time they aren't necessarily all that cheap, they do have the advantage that you can trade up as the student grows and becomes a better player. Second-hand instruments are another possibility. Some music stores sell second-hand instruments on consignment. Used instruments can be found on eBay and Craigslist. But buying and shipping instruments can involve some risk. Advise parents who shop online always to check the seller's rating and number of transactions on eBay, and always be sure that shipments are insured and that they must be signed for on delivery. Buyers should also ask about return policies. Some sellers may agree to let you return the instrument if it is not satisfactory. If you can negotiate a return, be sure to have the instrument immediately looked at by a technician.

Out of Tune

It's important to trust the piano tuner or technician to whom you refer your students, particularly if that person also sells pianos or works closely with a dealer. Some dealer-technicians are overzealous about trying to get your students to upgrade or to spring for a costly overhaul. Many students play on admittedly bad instruments, but the purchase of a piano, whether used or new, is such a major investment that it's only fair to be sure the student is really going somewhere before you (or a dealer) start pushing the family to spend thousands of dollars on a better instrument.

Piano teachers, in particular, need to quiz parents about the instrument they have and how it has been maintained. In some cases, a good-quality 88-key digital piano with pedal, touch control, and weighted keys is better than the behemoth in the living room that hasn't been tuned in decades and is, in fact, simply unplayable, especially in summer, when all the keys stick. As much as piano teachers hate to think of students practicing exclusively on digital pianos, many of them agree that digitals provide an acceptable instrument for a fraction of the price of a decent acoustic. Once the student reaches a solid intermediate level, however, an acoustic piano is essential for real progress in classical music. Parents should be aware of this at the outset.

Transfer Students

Transfer students are students who started their studies with another teacher but, for some reason, have now found their way to your door. Because music teaching is such a personal endeavor, it can be difficult for a student to make an adjustment to a new teacher. Transfer students thus arrive with their own collection of musical and learning baggage. Only one thing is certain: their previous teacher did things differently from the way you do.

Why Students Change Teachers

Sometimes students change teachers for obvious and unavoidable reasons that have nothing to do with their interests, abilities, or how well they were doing with the former teacher. Their old teacher retires. The student's family moves. Or the old teacher decides that the student needs to move on to a more advanced teacher, or one who can teach a different style.

Sometimes the reasons are not as clear-cut. In some cases, the student may have stopped lessons and now wants to resume music study, but with someone different. And sometimes the parents or student may simply feel things aren't working out with the old teacher, in which case, you'll hear something about "needing a change," or "new energy," or "they weren't connecting."

Finally, sometimes parents initiate the teacher change because they can't abide by or don't agree with the teacher's policies. They may have problems with the teacher's strictness (or lack thereof) with their child; with the practice expectations; or with the payment, make-ups, and refund policies. Generally, a parent won't come out and tell you about conflicts with a former teacher, especially if the conflicts were over business issues, so you may have to read between the lines.

Note also that sometimes the previous teacher is at fault. As you gain experience and make contacts in your community, you will probably learn the names of teachers who are so disorganized that they forget to show up for lessons, teachers who miss a lot of lessons for gigs and never get around to making them up, teachers who really are "mean," teachers who teach by rote to avoid the boredom and hard work of teaching music reading, and teachers who have habits (such as substance abuse) that are obviously inappropriate. Although you may be the recipient of "reports" about other teachers, don't ever engage in gossip or tell stories, and don't take sides. Just be a listener, take in the information with your own set of "filters," and move on.

Meeting the Transfer Student

During the initial meeting with a transfer student, you'll need to spend the usual time with parents going over your studio policy. This is perhaps all the more important with transfer parents. They might assume that you do things just like the previous teacher, when, in fact, your policies are vastly different. However, the bulk of the time should be spent with the student.

Transfer students are likely to be a bit older and, thus, more able to take part in a substantive conversation about their learning, music preferences, and previous experience. Remember to take in information without judging. If a student has had three years of lessons and is only in the second level of lesson book, don't ask why there has been "so little progress." Rather, you might ask the student and the parent whether they are "satisfied with" the progress, or something to that effect.

Transfer students should bring their most recent lesson books to an initial meeting. The books should serve as a familiar talking point—or playing point—for the student. And they give you a sense of the student's level of accomplishment. Ask potential transfer students about practice habits and attitudes. A particular student might not be progressing because the teacher doesn't inspire or motivate that student. On the other hand, teachers are only part of the equation. If the student resists practice, a new teacher may not be able to do much more than the old teacher did. It's important that students take responsibility for their part of the equation, which means that they understand your practice expectations and agree to meet them. Make it clear to the student that the two of you are starting out with a clean slate, that you assume the student is here because he or she wants to learn to play, and that to meet that goal, both of you will have to meet your responsibilities.

Evaluating the Transfer Student

Finally, you'll want to hear the student play. Let the student choose something to play; it will help him or her feel at ease. But don't be fooled! The student is likely to choose her best-worn recital piece or a favorite song she has played a thousand times. What you hear won't necessarily reflect her actual learning ability.

Be sure to chat a bit. Ask the student why he likes the piece, whether it was hard to learn, and how he practiced it. Ask him to show you other pieces he liked, as well as pieces he didn't like.

You may then want to do some evaluation exercises with the student. Try some sight-reading (start with easier sight-reading than you guess she can handle, then work up to harder pieces to find her true reading level). Then bring out a piece of music at a level or two lower than the level of the piece she played for you and ask how she would go about learning it. What is the key signature? (Does she know what a key signature is?) Time signature? How many beats does that mean per measure?

Out of Tune

Avoid the temptation to judge a transfer student or her former teacher too quickly. A complex array of elements have combined to produce the student who auditions for you. These include the teacher; the family; the student's age; the student's ability and learning style; the method used; practice habits; and family upheavals, other commitments and activities, and a host of other issues. It will take a while before a teacher can sort these all out and come up with a course of study that matches the student's learning style. For the first few weeks, go easy, with lots of review and "getting to know you time."

Some other ideas might include rhythm tapping or playback exercises; checking to see what he knows about scales, chords, and arpeggios; and doing a brief ear-training exercise to learn about pitch recognition. Finally, do something fun: a blues improvisation, or a call-and-answer, or a trading eights exercise.

Transfer Student Etiquette

Accepting a transfer student midterm from another teacher in your area is a tricky situation. In many communities, music teachers have collegial relationships. They may belong to the same professional associations, participate in the same competitions and recitals, and refer students among themselves. While it is certainly true that parents and students should have the right to study with the teacher of their choice, it's also not fair for them to blind-side a teacher with whom they have had a multiyear relationship by leaving with no warning in the middle of a term.

Unfortunately, parents are not always forthcoming about their reasons, which can put teachers in an awkward situation with their colleagues. A parent might insist that the previous teacher knows they are leaving and is "okay" with it. But if you ask the previous teacher, you will too often find that the teacher has no idea, that the student is leaving owing money, misses a lot of lessons, or has had a conflict on the subject of make-ups. For this reason, many teachers do network with each other regarding students who come to them midyear, especially if the student is coming from a well-regarded teacher. (If the student is leaving Mrs. Awful, you may feel that you don't need to worry too much about why.) At the very least, the other teachers appreciate the professional courtesy.

The only thing that can be said for certain about transfer students who choose to leave their current teacher is that something wasn't working: students who are doing brilliantly well with a current teacher, and whose parents show up on time and pay bills when due, are not students who transfer.

Trial Periods

In a few cases, you may have a feeling based on the initial meeting or conversation that you may not be the best teacher for a student. Some instances might include these: The child is very young, and you don't typically teach very young children (see Chapter 11). The student has a learning disability and you have no training in how to work with a student with that disability (see Chapter 12). Or the student might be interested in a style of music you aren't sure you can teach.

Implementing Trial Periods

A trial period is a time for the student, parents, and teacher to get acquainted and to make a decision. Suggest a trial period to evaluate whether the child "is ready" for lessons or whether you feel that you "have the skills to work with that student." Leave the door open so that *either party* can walk away without bad feelings.

The point of trial lessons is to find out if you and the student are a good match. Explain very clearly to the parents that not every teacher is right for every student, that you feel you lack training in dealing with … young students, autism, developmental disabilities … or whatever the situation might be, but you're willing to work with them for a month to see if you can help. Also add that you understand if they want to start with someone else. Make the trial period feel as mutual as possible.

Ending Trial Periods

Trial periods might go on for a month or so. That's usually enough time to get a feeling for the student, although you may choose to make the trial last a little longer.

The trial ends when one or both parties decide it isn't working, or when both parties decide they want to continue together.

Ending a trial period is tricky. No student should be excluded from pursuing music, and if the end of the period feels like rejection, you can permanently injure a child's confidence about his or her ability to learn to make music. It's difficult for parents, too, especially parents of children with learning challenges who may have a hard time mainstreaming their children and finding people willing and able to work with them. The best thing you can do is put the blame on yourself. Say all kinds of nice things about the child and what he has accomplished, but be honest about your limitations in being able to work with him. For example, you might point out that 4-year-old Matthew is bright and eager and learned to count in just one lesson, but that you almost exclusively teach much older and more advanced students. You feel Matthew is exactly at the level he should be for his age, which means that he really does need to work with someone whose studio is equipped with preschool equipment and who knows the kinds of games and exercises that are effective with children that age.

Then have some names on hand to give the parents. Never end a trial period without making a recommendation. Not only that, but be sure you have gone the extra mile and talked to the other teachers about the family you are recommending, to be sure they have room in their studios and are willing to take on the student you are sending them. Be sure the student understands that he is being passed on to another teacher not because he is a "bad" student, but because he is exactly the type of student Mrs. Wonderful loves to teach.

The Least You Need to Know

- Most prospective students inquire by phone. Keep a list of topics to cover.

- Call it what you will—an introductory meeting, trial lesson, or first lesson is a chance for both parties to evaluate each other.

- During the introductory meeting, leave time to present your studio policy and answer any questions. This is the time to prevent misunderstandings.

- Evaluate transfer students carefully to be sure that you are inheriting someone else's missed opportunity, not someone else's problem.

- Implementing a trial period is a good strategy if you aren't sure you are the right teacher for a particular student.

11

Teaching Preschoolers

In This Chapter

- ◆ The pros and cons of preschool music lessons
- ◆ Determining whether teaching music to very young children is a good match for you
- ◆ Curricula for young children
- ◆ Teaching young children in a group setting

All music teachers know three things about very young students. Everything is a challenge for them. They are learning machines. And they love music.

For a very young child, the world is full of mysteries and challenges. Tying shoes is a challenge. Remembering left hand and right hand is a challenge. Learning finger numbers is a challenge. Counting beats is a challenge. And, speaking of counting, When we say *1—2—3—4*, do we mean fingers or beats?

But children are programmed to learn. Everything they do, all day long, is about learning. When they are playing, they are learning. When they are eating, they are learning. When they are getting dressed, they are learning. When they are banging on a piano, they are learning, too.

And children love music. Put a child, a teacher, and music together, and you can have a winning combination. But that does not mean that teaching tots is the right decision for every music teacher, nor that every tot is ready for music lessons.

Understanding the Very Young Student

Loving music and being able to make it are two different things. Tiny hands struggle with strings and keys, fingers aren't strong enough to hold down notes, and coordinating two jobs at once—fretting and plucking, counting and playing—may be impossible. Fortunately, very young children don't concern themselves with such details as whether what they are playing sounds good. They are exploring. And exploring is what lessons for the preschooler are all about.

Wise Words

The most important thing to remember when teaching preschoolers is to assume they know nothing. Start from scratch and review each and every concept until you know it has been mastered, and then review it again. Be careful how you phrase things, as they will interpret what you say literally. Above all, notice the baby steps, praise everything to the hilt, and enjoy the learning experience.

—Susanne Gravel, music teacher, Oakville, Ontario, Canada

When Is a Child Ready for Lessons?

Whether a child is ready for music lessons depends on what kind of lessons we are talking about. It's hard to say how early is too early for private lessons. In some countries, such as Russia and China, children start music lessons at very early ages, particularly on violin and piano. However, cultural differences, such as parental involvement, practice discipline, and lesson frequency, come into play. What works in one culture may not work in twenty-first-century America.

So the real question is not whether the child is ready for music lessons. The issue for you to answer is whether the child is ready for the type of music lessons you plan to teach. What kind of music lessons do you think are useful and appropriate for preschoolers? What is a reasonable goal for a 4-year-old? Are you interested in teaching those kinds of skills and activities?

When you've decided what kind of lessons and programs you are interested in offering, evaluate the child to determine whether he or she is ready. A child who spends all day picking out tunes on the family piano, who begs for lessons, or who keeps demanding to know how to play a favorite song clearly wants lessons. Something is calling the child to the instrument, and indeed, that's how many children end up in a teacher's studio. But in other cases, readiness and interest are not so obvious, especially if the child is hiding behind mom's skirt.

For group lessons, you might simply require that the child be toilet-trained and able to follow directions in a class setting. For private lessons, however, you need to be sure children are ready for the sorts of tasks you will expect them to tackle. For preschoolers, these tasks might include the following:

- Can the child sit still for a few minutes at a time?

- Can the child pay attention while you are giving directions, and then follow a series of instructions?

- Is the child responsive? Eager?

- Can the child count?

- Can the child recognize letters of the alphabet? (This isn't required, but it's good to know whether a child can recognize letters before you introduce the concept of note names.)

- Does the child know left from right?

- Is the child coordinated enough and strong enough to hold the instrument and perform the physical tasks necessary to play it?

If you determine the child is not ready for private music lessons (or not ready for lessons with you), you have three choices. Suggest that the parents wait. Recommend a different teacher. Or suggest group lessons (which are discussed shortly).

Goals for Preschool Music

It's important for both parents and teachers to agree on the goals for early childhood music lessons. Is it just one more thing to add to the list between Baseball for Babes and Tae Kwon Do for Tots? Is it enrichment-oriented playtime? Indeed, many music teachers who work with preschoolers use specialized early-childhood learning materials that focus on music games, listening activities, singing, and rhythm. The joy of music is the biggest part of their curriculum, and instrumental skills is the smallest.

On the other hand, if the parents have a real expectation that this is the beginning of a formal musical education program involving regular practice, the teacher should closely evaluate whether the child is ready for that type of learning and what kind of help he or she will need from the parent. Another option is to take on only those few children who are clearly operating ahead of age and grade level, and who can work on their own.

There is no right or wrong approach. What is important is that both you and the parents agree on the goals you all have for the child and that those goals are appropriate for the particular 4-year-old in question.

Instruments for Very Young Students

A precocious 4-year-old might be able to pick out a nursery rhyme on the piano, but there is no way the child has arms long enough to play a trombone (let alone be able to blow hard enough to honk out a note!). Some instruments work well for young children and others are impossible. One of the most popular choices is the violin, which is not only small to begin with, but comes in half sizes, quarter sizes, and even one-eighth sizes! Child-sized instruments are also common for guitars, cellos, and violas, as well as percussion instruments.

Take Note _____

Young children are destruction machines. Instruments—even drums—are fragile. There is no end to the damage children can inflict on an instrument if they are allowed simply to bang on it. Children need to be taught proper care and respect for instruments. Putting them in cases, treating them gently, and always asking before touching an instrument that belongs to someone else are good lessons to learn.

Small electronic keyboards are another good choice for young children. This is not the time to be worrying about the sound of an acoustic piano and finger strength. Preschoolers will have an easier time sitting at a small keyboard, which can be placed at child height. Keyboards with multiple sounds intrigue children, although many youngsters simply jab at the buttons instead of trying to play notes. Still, this is just the type of music and aural discovery exercise that is most appropriate for this age group.

Boys and Girls

A distinct difference exists between the learning paths of the average preschool boy and those of the average preschool girl. Study after study points to the more active, whole-body running around and tearing-up-the-classroom learning style of boys versus the sit-still-and-figure-it-out style of girls. Developmentally, fine motor coordination occurs differently in boys and girls. Typically, preschool boys are slower than preschool girls to tie their shoes, cut with scissors, or color inside the lines, and they are slower at learning to control their fingers on instruments. These are stereotypes, of course; certainly, there are shy, task-oriented boys and rambunctious, physical girls. But stereotypes exist for a reason, and teachers experienced with pre-schoolers have certain expectations when faced with a group of 5-year-old boys versus a group of 5-year-old girls.

The sit-still-and-concentrate music lessons that work for older school-age students are unlikely to work for many preschoolers, whether boys or girls. This doesn't necessarily mean that the child isn't ready for music lessons; it just means that the teacher should probably have some drums on hand for channeling all that energy into a different learning activity. It also means that the course that is successful with a 5-year-old girl might not be the right course for her twin brother. Cognitive and coordination differences can be as much as six months to a year apart developmentally, so consider the needs of the particular student when choosing methods. Chronological age is only part of the equation.

The Role of Talent

Some young children arrive at music lessons with astonishing abilities. A 5-year-old might easily learn to read notes, to pick out tunes and harmonies by ear, or to display a sophisticated musical memory that retains multiple lines. Sometimes a talented child will seem to understand everything equally well. Fingers move easily, the ear is responsive, and music reading comes naturally. Other children excel in one area but not in others. For example, an academically gifted child may read music easily but lack a rhythmic feel. Another child may learn quickly by listening and by rote playing, but may struggle to read music.

The challenge for the teacher is identifying the strengths and giving these children enough pieces to let them move forward with those strengths, while also choosing supplementary material that focuses on weak spots.

Remember, however, that a young child with big talent is still a young child. If you're lucky enough to have one of these little prodigies in your studio, tread cautiously and don't be afraid to move slowly and deliberately. These are the years to make music fun and instill good habits. The big, flashy pieces can come later.

The Role of Parents

Preschoolers accept help from parents. This makes them different from many 7- and 8-year-olds, who stubbornly insist on doing everything themselves. It is worth noting that in the bygone classical music eras, rich families who were able to pay for a musical education hired music tutors not only to teach lessons, but to supervise practice sessions as well. Mozart was a genius, of course, but having *daily* lessons with his professional musician father certainly didn't hurt.

If parents are committed enough to a young child's music education to be bringing the child to private lessons, those parents need to be part of the process. Indeed, some teachers agree to take on young children only if the parents agree to certain types of participation, such as supervising practice or taking notes during lessons. Average preschoolers need supervision; they cannot practice on their own effectively. Parents who don't know anything about music need to be willing to learn enough to keep up with their 4-year-old, at least until that 4-year-old pulls ahead and can work independently.

Should You Teach a Very Young Student?

From a business perspective, teaching preschoolers certainly makes sense for the independent studio owner. Day programs for preschoolers are in high demand, parents love early music education classes, and teachers can work during hours when it is otherwise difficult to find students.

However, all of this is secondary to the main question: Are you well suited to working with young children? Children at this age have fingers in their mouths as often as on instruments. There may be tears, and there will certainly be challenges holding a young child's attention and trying to get fingers to coordinate. These realities are natural parts of the learning process; a teacher who sees them as inconvenient problems to be overcome on the way to the "Moonlight Sonata," is probably not going to enjoy the journey. And the child probably won't, either.

The ideal preschool music instructor needs to be at least as much a nurturing care-giver as a musician. And she must be patient—more patient, even, than a teacher of more traditional elementary-aged students. Not everyone is cut out for a thousand shaky renditions of "Twinkle, Twinkle, Little Star." Other job requirements include an affinity and affection for young children, some training in early childhood educa-tion, and a sense of humor. The ability to play Paganini on the violin? Not so much.

Teaching a 7-year-old and a 70-year-old has more commonalities than teaching a 3-year-old and a 7-year-old. Pedagogically, the 7-year-old and the 70-year-old can actually use the same introductory books (as long as the 70-year-old has a sense of humor about childish illustrations and kiddie music). But a 3-year-old can't learn from a book designed for 7-year-olds any more than she can solve calculus equa-tions. Once students reach first or second grade—usually at about the time they start to read—they can generally be taught using standard methods. But before then, only the most exceptional preschoolers and kindergarten students can use a method meant for an older student.

> **Wise Words** _____
>
> I am mentally preparing myself for the 5-year-old mind. I want to come down to their physical limitations and up to their sense of wonder and awe.
>
> —Dr. Shinichi Suzuki, music edu-cator and founder of the Suzuki Method

Very young children are not simply younger, smaller music students. The differences between 3-year-olds, 4-year-olds, and 5-year-olds are striking. Even a method meant for a 5-year-old may move too fast and require physical coordination impossible for a 4-year-old. At this age, children grow and change rapidly, and their cognitive levels vary tremendously. You will have to change with them.

For the teacher, this means more than simplifying or slowing down the standard teaching approach. Very young children need an entirely different curriculum, with elements presented in a completely different order. Some teachers intuitively figure out how to work with young children, modifying and developing curriculum and games to teach to their abilities. But trial and error is a tough teacher.

College courses in early childhood education can smooth the road for a teacher who wants to work with preschoolers. Training is also available privately, through music educators' organizations (often at annual conferences), and also through organizations and curriculum programs. One for-profit example is Kindermusik, which sells teacher training, licensing, and curriculum materials. A nonprofit example is the Suzuki Association of the Americas, whose purpose is to "support, guide, and promote Suzuki education."

Programs and Curricula for Young Children

On some instruments, notably piano and violin, the methods for preschoolers fully assume that even 3- and 4-year-olds can make actual instrumental music. Some of these methods focus on very simple tasks such as learning one note, then a second, then a third. Most use well-worn recognizable nursery rhymes and tunes that children recognize or find instantly appealing. Some have an intense listening element and may have children playing along with CDs (even if it's just playing one note in rhythm). Additionally, some early childhood methods focus on ear training and rote playing, believing that, just as in learning to speak and learning to read, the action should come before the symbol. This makes sense when you consider that most of these young students are at the prereading stage.

> **Facts and Stats**
>
> There are 19 million children under the age of 5 in the United States. Roughly one quarter of these children (nearly five million) are enrolled in an organized program such as a nursery school, day care, or Head Start. Many of these programs offer group music lessons. This translates to job opportunities for independent music teachers who have been trained to work with young children.

Many music teachers feel that at the preschool age, students can best work on activities that teach such musical goals as rhythm and pitch recognition instead of specific instrumental skills. Games and musical activities that may not on the surface seem to have much to do with making music can help develop hand positions and familiarize students with moving around the instrument.

As with any curriculum choice, the teacher can (depending on the instrument) follow a method, adapt a method, or make up her own method and activities. Here are some popular ways to adapt your teaching to working with preschoolers.

   ◆ **Following Suzuki programs**—Based on the teaching philosophy of Shinichi Suzuki, the Suzuki program puts ears ahead of eyes. It is best known as a violin program, although it is also available on guitar, piano, and recorder. Some teachers use elements of Suzuki training folded into their own curriculum. Courses on how to teach the program are available worldwide.

◆ **Using teaching materials designed for preschoolers**—Many authors of popular method series have put out versions for younger students. A few independent teachers have self-published methods for teaching young students, particularly on piano. These are reviewed in piano teaching literature. (See the Appendix for more information.)

◆ **Developing manipulatives and "off-chair" activities**—In addition to written material and CDs, many teachers of young children use teaching aids and games to present and reinforce new concepts. Examples include a floor-keyboard mat on which the student steps on notes, and a game in which a teacher and student toss a ball back and forth while counting rhythms.

The key to making lessons work for young children is to keep the lessons varied and interesting and to take into account shorter attention spans. In addition to using materials specifically deigned for preschool children, teachers should do the following:

◆ Keep the lessons moving. Don't stay on any one task for too long, and be sure to break tasks into achievable pieces. If a task seems too difficult, break it down further, or go on to something else.

◆ Have reasonable practice expectations. That might mean five minutes at a time. At this age, the benefit is in establishing routine and having fun. There will be time for hard work later.

◆ Offer extravagant praise, stickers, and small rewards for jobs well done.

◆ Focus on what children can do, and always give them assignments they can easily master so they experience success.

Group Lessons for Very Young Students

Group lessons for very young children can focus on either a single instrument (for example, a group Suzuki violin class) or on general music skills (as in a Kindermusik class), which teaches rhythm and pitch recognition, encourages moving to music, and introduces instruments. Teachers can either affiliate with a formal program or make up their own curriculum.

Programs range from well-known national programs such as Kindermusik or Musikgarten to local programs developed by entrepreneurial teachers. Programs might offer any combination of the following: teacher training, curriculum materials, perhaps some advertising and marketing support, and a facility to teach in.

These formal programs are a good choice for new teachers because they save a lot of time reinventing the wheel. Teacher training programs offer invaluable information about lesson planning and pacing, classroom management, and games and activities that have been modified over time. Some of the better-known programs (either locally or nationally) have name recognition among parents, which helps with marketing and also helps establish a new teacher in a community. Some programs may offer you a fully outfitted place to teach (important if you're talking about a kiddie keyboard program that requires multiple digital pianos and a lot of space). This can be a consideration if your home is not childproof or if zoning laws don't allow you to teach six kids at a time.

> **Out of Tune** _____
>
> Don't ignore children's health issues! To keep a healthy studio (and that includes yourself), be hyper-vigilant about childhood illnesses. Ask parents to keep young children home if they have colds and runny noses. Use antibacterial wipes on instruments and toys, and ask parents to help children wash their hands when they come into the studio.

Pros and Cons of Group Lessons

The biggest advantage of group music lessons is that they are fun. Children learn by playing, and children practice what they enjoy. Group lessons allow children to focus on broader musical activities that are easier (and, hence, more fun for them) to learn. It is far easier for a young child to chant *1—2—3—4* to a march than it is to make a note on a guitar.

Group lessons have an educational advantage. They are ideal for teaching rhythm— counting, doing clap-backs, feeling rhythmic pulse, and learning about whole notes and half notes and what beats are. Rhythm is such a primary part of learning music. Any program that can help instill it gives children an enormous leg up when they start formal studies. In the case of teaching rhythm, the value of group lessons may exceed that of private lessons because the skill is more easily learned by children of this age in a group setting.

Group lessons can also include listening activities during which students listen to different styles of music or learn to identify different instruments. And, of course, group lessons introduce the idea that we enjoy music with each other—players and listeners, both.

Thus, there are very few disadvantages to group music lessons for preschoolers. Even a young Mozart can benefit from pitch recognition and note-naming games, rhythm activities, and simply fun with music. Nor are slower students likely to get left behind in a marching and counting game. The only negative would be if this were the only type of lesson available to a child who is ready and eager for private lessons.

Group Lesson Structure

As with private lessons, group lessons for young children must include lots of varied activities, each one lasting for no more than a few minutes. Many such groups start with a hello song, with students going around the room chanting or singing, each one introducing him- or herself in turn.

The class can be divided into units of active time, rhythm time, singing time, marching time, sitting still and figuring things out time, and listening time. With very young children, parent "assistants" can be marshaled to help keep things moving—or not moving, as needed.

The Least You Need to Know

- ◆ Preschool students love music, but lessons are often more a matter of play and exploration than formal learning.

- ◆ Before taking on preschoolers, consider whether you have the patience and sense of humor needed for the job.

- ◆ Group lessons are an excellent way to teach basic rhythm and pitch skills in a low-pressure, fun-filled setting.

- ◆ The most important element for preschool music lessons is fun.

Chapter 12

Teaching School-Age Students

In This Chapter

- ◆ Understanding the elementary-age music student
- ◆ The challenges of the middle school student
- ◆ Motivating and energizing the high school music student
- ◆ Determining whether you are suited to teach music to special needs students

School-age children are the bread and butter of a music teacher's life. Year after year, 7- and 8- and 9-year-olds enter your studio. Some stay a year, others a few years. And a smaller number stay until they graduate from high school, having turned from little kids into young men and women.

In between that first nervous, exciting lesson and the final bittersweet goodbye, you will encourage, threaten, cheer, and despair as they learn, don't learn, practice, don't practice, perform well, perform badly, learn their notes, learn to count, learn to express themselves, and finally (if you can just get them to practice a little more) become musicians in their own right. It is a long and cacophonous road from that first middle C to the "Moonlight Sonata." This chapter covers a little bit of what you can expect on that journey.

Elementary School Students

Most parents who call about music lessons do so either because their child has expressed an interest or because the parents have decided that learning music is something that should be part of a child's education. The choice of instrument may be the student's preference, or it may be that there is a piano in the house, that Uncle Jim plays clarinet, or that Mom always wanted to play guitar. For whatever reason, they find their way to you.

Typical Challenges

Typically, parents interested in lessons for young children choose an instrument such as piano or violin, for which there is a long tradition of methodology appropriate for young students and, in the case of the violin, one-eighth-size instruments for the tiniest fingers. Additionally, some students choose guitar (where small instruments are also available) and percussion. Those students or parents who have their sights on tubas, bassoons, or even French horns—they'll just have to wait.

Once children are in elementary school, there may also be a school music program through which children can choose instruments. Typically, a band director will do a show-and-tell for students, who then sign up for group lessons and rental instruments. Who knows why one child is fascinated by the sound of a cello and another is transfixed by a flute? But as far as children are concerned, not all instruments are created equal. Different instruments have different requirements.

Three things go into choosing the right instrument for a child, and before accepting a child as a student, you need to make sure all three are in place.

- First, and perhaps most important, is the child's own interest in the instrument.
- The child must have the physical size and coordination to handle the demands of the instrument.
- A practice instrument must be available in the student's home.

Learning Issues for Elementary Students

The biggest challenge in teaching music to an elementary student is prioritizing learning tasks. Every music teacher has had the experience of teaching three beginners the same piece—and teaching three entirely different lessons. Depending on the instrument, learning music involves coordinating some combination of eyes, ears, hands, breathing, mouth, feet, and intellectual understanding, just for starters.

Each student puts these elements together differently. No one can learn to read notes, count beats, put the right fingers in the right places, use two hands at a time (not to mention a bow, or their breath), play softly, play loudly, slow down, speed up (intentionally, that is), shape a phrase, pedal, mute, and articulate correctly all at the same time. So the teacher needs to figure out which of these to teach and in which order.

Wise Words

Meet with the grade school and middle school music instructors. Find out how they present rhythms and intervals. At the private lesson, you can keep the terminology the same or be able to explain a musical term using language they've heard at school. An added bonus to your effort is that the school music instructors will most likely give you referrals, having met you and knowing you are proactive in your teaching!

—Vickie Steenhoek, music teacher, Windom, Minnesota

The teacher's job is to identify the student's strengths and use them to introduce music that the student can learn and will enjoy playing. It will quickly be very clear which of your students are good readers and which are resistant readers, which are aural learners and which have trouble with pitch recognition, which have a natural sense of rhythm and which march to the beat of a drummer only they can hear. Tap into their strengths to get them practicing and playing, and from that positive place, introduce the tasks on which the student will have to work a little harder to master.

Practice Issues for Elementary Students

Most music teachers try to establish practice expectations right from the start. This is easier said than done. Young children have little concept of the idea of practice, beyond, perhaps, doing something over and over again. If they like a piece of music, they will happily play it 100 times in a row—correctly or incorrectly. They have a poor concept of time as well. Three minutes can seem like an eternity to a fidgety 7-year-old.

The other issue is that, during the first few months, it often takes a half-hour lesson to teach a very small amount of music. To expect a student to go home and repeat that small amount of music for half an hour a day for six endless days is, in most cases, unreasonable. You would have to have an extraordinarily patient, obedient, and motivated child to get three hours of practice on "Mary Had a Little Lamb," or "Old MacDonald." For typical 7- to 8-year-old beginners, 15 or 20 minutes of practice a day is about the most a teacher can hope for.

It is important to note that young children enjoy repetition of something they like (which often translates to something they can easily accomplish). The teacher's job, therefore, is to capitalize on this tendency and to assign jobs that are easy to understand. Rote exercises that are easy to play and easy to remember are terrific. If the tune is catchy, so much the better; children will repeat tasks that they enjoy.

> **Take Note** _____
>
> Young children may not read fluently until fourth grade or later. When you write instructions for young children, use your best block-letter handwriting, and use the simplest instructions and words possible. It even helps if you go over the words with the student (which helps their reading as well as their music).

Simply telling a child to "go home and practice" doesn't work. Most teachers will assign a list of pieces to be learned. (As time goes on, this list will expand to include memorizing tasks, studies, scales, and theory homework.) While most teachers use assignment books, some 7-year-olds (and even 8-year-olds) are not yet reading fluently. So you have to tell them to first open their practice book, then ask Mom or Dad or Big Sis to help them read what it says to do.

You can give practice assignments in three basic ways: by time, by the number of times a task is repeated, and by an evaluation that the work is done to satisfaction.

- **Time**—The simplest way to tell children to practice is to give time requirements. For very young preschoolers, 5 or 10 minutes may be a reasonable practice goal. For typical beginners in the 7- to 8-year-old range, 15 or 20 minutes a day will lead to noticeable progress and to a "circle of achievement": more practice leads to the student being able to learn more fun pieces, which leads to the desire to practice.

- **Task**—Another way to assign practice is break the job into specific tasks, which are then repeated a certain number of times. For beginners, this may involve playing one line at a time, three times, or two measures at a time, five times, or the right hand three times and then the left hand three times (for pianists).

- **Goals**—The goal of many music teachers is to teach students to practice to a standard. They want the student to learn to practice a page as many times and for as long as it takes to be able to play it well. An objective goal can help. For example: Be able to play with the metronome at 96 beats per minute three times in a row with no mistakes. Or, be able to play the scale at mm = 100 with your eyes closed.

Sometimes students don't practice because they are "confused." In truth, very few of these children truly are confused. They are better described as not yet able or still unwilling to take the mental leap needed to figure out how to get started working on the assigned tasks. "I'm confused" is what children say when they want an adult to spoon-feed them the answer.

But it is the music teacher's job to help students find the answer for themselves— to lead students through the thought processes necessary to figure out the note so they can practice independently. If a student didn't practice a piece because she was "confused" about the starting note, she is probably expecting you to tell her the note and how to find it on the keyboard, make it on the flute, or pluck the correct string on the guitar. They expect this response because it's the response they get from most adults. But it's the last thing they need from their music teacher.

 **Take Note**

Go over an exact practice plan with each student at each lesson, starting with opening the assignment book, finding the right page, and going down the list of tasks. For young children, drawing boxes to be checked off each time a task is accomplished helps make students accountable and gives you at least an approximate idea of what's going on at home.

For beginners, the crucial skill is the skill of learning itself. This means teaching a step-by-step process of approaching a piece of music. Students may learn to interpret and tap a rhythm of a piece first, then say the notes (following whatever method you use for teaching note reading), then say the notes in rhythm, then tap the rhythm while saying the notes, then finally play the piece. This approach is time-consuming at first, but it sets forth a methodical way of learning that the child will, over time, internalize.

Motivating Elementary Students

Elementary-age children are often motivated as much by extrinsic rewards as they are by the intrinsic reward of a job well done. Music teachers, who experience the joy of their art as its own reward, may have difficulty adjusting to a young child's enthusiasm for a colored sticker. But make no mistake: children, especially young children, respond to tangible measures of progress—a new book, a certificate, a sticker. The reward can be as simple as a smiley face drawn on their assignment book, or it can be public acknowledgement at the year-end recital. Some teachers keep a reward box of trinkets, such as pencils decorated with musical motifs, little statues of composers, or even (with parental permission) candies or gum. Other teachers maintain progress boards on which students' earned points are posted each week for completing certain tasks, such as memorizing songs, practicing assignments, performing for family, or learning a piece on their own.

> **Out of Tune**
>
> Never discuss one student's progress with another. Students are motivated by making progress in their books. They are keenly aware of which level book they are in, and if they happen to be in school with other students from your studio, they are often just as interested in what level those students are in. Answer queries about other students with something like, "You'll have to ask Johnny what book he's in. I wouldn't gossip about you with him; I'm not going to gossip about him with you."

Finally, never underestimate the value of good, honest praise. Kids know when they've done something right and when they've practiced. Always notice their achievements and comment on them.

Sports and Activities Schedules

Scheduling conflicts can be difficult if most of your students are in elementary school. Elementary school children frequently participate in many extracurricular activities. Parents of children this age are still trying to figure out what Johnny is good at, whether Suzie really likes ballet, and whether third-grade Anna needs tutoring. Parents are struggling to prioritize, sometimes running from the latest new activity to an even newer one. They've heard that music is good for math and that music students score better on tests; they also know that Sammy enjoys soccer, and Marie loves hip-hop dance. How much is too much? Most parents of elementary school students haven't yet figured out the answer.

The problem for music teachers is that many activities take place for only a few weeks at a time. Ten weeks for soccer, six weeks for the school play, one week for nature camp. This wreaks havoc with schedules. Some children are so overscheduled that it's a wonder they have time to brush their teeth and do their homework. Obviously, not only are these children likely to miss lessons, but they also don't have time to practice.

Introductory interviews (we talked about these in Chapter 10) are the place to discuss scheduling and priorities. Generally, once parents understand that music lessons are a regularly scheduled weekly commitment that cannot easily be rescheduled, they prioritize lessons and show up as planned. Or, they decide not to do them at all.

But it's not just about coming to lessons. Overscheduling is a much bigger problem because overscheduled students don't have time to do anything well. Addressing this issue isn't a matter of prioritizing music above everything else, but it is a matter of being honest and direct. It's not possible to learn an instrument without regular lesson attendance *and* regular practice. Parents need to understand this when they make commitments to their children's activities.

The Role of Parents

Parents of elementary-age music students can have an enormous influence on the success of their children. As with preschool children, some parental involvement is sometimes necessary. Many teachers of younger students ask parents to sit in on lessons and simply pay attention. Others expect parents to act as practice coaches (depending on the relationship between parent and child—not all children at this age accept parental help).

Take Note

A parent doesn't have to be a musician to encourage a child to practice. Parents can ask to hear a prelesson family "recital," can ask to hear their "favorite" songs played "just once more, please," and can encourage their child to play for Grandma, Grandpa, or the family pet. A regular standing family performance is one way to integrate music into family life and keep tabs on how the child is doing.

Beyond assisting with practice and making sure that the assigned tasks have been completed, the best help a parent can give a child is to make sure the family has a sane schedule with a regular time for practice. Many families find that before and after dinner, or after breakfast and before leaving for school works well. Children need routine, and the earlier the habit of regular practice is instilled, the better.

Muddling Through Middle School

Middle school starts in fifth or sixth grade, depending on the school, and goes through eighth grade. No longer young children motivated by stickers, kids in middle school are sandwiched between childhood and full-fledged teenager-dom. One week, you may get the goofy little kid who can be teased and cajoled into a better performance. The next week, you may get the stereotypical moody, glum teenager.

Middle school is typically the time when beginners become intermediate players, and some start showing real chops. The most talented might even be trying to play advanced repertoire. At this stage, the school band is starting to sound pretty good and the jazz ensemble doesn't take just anyone who walks in the door. Students may come to their private lessons clutching solos or telling you they've joined the orchestra and need to learn 20 pages of music by next week. Or maybe they want to accompany the school chorus; can you help them learn their part?

They may also start developing pronounced tastes in music and be more than willing to tell you what they "love" and what they "hate." You may find yourself chasing down the scores for the power ballad by the latest teenage heartthrob.

Typical Challenges

Scheduling remains a challenge for this age groups, although it's not quite as bad as elementary school. By fifth or sixth grade, and certainly by seventh and eight grades, many children have settled into a smaller number of activities, although the commitment to those activities may be more serious.

In seventh and eighth grades, students are dealing with increased expectations in school, as well as changes in their bodies and hormones that affect moods, attitudes, and energy levels. Peers become increasingly important. If you're lucky enough to have kids with friends who are musical, there's more motivation to keep going, but peer pressure can work the other way, too. It's not unusual for children at this age to become suddenly and completely overwhelmed. Music can be a refuge for them, or it can add to the pressure. Add parents haranguing about practice to the mix, and the student may decide it's all too much and the only answer is to quit. For the teacher, this means walking a fine line between encouragement and coddling, between setting reasonable expectations and tipping over that invisible emotional line that drives so many young teens.

Although many students start music lessons at the age of 7 or 8, a few wait until middle school—especially on larger wind instruments. If you have middle school beginners, especially in the higher grades, be careful in your choice of method books. Kids in middle school are very intent on not being perceived as little kids, so you'll want to avoid the babyish-looking books with bright colors and pictures of teddy bears.

Practice Makes ... Permanent

At the solid intermediate level, the quality of practice becomes increasingly important. Quantity is important, too. As songs get more difficult, the amount of time required to learn them increases. But quantity is only part of the equation. The saying that practice makes perfect isn't entirely true. Rather, practice makes permanent. And only perfect practice makes permanently perfect.

This is where a student who has been taught methodical practice methods has a leg up on students who are in the habit of simply sitting down, banging or tooting or bowing their pieces a few times, and declaring their practice a success. And, as every teacher knows, the result of playing something incorrectly 100 times in a row is to learn it incorrectly.

Correct practice is something that intermediate-level middle school students tend to resist with all their might. (To be fair, many adults resist it, too.) Yes, some students enjoy the process, almost making a game of noting the progress, and finally getting to that point where they can fly through a piece and it's fun. But more students get frustrated. They are impatient. They want to play the piece, not struggle with it, and nothing comes quite as quickly as they want it to.

Take Note

Teach students to use the metronome to work on technique and fluency. Students should learn a piece until they can play it at half-speed with the metronome. Then the practice process is to play the piece (or a section of it) three times in a row with no mistakes. Once that is accomplished, the student moves the metronome up a notch and does it again. If a mistake is made, the student has to start the count from the beginning.

A methodical teacher approaches introducing each piece the same way. What is its time signature? What is its key signature? Is it major or minor? How can you tell? Are there clef changes, key changes, or time signature changes in it? What is the musical "story" of the piece? Does it have repeated patterns? A series of chord progressions? A motif that repeats several times starting on different notes? Scales? Arpeggios? At times you may sound like a broken record. For pianists—"One hand at a time." For everyone—"One line at a time, one phrase at a time, one measure at a time. Count out loud" (unless you're a wind player, in which case you'd better be deliberately counting in your head). "Work with the metronome at a slow speed, at a medium speed, at a fast speed." "Do it again. And again. And again."

Motivating Middle Schoolers

Many middle school students who have been taking lessons for a few years have reached a level where playing music can actually be recreational. A guitar student who has been taking a few years of lessons is probably capable of accompanying songs, or even soloing over a band. A pianist might be able to accompany friends or choruses, or play in church. A violinist might handle fiddle tunes, and horn players might be able to improvise.

Middle school students are starting to develop a firmer sense of their own musical personalities. They are choosing music for their iPods, and they are starting to define themselves by what music speaks to them. With their newfound skills, some middle schoolers are apt to march into lessons wanting to play everything from pop songs, to jazz tunes, to a song from a movie score. For the teacher, this is all good, although one challenge can be keeping them on track. Although it's fine to veer off into the "fun" stuff, the typical intermediate player still has a lot to learn about technique, and there's a lot of hard work that still needs to be done. Balance is the key issue, as well as the judicious doling out of "reward" pieces.

To keep middle school students on task and in balance, consider these guidelines:

◆ Careful selection of repertoire is essential. Look for balance between big-sounding pieces they can learn quickly, reliable "student savers" (pieces that virtually every student loves to play over and over again, and which can help revive flagging interest), pieces they can be assigned to learn on their own, pop pieces, and challenge pieces.

◆ Understand the student's musical tastes. Not to encourage a stereotype, but (some) girls and (some) boys gravitate to different music. Let's say you have two students, a 12-year-old boy and a 12-year-old girl. Who's going to want "Dancing in the Moonlight"? Who's going to choose "Indian War Dance"?

◆ Encourage students to play in any ensemble they show an interest in—anything from playing with the rock "band" they formed with their friend down the street, to playing the glockenspiel in a school symphony orchestra ensemble. If they are playing music with other people, they are more likely to have fun and more likely to keep playing.

The Role of Parents

Parents of middle schoolers are walking the same tightrope as teachers are—trying to be encouraging without being off-putting, supportive without domineering. Most middle schoolers are reluctant to accept help from parents. The student may even scoff at the parent's comments, especially if the parent is not a musician. But parents can still help by creating sane family schedules that include space and time for music.

Another way parents can help is by taking their children to live music events. It doesn't matter whether it's a coffeehouse, a rock concert, a symphony orchestra, or a band in the park. You can post news of kid-friendly concerts and student discounts on your website or on your music room door. Or you could even organize a field trip yourself.

High School Students

By high school, most kids have developed strong preferences about the music they like (although these preferences can certainly change). They are starting to figure out who they are and what they want to play, and they need a good reason to play anything else. But students who stick with music through high school are doing it because they want to; very few parents force lessons on high school students.

Typical Challenges

For high school students, the challenge is to keep them motivated and interested at a time in their life when the world is becoming much more complex, and peers and popular culture are tugging them in various directions.

Music is incredibly important to most high school students, many of whom identify themselves by what's on their iPod. A classical music teacher could do worse than to take a break from Beethoven and teach jazz chords, modes and scales, and syncopated pop rhythms. In fact, this is a great way to teach music theory. This is not to suggest that a talented student who is considering a music major abandon the classics. But marginal students, or those who are wavering, can be energized by playing music they like.

High school students continue to have a strong peer orientation. Encouraging and actively helping students to play in ensembles, even if it's a punk band, can keep them in music throughout their high school years. Playing in a concert band, marching band, jazz band, or orchestra, are all social experiences as well as musical ones.

> **Take Note** _____
>
> Some students start lessons in high school and think that because they are in high school, they shouldn't have to do all the same beginner things little kids have to do. Therefore, select your method very carefully. For a high school kid, a year spent in baby books is not going to be motivational; it's going to be endless. As the teacher, after assessing the student's strengths, learning style, and goals, you may decide to throw in a little "music candy"—easy chords, easy improvisation exercises, play-along CDs in a style they like—to get them going.

Sports and Academics

In high school, most kids have settled into a routine of things they do and things they don't do. They won't be running off to try Afro-Caribbean drumming one week and ballet the next. But just as their extracurricular activities settle down, other issues pop up. Many high school kids have a lot of homework, not to mention college entrance exams, driver's ed, and visits to colleges. The extracurricular activities they do may take up more time than ever, and they may have after-school jobs, along with employers who demand that they come in on short notice, regardless of their music lessons.

> **Take Note** _____
>
> Evening lessons tend to work well for scheduling high school students. Many teens are up late, and by evening they are likely to be home from part-time jobs; many states don't allow teens under 18 to work past a certain hour. But avoid Fridays and weekends; no way can music lessons compete with football and basketball games, or the school dance.

High school kids either participate in sports at a committed high level or don't participate at all. The committed athlete, however, can drive a music teacher to gray hair, especially if it's a student with musical talent. Team sports can have brutal training schedules, coaches who refuse to accept excuses for absences, and unpredictable game and tournament schedules.

You can, of course, turn down a student whose sports schedule is so relentless that music lessons are missed week after week. If a new parent approaches you saying that they're changing teachers because the old teacher is "inflexible" about sport-related absences, you have a pretty clear idea of what lies ahead. It's a little harder when you have had a long-term relationship with a good student who simply wants to do too much. The best strategy, if you want to keep such a student and stay sane, is to schedule them for an unpopular time later in the evening (the last lesson of the day), and figure that they will be a part-time student.

The Role of Parents

The role of the parents of high school musicians is pretty much relegated to chauffeur and banking duties, along with making sure the student doesn't miss too many lessons.

Most parents of teens in high school won't insist that they continue to take music lessons if the student clearly wants to quit. The only exception might be if the student is starting to be an advanced player or has already reached that level. This isn't to say that a 16-year-old who is playing Chopin etudes should be encouraged in a performance career. But a student who has reached this level has so much ability, and there is so much more to learn. Sticking with it at this stage can make that difference between true musical competence and "I wish my parents hadn't let me quit."

Special Needs Students

Special needs students are students, of any age, who are somehow off the path of mainstream learning. They may have attention deficit hyperactivity disorder (ADHD), suffer from anxiety, or be somewhere on the autism spectrum. They may have developmental delays or dyslexia, or problems with vision or motor skills.

Wise Words

I've found that kids with ADD/ADHD often need to be doing some kind of physical movement in order to pay attention. But their fidgeting can make it difficult to get things done. What I'll sometimes do is give the child a small squishy ball to hold and play with while I'm talking. His need for movement is satisfied by playing with the tactile toy, and he can consequently pay better attention to what I'm saying.

—Libby Wiebel, singer, songwriter, piano instructor; Falls Church, Virginia

As with most learning and development issues, special needs exist on a continuum, ranging from students who are just a little bit off the "normal" learning path, to students who need an entirely different approach. Some special needs students will never be able to do much more than pick out a simple children's song; others are fully able to learn, if taught in a way that they can absorb and apply.

Should You Teach Special Needs Students?

Not all music teachers are qualified, by either training or temperament, to teach special needs students. In many cases, teaching special needs students is not about musical achievement, but about exposure to music—about the journey, not the destination.

The two main requirements are patience (again, that word) and creativity. Teachers need to be able to find ways to engage students and keep their attention. They need to be able to identify the learning tools and strategies that will work. And they need to enjoy (and ensure that students enjoy) the process.

The Role of Parents

Sometimes parents don't tell teachers about special needs, especially if they aren't immediately obvious. Some parents want to start their kids off with a clean slate, or they may be afraid that you'll reject their child. If the child is being mainstreamed, it may be difficult to figure out what's going on. Other parents acknowledge that a teacher can do a better job from the start if she knows what she's dealing with because, among other things, the teacher may have a collection of appropriate materials that won't frustrate the student.

Out of Tune

Never try to diagnose a learning disability! Music teachers are in no way qualified to say to a parent, "I think Johnny is dyslexic." Instead, ask the parent how the child is doing in school, and perhaps suggest, "I've noticed that Johnny has trouble following the notes when they go up or down. Is there something I should know about his reading, or something you would recommend I do?" If the answer is negative, a gentle suggestion to get the child tested for vision or reading problems might pinpoint not only musical issues, but academic learning issues as well.

Communication with parents is essential. For instance, you might have a child who says he needs to go to the bathroom several times a lesson. Is it true that he needs to go? Is it a behavioral issue? Is he trying to get away from the lesson? Is it physiological? A parent can tell you what's going on and how you should respond. Similarly, a parent should feel free to let you know if any assignments you give the child are frustrating, are too hard, or require more than he can give. (Of course, your "typical" students probably already complain that the music you assign is too frustrating, too much, and too hard. But in a special needs case, it might actually be true.)

The "usefulness" of the parent at home during the week varies, just as it does with the rest of your students. Depending on the situation, it might help if the parent sits with the child during practice sessions. Or the child might resist being watched over. The practice routine is something that you, the parent, and the child will have to work out.

Making It Work

Entire college degrees are focused on teaching special education. For the private music teacher with one or two such students, the following techniques may help:

♦ Set expectations. Expectations for special needs students may be completely different from the expectations you have for mainstream students.

♦ Assign short practice pieces. Look for jobs that make the student feel successful.

♦ Choose appropriate teaching material. A special needs student may need completely different material, either easier material designed for younger students or a methodology that follows a different learning path. For example, a student might need rote pattern repetition rather than note reading.

♦ Alter materials. Give visually impaired students music written with bigger notes; an enlarging photocopier will take care of this. Color-coding may also help students who are having trouble making sense of the dots and lines.

♦ Abandon tasks that are too hard. Frustration serves no purpose.

♦ Use plenty of off-chair and away-from-the-instrument activities. Vary the lesson and make things fun.

♦ Assign very small tasks for at-home practice. Give copious praise for doing them.

A special sense of accomplishment accompanies working with some of these children. And parents talk. If you are enthusiastic and good with special needs students, don't be surprised to find others finding you. And don't be afraid to ask for help. A local college course in special needs education is a good move for teachers who find themselves working with these special children.

The Least You Need to Know

◆ Start with your elementary school students by establishing (perhaps multiple times) expectations for practice and lesson attendance. You will reap the rewards later.

◆ Middle school students need support and encouragement, or they can be overwhelmed with growing demands on their time.

◆ High school students generally continue music lessons of their own volition, but add some music candy to their regular diet in the form of popular repertoire and cool jazz techniques to keep them interested.

◆ Teaching special needs students can be rewarding, but success depends on establishing good communication with the parent and being flexible enough to modify expectations and teaching methods for each student.

Chapter 13

Teaching Adult Students

In This Chapter

- ◆ The adult student's goals, and matching them to abilities and practice habits

- ◆ Adult learning issues, including finger stiffness, slow progress, and frustration

- ◆ Learning methods for the adult beginner

- ◆ Repertoire and technical studies for the returning more advanced adult student

Adult students come in all ages and from all occupations. Some have had musical training, some haven't. Some are quick, some are slow. About the only thing they have in common is a little bit of free time and the desire to learn.

Sometimes adults with prior musical training take up a second instrument; the most common choices include violin, cello, and saxophone. But the vast majority of adult students study piano, voice, guitar, or bass.

How Teaching Adults Is Different

There are so many differences between teaching an adult and a child that it's impossible to list them all. Adults have stiffer hands, they are self-motivated but can easily get frustrated, and they can be incredibly impatient with themselves and overly critical. But with all the differences, it's nonetheless true that the actual process of learning notes and counting rhythms is actually quite similar for adults and children. And one thing that children and adults certainly have in common is that learning music is a challenge. There's no way around it.

Teacher-Student Dynamics

The dynamics of the teacher-student relationship are necessarily different with adults. Adult students are likely to bring their long-standing musical and learning baggage to their lessons. Sitting with their instrument, they may feel as vulnerable and exposed as a young child. They may think themselves "stupid at music theory," or as "having a bad ear" or "unable to sing in tune." They may have memories of frustration—or memories of success—and neither set of memories may be entirely accurate.

And, just as with children, adults will come into your studio with a long list of reasons why they didn't practice. (They will also tell you, as earnestly as a child, that they "played it perfectly at home.") And they will express annoyance at having to practice in sections, slowly and repeatedly.

The challenge for the teacher is to deal with these very childlike problems in a way that is appropriate for an adult. Successful teachers of adult students are those who choose interesting repertoire that the students want to play—pieces that are a good match for the student's practice commitment and abilities. The teacher of adults also needs to support adult students emotionally while they struggle through the early awkwardness of trying to teach middle-aged hands to do things they have never done before or have long since forgotten.

Scheduling

Scheduling adults is a completely different breed of animal from scheduling children. Many adults who have time for music lessons have unorthodox work schedules. They might be stay-at-home moms, they might work part time, or they may be retired. It's not unheard of for someone with a 9-to-5 schedule and family responsibilities to take music lessons, but it is unusual because of the time commitment.

Adults are not usually on a school-year schedule (although if they have school-age children, they may be governed by the ebbs and flows of school holidays and vacations), so they are able to come to music lessons at times that are not possible for children. Evening hours, for instance, don't work for 7-year-olds, but an after-dinner lesson often works for an adult. Similarly, adults who have flexible or nontraditional work schedules might be available during the day. Thus, adults fill in hours that a music teacher might otherwise not be teaching.

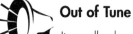 **Out of Tune**

It usually does not work for two students to share time slots by taking biweekly lessons on an alternating basis. There are always cancellations, which throw everyone off. If the lessons can't be made up, biweekly lessons then turn into monthly lessons, and finally into no lessons at all.

Many adults request biweekly lessons. Whether this will work depends on the student's commitment, the teacher's schedule, and also the level of the student.

If you have an available time slot and are willing to schedule biweekly lessons, make sure the lesson is long enough to cover two weeks of practiced work—at least 45 minutes, and preferably an hour. Biweekly lessons are a much better choice for advanced students than for intermediates because advanced students can generally go home and work on technical or interpretive issues independently and find creative ways to solve problems. With intermediates, meaningful practice depends on whether students are able to work independently. Biweekly lessons are not generally appropriate for beginners, who need a lot of handholding and reinforcement.

Policy Issues

Some teachers apply the same scheduling and payment policies to adults as they do to children. Many other teachers feel that they can be more flexible with adults because adults use time slots that are not otherwise in demand. Be aware, however, that some adult students attend lessons religiously and some cancel on a whim. This affects both your business and the amount the student can learn. If you teach only a handful of adults, you may not consider this a problem (and you may even welcome the occasional hour off). However, if a high percent of your students are adults, having to deal with constant scheduling changes and make-ups can become unwieldy, in which case you need to lay down the ground rules of what works for you and what doesn't. Here are some policy choices to consider.

- Apply the same policies across the board to adults and children alike.

- Apply the same policies to adults who must be scheduled during the in-demand after-school hours, but be flexible for adults taking lessons in nonprime slots.

- Charge adults by the lesson and let them cancel whenever they want, but charge a higher per-lesson rate for students who are not committing to a fixed annual tuition.

- Allow cancellations, but ask for 24 hours' notice except in cases of illness or emergency.

- Charge by the month according to the number of lessons scheduled, and offer make-ups only if they can be rescheduled during the week the lesson is missed.

Some teachers write up a separate policy for adult students, which minimizes confusion and makes expectations clear.

Beginning Adults

The term "beginning adult" covers a wide range of interests and abilities. As with children, adults vary widely in how they take in and process information. Aptitudes vary. Some have listened to music their whole lives, and it shows in their understanding of musical styles. Others seem to be starting from square one.

Typical Challenges

Three factors affect how you teach adults and how well they progress—their aptitude, their goals, and their ability to stick it out. Many adults say they just want to be able to "sit down and play and have fun," but that isn't as easy as it sounds.

Some students may come in with a great ear and be able to pick out chords and tunes on a keyboard; others may have fingers so stiff that it takes weeks before they can plunk out a three-note chord. Some students have the kind of "music smarts" that make them easily able to grasp concepts of music theory, such as how scales are formed, how chords are made, and how chord extensions and alterations are named. And others can get stuck on the simplest concept, never quite managing to master the difference between sharps and flats or major and minor.

For the teacher, the first challenge is aligning goals with aptitude. Even with a seemingly adept adult, start slowly. Before you barge in with stacks of chord charts or scales or explanations of modes, make sure that you understand how the student processes information. You will need to present material very differently to different adults. Individuality of learning styles is something adults have in common with children.

Finger Stiffness

While young children's hands are floppy and soft, adults can have a grip of steel. They have spent most of their life not playing an instrument. For an adult to play a fluid, correctly fingered scale is about as impossible as most of us getting up and doing a back flip. With additional issues such as arthritis, the problem is exacerbated.

Knowing some basic rote exercises that don't involve complicated notation can help a lot, if the adult is willing to do them. Choose exercises that focus on one issue at a time. They should be simple to remember (but write down instructions, just in case), and you should give specific instructions. For example: "Play five times starting on each string." "Play three times with your eyes closed."

You may also need to modify tasks to make them more achievable. Guitar teachers can use "cheater" chords. Piano teachers can modify left-hand chords so that the student plays two notes instead of three. You may just have to accept that a complete chord isn't going to happen for a while.

Adult Frustration

Frustration can be intense for adult students, regardless of ability or prior study. Children can happily bang out "Twinkle, Twinkle, Little Star" week after week. In fact, very young children thrive on repetition; just ask any parent who has had to read *Goodnight, Moon* a thousand times. Adults, however, aren't so easily satisfied. They don't want to play "Twinkle, Twinkle, Little Star" over and over, and they aren't placated by stickers. They know what "Stairway to Heaven" sounds like, and they know that when *they* play it, it doesn't sound like that.

Adults are used to using their minds, and many adults—especially adults who have experienced academic and intellectual success in other fields—think that if they understand something, they should be able to do it. Unfortunately, learning to play an instrument doesn't work that way. A student can understand the circle of fifths and all the key signatures, but still be unable to find the chords with her fingers. It takes practice, drills, and long hours of repetition to transfer intellectual understanding into the fingers, and even more hours to make hand placement automatic and natural. Often the end isn't in sight—or, more accurately, there is no end, because learning an instrument is a lifelong process that never ends.

Senior Adult Frustration

With senior learners, all the same challenges apply, but they may be multiplied. Some seniors have more trouble learning and retaining new material, so if the music is entirely new to them, the learning curve may be steeper. Fingers and joints are often very stiff and uncooperative. In many cases, the seemingly simple goal of just being able to sit down and play some favorite songs or hymns may be two or more years away.

> **Out of Tune**
>
> Nothing is more frustrating for a student than being given an "easy" piece and not being able to learn it. Teachers need to examine carefully any assignments given to students to be sure that the student can handle each skill demanded by the piece. Many commercially published arrangements are sold as "easy" when, in fact, they aren't easy at all.

Be aware that many senior beginners don't have lofty musical goals for themselves. They just want to play songs they like and enjoy the process of making music, even if on a beginning level. They don't expect to sound like rock stars or classical concert artists. For the teacher, knowing where to look for pleasing but simple arrangements is paramount. You may have to adapt or rearrange some music.

Choosing Adult Materials

The two instruments adult students gravitate to—piano and guitar—are the two instruments with the biggest selection of introductory learning books, starting with children's method books and including methods for classical, popular, and jazz music; play-along-with-the-CD music; "teach yourself" books; and method books specifically designed for the older learner.

We'll talk specifically about method books in Chapter 15. For adults, the choice is important, and it shouldn't be made too quickly. Not all teachers use method books with adults. And some teachers use method books with one adult and not another. It depends very much on a student's goals and natural abilities. Some students may come to beginning guitar lessons already able to read music from playing trumpet in the high school band. Or they may have a coordinated fretting hand from a few years of beginning violin. Or they may not be interested in learning to read music and may want to know how to make and strum chords instead. When faced with students who come in with spotty musical knowledge—knowing this but not that, being able to do one thing but not the other, wanting to learn this but not that—some teachers prefer to make up their own method as they go along, tailoring it to the student's interests.

Wise Words

I feel that a lot of the 'adult' method books move too quickly for the average adult student. Most adult students have full-time jobs, kids, dogs, houses, etc., to pay attention to. Sometimes practice falls by the wayside just as a course of everyday life. When I have an adult like this who can't handle the pace of the adult book, I'll sometimes supplement with or switch them to a children's method book. The children's methods move slower and have a lot more reinforcement of concepts. And most adults aren't offended by using a kids' book at all. In fact, it comes as a relief.

—Libby Wiebel, singer, songwriter, piano instructor; Falls Church, Virginia

For absolute beginners who seem a bit befuddled, a method book offers an organized, step-by-step approach that keeps everything in order. Some adults neither understand the elements of music notation and organization on an intellectual level nor have an instinct for the sound and feel of their chosen instrument. Such students can learn to play, but it takes a long time, and a lot of patience, not only on the teacher's part but also on the student's part. And it takes dedicated practice that is hard to sustain in the face of such slow progress unless the musical material being learned is rewarding and fun.

Practice Issues for Beginning Adults

Because frustration is such a huge issue for adults, teachers need to be up front about practice. Let the student drive the train, but be certain that the student understands where it's going. If the student will be satisfied with slow and incremental progress over many months, then an irregular practice schedule is not doing any harm. But if a beginning piano student wants to learn the first movement of "Moonlight Sonata" after one year of lessons (assuming he is capable of it—most students aren't), he needs to know that he's probably looking at an hour a day of practice, if not more.

But remember, these are adults. It's up to that student to actually put in that time and achieve that goal. Your job is to try to make sure that the goal is reasonable, to give her the supplemental work she will need to have the skills to reach it, and to be as honest as possible about the amount of work required.

What's reasonable? As a rule of thumb, if an adult puts in a solid half-hour a day about five days a week, then progress is satisfying and noticeable. In a sense, practicing an instrument is exactly like working out every day. You can work out for 2 hours one day, but the next day you may not have lost an ounce of weight. And if you work out for 2 hours one day and then don't work out for a week, you lose the benefit of having done anything at all. Both exercise and musical progress are long-term goals, and people fail for the same reasons—lack of visible progress, lack of faith in the process, and frustration.

As the teacher, your job is to be head cheerleader, not to be disapproving or punitive about practice. Adults take lessons voluntarily; if you make it too demanding, they will quit.

"I Could Have Been a Contender"

Assessing the returning adult can be a challenging process. Two adults may use completely different language to describe the exact same level of accomplishment. For instance, one adult might confidently state that she had 12 years of lessons and played Chopin and Beethoven, and then demonstrate her skills by confidently and unmercifully butchering Mozart's poor little "Sonata in C Major" (the one played by any child who reaches a solid intermediate playing level).

Another student might apologetically describe herself as someone who took lessons as a kid but forgot almost everything, and might have to start from scratch. She, too, also mangles Mr. Mozart, although the thrashing is perhaps not as thorough.

The first student lays out an ambitious course of study: she wants to play Beethoven's "Appassionata," and while we're at it, can she do the "Revolutionary Etude" of Chopin, too? The second student lets the teacher choose the repertoire. What to do with these two students?

With the first student, you'll have to find out how much of Mr. Mozart's butchering was the result of years away from the piano. Sometimes the problem may simply be that the student hasn't played for 20 years. She may once have been a good pianist, and she can regain that level with practice. Or it could be that she has an exaggerated remembrance of her abilities. You'll have to be the one who figures out where she is now and how well she seems to be progressing, and then gently tell her exactly what to expect on the road to being able to play the major piano works.

With the second student, you have a recipe for less frustration and more progress because you can start with manageable works, identify problem areas, and assign etudes and technique work to address those problems. Then you can make a selection of appropriate repertoire that will take the student forward technically, but can also be played musically.

Out of Tune

It can be hard to steer students away from the big virtuosic warhorses. But unless students have the technique to handle them, and the patience and work ethic to put into learning them, the big technical showpieces can turn into a mire of frustration. Have a few alternates on hand that have the same big sound, but perhaps not so many notes and difficulties.

Technique Issues for Returning Adults

Technique issues are a recurrent problem among returning adults. Sometimes the student's earlier teachers didn't focus on technique. Sometimes the students ignored it. It's often hard to tell whether the poor technique you're seeing is the result of disuse or whether it was never there to begin with. Many retuning adults don't remember their early lessons, or perhaps they've just blocked out the memories of having worked through standard tomes such as the Hanon piano drills or the Sor guitar exercises. In the end, what is important is that you be able to evaluate the student's current abilities and give enough remedial technique drills so that the student can achieve what he or she wants.

Even students who once reached a fairly advanced level of repertoire may have gotten there with substandard technique. Or they may have the memory of having played big concert pieces in their minds, but that memory may not exist in their fingers. Technique issues can stop students from achieving their goals or, even, from being able to return to music they once knew.

For returning students, depending on the level and the time away from the instrument, technique problems might include stiff fingers, stiff wrists, stiff arms, poor finger position, and the inability to move smoothly from position to position. In wind instruments and voice, breath control may be weak or lacking altogether. And basic skills—creating a vibrato on a violin, bending and hammering strings on a guitar, correctly fingering scales on the piano—may be completely forgotten.

It is not in the least unusual for a student to come into a lesson—the first one in 20 years—with a stack of books she used to play out of and be unable to play a single piece. For the teacher, this means being very conservative about where to start. Don't be afraid to review, or to choose easy pieces to evaluate reading, rhythm, and technique. It is far better to start too slowly than too quickly.

Take into account the student's current goals as well. A student who once played Bach's "Two-Part Inventions" on the piano might be unable to voice the parts properly. However, if that student is coming to you for lessons on how to play from a fake book, voicing Bach fugues is probably not necessary, at least for now.

The thing to remember about adults is this: they are in your studio for their own goals and reasons. Your job is to help them meet those goals, if possible, assuming they are doing their part to meet them, too.

Coachability

Athletic coaches talk about whether a student athlete is "coachable." Talent is one thing. The ability to accept and apply instructions is a different, equally important, skill. The same can be said of music. Some adults are more difficult to teach than others.

Some adults are difficult to teach because, no matter what you suggest and demonstrate, no matter how much you cajole, they go home and do the same thing they have always done. What teacher hasn't been frustrated to the hair-pulling-out stage by an adult who fumbles through a piece, occasionally correcting mistakes but never going back to work on eliminating the problem? Adult students can be every bit as reluctant as young students to practice one measure at a time, one phrase at a time, one section at a time.

Some adult students have very strong ideas of what they want to do. They are coming to lessons to learn that particular thing, and they are not interested in being told they should be focusing on doing something else first. Often problems arise when students want to play a piece of music that is way beyond their technical skills—usually big, noisy encore pieces with a strong flash factor. I recall an instance when an older gentleman wanted to work on Chopin's "G-minor Ballade," a concert-level piece with flashing octaves and flying fingers. His technique wasn't up to the piece at all, although he could get through enough of the notes that the piece was recognizable.

Playing it a thousand times would not have helped. What he needed to do was go back and practice basic exercises—arpeggios in all keys with proper legato, scales in double octaves, runs in strict metric timing. Instead, each week brought forth the same mistakes, only more entrenched, because you learn what you practice, and he practiced his mistakes. Worse, this student treated the elegant, quiet parts of the piece as an annoyance, merely as a bunch of notes to be hammered out between the flashier faster parts. And he flatly declared himself "not interested" in issues of phrasing or expression. He was quite convinced that most of the audience wouldn't hear the difference, so why should he care? Lessons ended, because there was no point in continuing. He knew he wasn't playing the piece the way it was supposed to sound, but he wasn't willing to do anything other than play it over and over again the same way.

This is, of course, an extreme case. More commonly, the problem is that the student has not been educated to hear the subtleties of dynamics and expression. These can be taught to a willing student, but not to an unwilling one. For a teacher, lack of musicality in a returning student who wants to tackle great works of art can make for a very long hour or a very short student-teacher relationship.

> **Take Note** _____
>
> Encourage students to listen. With YouTube offering multiple versions of just about every piece ever written, there's no reason not to explore interpretation. Save some lesson time for discussing interpretation, phrasing, and dynamics. Most students who listen to the great performers will sooner or later internalize their musicality and strive for it in their own playing.

Practice Issues for Returning Adults

Returning students have the same practice problems as every other music student, ranging from your youngest preschooler to yourself. No one practices enough, and everyone takes practice "shortcuts" that aren't shortcuts at all.

Beyond the problems (discussed in more detail in Chapter 14) that are common to everyone, here are some effective tips for working with a returning or more advanced adult student:

◆ If the student is expressing frustration, it sometimes helps to look in detail at how the student is working on the piece. Look especially at fingering.

◆ If poor practice habits are involved, the teacher can sometimes work through one or two phrases with the student in detail, showing exactly how to address each issue.

◆ Identify ongoing and limiting technical problems, and prioritize which issues to work on. Then choose repertoire that focuses on those issues.

◆ Try to determine whether the student has physical limitations that are simply not going to be fixed. Just as a 200-pound middle-age woman is not going to become a prima ballerina, some fingers are never going to be able to play "Variations on a Theme of Paganini"—or, for that matter, anything by Paganini himself. Choose repertoire that the student can master.

◆ Match student expectations and practice to repertoire. Teachers need to get a sense of the practice commitment to know what and how much to assign. Better to assign a short, easy piece that can be mastered in the amount of time a student has to practice than a piece that will take months of 10-minute here-and-there practice sessions.

Sometimes the teacher of the adult student needs to accept that an adult student's performance of a well-loved piece may sound perfectly dreadful to us, but that same performance may give that student enormous pleasure. The student may know he is missing notes, or flubbing legatos, or fudging the fast runs, or playing the whole thing at only half the suggested tempo. But if he gets satisfaction out of playing the piece, uses that piece to express his feelings, and feels a sense of accomplishment, then, as teachers, we are doing our jobs.

The Least You Need to Know

◆ Adult methods may not be the best way to teach adult beginners. Sometimes kids' methods help adult students progress at a better pace and are less threatening.

◆ Be honest with adults about practice requirements because adults who do not make satisfying progress will quit.

◆ Returning adults may be overly ambitious about what they want to play. Provide some alternative suggestions that have the same feel but are more manageable.

◆ Try to get adult students to listen to great performances of the music they want to play so they have a model.

Chapter 14

Solving Common Studio Problems

In This Chapter

- Reluctant students
- Practice problems
- Teaching parents to help you teach their kids
- Troubleshooting business issues
- When it's time to let a student go

Studio problems come in two basic flavors: educational issues and business issues. Educational issues tend to fall into certain predictable categories: lack of practice, poor motivation, learning difficulties, reluctance to take on a challenge, coordination issues, counterproductive or inappropriate behavior in lessons, and inability to pay attention. And just when you think you have it figured out, a student will surprise you with a challenge you haven't yet seen.

Business issues make up a shorter list. They include nonpayment, absences, and scheduling problems. However, if you have implemented a good studio policy, these are usually much easier problems to address, although doing so is not necessarily pleasant.

Whether the problem is educational or business oriented, it affects how you deal with students and their parents. You're not human if you don't have trouble relating to a student who seems to have talent but *never* practices. Similarly, your relationship with a steady-paying student will be different from the relationship you have with a student whose family you are constantly "chasing" for payments. Again, you're not human if these external factors don't affect your relationship with the student. In this chapter, we'll figure out how to deal with students equitably in spite of common music studio problems that may put a strain on teacher-student relationships.

Educational Issues

Of all the issues that have ever faced music teachers across the span of centuries, one is a constant: lack of practice.

No matter how much children enjoy music, no matter how much they like plinking out "Heart and Soul" and "Chopsticks," and the first nine notes of "Für Elise" or the first phrase of "Stairway to Heaven," no matter how much they enjoy Guitar Hero—actual practice is something else entirely.

Practice is "hard," practice is "boring," practice is something "I forgot."

Not Practicing

In Chapters 11, 12, and 13, we talked about various amounts of practice time for students of all ages at different levels. We also discussed ways to help students develop effective and regular practice habits. But what if all the teacher encouragement and parental nagging doesn't help? What if the student is simply not practicing?

If you have included a student "contract" in your studio policy, now is the time to bring it out. And if you haven't, now may be the time to say to the student, "We need to come to an agreement on this, because otherwise you are going to be playing 'America the Beautiful' for the next 17 years. And I don't know about you, but I don't want to hear this song every week for the next 17 years, especially because, if you would practice it correctly for one week, you could move on to something else."

Your success with this approach, of course, will vary, depending in no small part on just why and how strongly the student is resisting practice and whether he even wants to be taking music lessons. A child who enjoys lessons and music but dislikes practicing may be reachable. A child who wants no part of music lessons is a whole other problem (which we'll get to a bit later).

Teachers use a combination of encouragement, threats, rewards, and sheer bribery to get kids to practice. While no strategy works with all children, some of these work for some children:

- A log for minutes practiced *each day.*

- Reward stickers for meeting weekly practice goals.

- Reward stickers for well-played songs.

- A parent's signature on a daily practice log.

- Careful repertoire selection. Every instrument has a repertoire of "student savers"—pieces that are so much fun to play that even a resistant student will play them over and over.

 Take Note _____

Have problem students sign a practice "contract" for a certain amount of time. The contract should include how much practice, when, how many missed days are "allowed," and specific tasks that must be done and logged at each session. This allows the student to take responsibility and may help the teacher identify problem areas.

- Bribery. A student who is dying to play "Star Wars" or "Pink Panther" or the "Peanuts Theme" will be allowed to do so after meeting a specific goal.

- Probation. A probation period needs to be very clear. It needs to have a firm end point, at which point the student is either "off probation" or out of your studio.

With older students, reason occasionally works. A stern "What are you doing here?" in an adult-to-adult tone can catch an underperforming teen off-guard and serve as a wake-up call. The response will usually be a blank stare, but you can continue by saying that you don't understand why they're coming to lessons if they're not going to put in even minimal effort. Ask them if they like music. Ask if they want to be able to play the instrument so that they can enjoy themselves and express themselves. Ask them what they want to play (and listen to the answer). If you have a good relationship with the student, you might see a turn-around.

Sometimes, however, students and parents aren't forthcoming about practice problems. Family difficulties, schoolwork issues, and emotional ups and downs (typical of young teenagers) are frequent triggers for students to slide backward, especially in the late middle school period. Sometimes teachers need to know when not to push and when to take the pressure off, let students enjoy their lessons, and coast for a bit.

Incorrect Practicing

Incorrect practice is almost as endemic a problem as lack of practice, and probably even more detrimental to musical progress. Practice is "hard"; correct practice is excruciating.

Correct practice is an ongoing battle, and too often the student's performance clearly demonstrates that by "Yes, I practiced" the student means, "Yes, I stumbled through this piece and I'm not sure whether or not I am even playing the right notes because I never actually took the time to stop and think." It is completely normal to want to plough through an entire piece. We teachers are as prone to doing it as our students are. We also know from experience that it simply doesn't work. There's no getting around the fact that pieces must be learned one section at a time. It is very obvious to an experienced teacher just exactly what kind of practice is being done at home.

Facts and Stats

A recent study concludes that it takes a person 10,000 hours of practice to become a master in disciplines such as music, sports, and chess. The research took place at Berlin's Academy of Music, where researchers studied violin students who began playing at the age of 5. Practice time started at two to three hours a week, then increased. Researchers concluded that practice time, not talent, made the difference between being good and being brilliant, and that 10,000 hours was the magic number.

Sometimes the student doesn't understand something. Stop at the problem area and have the student show you how he or she would work it out if you weren't there. Watching a student try to "practice" can be excruciating but instructive. Avoid the overpowering temptation to jump in and help with a pointed question or a whispered "That's a C!" What you need to find out is where the stumbling blocks are. You may have thought you sent the student home knowing where all the starting notes were, how to figure out any notes he or she didn't know, and how to tap the rhythm or write in the counts, only to find that the student is randomly plucking notes out of thin air, guessing at the rhythm, and desperately hoping that something, somehow, will sound right.

About the only way to fix this is to break down the practice process into step-by-step modules and repeat them in your lessons so often that the student can recite them by heart. Even so, working this way requires focus and mental energy. There's no guarantee that your student will play by the rules once he or she gets home.

Task-Related Difficulties

Learning to play an instrument is a process involving several different learning streams at once. It makes learning to read look like a walk in the proverbial park.

Task-related problems may include any or all of the following:

- Inability to count out beats
- Inability to keep a steady pulse
- Inability to internalize rhythm
- Inability to read notes
- Incorrect hand positions
- Incorrect fingerings, or tendency to forget fingerings
- Incorrect breathing
- Incorrect bowing
- Incorrect hand positions
- Incorrect body posture
- Incorrect arm weight
- Lack of coordination
- Poor tone production
- Lack of phrasing, or inappropriate phrasing
- Inability to articulate adequately or properly
- Inattention to dynamics or inappropriate dynamic changes

And, of course, the more difficulties a student has, the more difficult it is to practice, and the less fun it is to try to play.

It's crucial that the teacher identify where the major difficulties are and where the student's strengths are. Focus on fixing one issue at a time. A student who is floundering is not going to be able to fix rhythm, pitch, breathing, bowing, tuning, pedaling, and articulation all at once. If the most important problem is rhythm, focus on rhythm and give the student easy assignments that will let him or her experience some success with rhythm. Many method series come with lots of supplemental material—not only technique and theory books, but performance books and repertoire books of music in various styles. Let the student learn new pieces at an easier level to give some sense of control over what he or she can do well, while focusing on pieces that address the deficiencies in lessons. And don't be afraid to go outside the method books you are using to find supplemental works, drills, exercises, etudes, and fun pieces. Stay on easy works that address the problem rather than moving on to more difficult pieces the student isn't ready for. But look for works that sound harder than they are to give the student a sense of accomplishment.

Out of Tune

Watch out for students who use their strengths to compensate for weaknesses. A child with a terrific natural sense of rhythm might be able to mimic complex syncopations after only a few hearings, but might be unable to figure out how to play these rhythms from a piece of printed music. It is the teacher's job to pinpoint when this is happening and make sure the student learns to count the rhythms. Otherwise, the student will never learn to play independently.

Often a practice problem is a reading problem. Some students can fool you into thinking that they can read music when they can't. And then they go home and can't figure out how to practice. A student with innate aural skills may be able to hear a piece and replicate it immediately, or replicate it closely enough that by trying adjacent notes, he or she will find the right ones. So the first rule is this: don't demonstrate how pieces sound for these students! Instead, give them "learn on your own" material at an easier level so that they work through the process of learning music. Be sure to pick obscure tunes that they're unlikely to have heard before.

Behavior Issues

The music teacher occupies a unique role in a child's life. The one-on-one time we spend with students over many years creates a familiar relationship that may include goofiness and true mutual affection. But familiarity can lead to overstepping boundaries.

Students are not always "in the mood" for lessons, and they are not always in the mood to try hard, think hard, or work hard. They get frustrated, get bored, and sometimes just flat-out dislike a piece. There may be sulking and eye-rolling at being presented with a piece that looks "hard," deep sighs at being asked to practice a piece for another week, expressions of boredom, resistance to trying something new, and declarations that they "hate" a song they haven't even tried yet. There may be fidget-ing, noodling while you are talking, and all manner of inattentiveness. It's normal, and it usually isn't personal. Kids want to see what they can get away with, and indeed, the more comfortable they are with you, the more they test the relationship, perhaps to see exactly what it's made of.

Obviously, they can't learn while they are working so hard to not learn. So it's your job to put a stop to it. How you deal with these behavior problems depends on your personality, your relationship with the student and the parent, and your overall feel-ings about what is going on. And in a few cases, it may also depend on whether you want to continue working with that student.

An example from my own studio seems both typical and instructive. A 5-year-old, at his first lesson, fidgeted ostentatiously and did his best to be completely unreachable and unteachable. And then, after about 3 minutes, he said, "Bored." (And, I should add, his tone of voice would make him the envy of any teenager trying to make a one-word point to a grown-up.) Up to this point, I had been my gentle teaching-a-very-young-child-carefully self, so when I said "Pardon me?" in a very stern tone of voice, he looked surprised and said, "I'm bored," but in a much smaller voice this time. To this I sternly replied, "Do you want piano lessons or not?" He nodded. I said. "Are you sure?" He nodded. He was then informed that rude behavior was not acceptable, and that was that. If he changed his mind and didn't want piano lessons, that was fine, and he was to go outside and tell his mom he was finished. Or he could stay and behave. His eyes got very big. I asked him if he understood, and he nodded. And that was the end of it. There was never another hint of rudeness.

Take Note

It's a last resort, and you should use it sparingly, but ending a lesson early—suddenly and firmly—is one of the most effective ways to put a stop to rude behavior. "Okay, this lesson is over," said in a calm and completely definite voice will snap a student to attention. But you have to mean it, and you *have* to carry through with it. Tell the student that you are not angry, but that his or her behavior is completely unacceptable. Chances are that if the child has the slightest interest in continuing lessons, you won't have to have the same conversation again.

Each teacher develops a unique personal style to deal with various levels of student rebellion. Minor rebellions can often be handled with humor and understanding, and a teacher who is generally good humored and funny and supportive will be all the more effective when and if she has to be stern and strict.

When the Student Hates Music Lessons

Sometimes you will be faced with a student who simply does not want to take lessons. Period. This can range from students who actively hate lessons but are being forced to take them by their parents, to students who don't mind obediently sitting in a lesson, and maybe even having fun, but who simply are not motivated to practice or who actively resist practicing.

It's sometimes hard to know exactly what's going on because what a student says about liking or not liking music lessons may have nothing to do with music lessons at all. It may have to do with rebelling against being told to do something, or it may be that the student doesn't want to have to practice in an older brother or sister's shadow. It may also have to do with being afraid of failure, or being reluctant to work hard, or not liking the music the teacher has chosen, or being frustrated with a lack of progress.

The problem for music teachers is that we understand that there is, for so many students, a pot of gold at the end of the rainbow. We know how much the ability to make music can add to a human's creative and artistic inner life. The list of reasons to take music lessons is long and well studied, ranging from improving math scores to establishing a pattern of hard work and stick-to-itiveness. One study even showed that, percentage wise, the group of applicants most likely to be admitted to medical school is music majors! Not to mention that all of us music teachers constantly hear the adults around us saying that they wish they hadn't quit music lessons.

So for us to suggest that a student end lessons truly requires that we believe a particular student is a "lost cause"—someone who actively resists, someone who might even be emotionally damaged by being forced to keep doing something he or she so actively dislikes. It's especially difficult for us when we see this happen with students who have ability and seem to enjoy music, but who just won't participate in their own learning process.

If a child is being forced to take lessons, occasionally it works to say, "Look, your mom said you are taking music lessons until the end of eighth grade, like it or not. So we are stuck with each other, unless I decide to boot you out of here, in which case I'm going to give your mom the name of the strictest teacher I can think of, and maybe she can do a better job. But if you're going to stay with me, we may as well make this easy for each other. I will let you play 'Raiders of the Lost Ark,' and I will not make you play those etudes that you hate. And in return, you will give me 20 minutes of decent practice 5 days a week. And we will try to have fun. Deal?"

If that doesn't work, there probably isn't much more you can do. If you're willing, you can, of course, continue to teach basically the same lesson week after week, in which case there's no problem (and probably a spot in heaven for you). If you aren't willing to essentially be a babysitter and playmate, simply say to the parent, "Jenny has been adamant about not wanting lessons. I am willing to teach her. I've done my best to motivate her and make this enjoyable by giving her fun songs. But I cannot make her practice. It has to be your job to get her to the piano for this minimum amount of time, or we can't continue." You are not, after all, a miracle worker.

Educating Parents

Parents don't mean to be problems. Quite the contrary, most parents are desperate to do the right thing for their children, and they appreciate any guidance you can give. Even if you are a beginning teacher just out of college, to them, you are the expert and the authority on how their child is learning music. And part of your job is to help educate the parents about how they can help.

Parent problems come in two main varieties: expectations that are too low, and expectations that are too high. The former is far more common than the latter.

Nonmusical Parents

Parents who have no musical training of their own are stepping into a whole new arena when they bring their children for music lessons, invest in an instrument, and spend perhaps $1,000 over the course of a year, after which their child may or may not be able to play much more than a simple little ditty. It is an act of faith on their part, and they are putting their trust in you.

Part of the problem is that nonmusical parents don't understand that the commitment to learning music involves years, not months. Very few other things that children do require the same type of daily exertion, one-on-one study with a teacher, the slow and sometimes frustrating progress, and plain old hard work. It is not at all uncommon for a parent to think that the weekly lesson is "practice." Don't assume that parents know anything at all about the process of learning music. Some may even need to be told that they have to supply an instrument for the child to practice on!

It's also common for parents to tell you that they want "to try it out" and "just want him to have fun." Indeed, they may have chosen you because of your reputation as being "fun" with kids. That's all well and good; most teachers start out with high hopes of communicating the joy of music to their young students. But we, too, run smack into reality when we learn (yet again) that, as it was for us, it is for them: learning music takes work. In a very real sense, part of our job is seducing the students, and their parents, into agreeing to a routine that will give results, even if it takes more work and commitment than they probably thought they were signing on for.

The Stage Parent

On the other end of the spectrum are parents who have overly high expectations. In some cases, the parents have had some musical study themselves and want the same for their children. Sometimes these parents think their children should make the same progress at an instrument that they did. Or they push their children to start lessons too early, or sit over their children when they practice (even when such help is no longer needed). They may dictate an amount of practice per day. And they may take all the joy out of it.

Again, communication with parents is key. If the child truly is talented and interested, then the teacher can ratchet up expectations and suggest, perhaps, 45 minutes of practice rather than half an hour. You can make more performance opportunities available, suggest listening activities, and give the parents regular feedback. Entering children in music festivals and evaluation programs (see Chapter 17) is also a good way to motivate the student and to show the parent tangible "evidence" that the student is progressing.

Fortunately, most parents don't envision an international solo concert career for their children. As misguidedly optimistic and ambitious as many parents are about their children's chance to play in major league sports, they don't usually have the same aspirations about musical careers. And that's a good thing. It cannot be the parent's aspiration that sets a musical career in motion.

Boundaries and Cultural Mores

Teaching music is an intensely physical activity. Students must be shown how to hold instruments, how to touch them, how to breathe into them. Physical posture, the weight of an arm, the position in which an instrument is held, the tilt of the head, the shape of the wrist—all of these are physical skills.

Unfortunately, we live in a time in which teachers of all subjects are trained and cautioned not to touch students, in order to avoid any sort of real or perceived impropriety. This makes it difficult for music teachers, who may need to help a student reposition a hand, hold an instrument, or put weight into a bow arm.

Setting and Maintaining Boundaries

Setting boundaries starts with the attitude a teacher communicates to the student. With all students, but especially older ones, ask before you touch! This is also important from a teaching perspective. If you simply grab a student's hand and try to reposition it, the student will almost always tense up, or maybe even strain to keep the hand where it is. Ask if you can show the student how to hold the hand, put weight down into the keys, put fingers on a bow, or hold the instrument.

Piano teachers generally are closest to students, so a few specific words are in order. Don't sit too close to older students; give them some personal space. When playing duets with younger students, you can be playful. For example, make a game of pretending to nudge the child off the bench, or say, "Hey, we've got to share some space here. You stay out of my territory and I'll stay out of yours." With middle school or high school students, maintain a little more distance. If you don't have a duet bench, use two chairs for duets rather than squeezing onto a standard artist's bench. Often you'll find that for short or simple pieces, you can play from a standing position or from a separate chair.

Obviously, the problem of mixed messages is not especially serious for a middle-age woman teaching a young child. But what about a 20-something male piano teacher instructing a 16-year-old girl? Duets might be best left off the lesson plans. If you're a younger teacher, take special care to maintain an appropriate physical and emotional distance with students of the opposite sex. Dress a little more conservatively than you normally might.

With adult students, you're on your own. Two consenting adults can get into all sorts of trouble, and unlike medicine or psychology, there aren't any ethical rules against it for music teachers. Single women, however, might think twice about scheduling adult male students to come into their home when they are alone. Usually, of course, there are no problems (beyond the ordinary challenges of finding arpeggios and identifying chords). But listen to your gut. If a prospective student makes you nervous, you can always decline to teach him.

Open Door Policies

Open door policies are perhaps the most effective way to prevent miscommunication or misunderstandings and establish transparency. Even if you prefer for parents of older students not to observe the entire lesson, you should always make it clear that parents are always welcome to pop their heads in the door for a few minutes to see what's going on or ask questions.

Students and parents in our studio are invited to walk in unannounced, even if they are early for their lessons. It is common knowledge that our doors are unlocked during lesson hours, and we request that students (and parents) come in without knocking.

Business Issues

The other set of issues that can derail a student-teacher relationship is business issues. Most music teachers would agree that the measure of a good studio policy is never having to use it at all. By explaining your policies carefully at the outset and running a consistently managed studio that adheres to these policies, you may never have to do much more than say, "It's in the studio policy—do you need another copy?" or "Would you like me to go over it with you?"

Enforcing a studio policy really isn't a matter of sticking up for your legal rights or going to court. If a relationship plummets to that level, there's more than a poor studio policy to blame. Simply put, most teachers don't go to court and don't wield the studio policy like a legal contract. It's simply not worth it. And actionable disagreements between students and teachers are few and far between.

However, you do have the right to run your studio the way you see fit, and that includes dismissing students (and parents) who are not upholding their end of the deal.

Out of Tune

Even the most tightly worded studio policy is probably not legally binding (not to mention that, even if it were, you don't want to be threatening your student families with lawsuits over missed lessons). Always give the parents the benefit of the doubt. The vast majority of parents who don't adhere to studio policies didn't bother to read them, don't understand them, or have long since forgotten them. In case of disagreement, a friendly "I just need to go over something with you quickly" approach is much more effective than beating them over the head with a studio policy.

The business issues that generally cause parents and teachers to part ways are late payments or nonpayments, rescheduling, and make-up lessons. And because all of these issues should be thoroughly covered in your studio policy, dealing with them is simply a matter of addressing them as soon as they become a problem and stating calmly and clearly what you require so that you can continue teaching the student.

Late Payers and Nonpayers

People pay late because they are having difficulty juggling their budgets, or because they are inconsiderate or forgetful. Even if you're a brand-new teacher with only half a dozen students, you probably already know who is going to walk in the door every month with a check and who can just as reliably be counted on to arrive empty-handed. Regardless of the reason, a music teacher cannot keep teaching a student if the lesson fees are in arrears.

Requiring students to pay in advance—say, by the month—gives teachers a bit of an edge because if you insist that parents keep current with payments, you aren't likely to be chasing down large sums of money for services long since rendered.

A direct approach is best. "It's creating a real problem for me to have to chase down overdue payments. Please try to remember that payments are due on the first lesson of the month. Would you like me to e-mail you a reminder?"

A friendly phone call to remind a chronic late payer to bring the check is usually effective, but it puts the burden on the teacher. If you're willing to make the calls, always ask first if they'd like you to phone.

Lesson Skippers and Schedule Changers

Chronic lesson skippers and lesson reschedulers shouldn't be a problem for a teacher who enforces a studio policy. At least, that's the theory. Chances are that if the family is absent a lot, you are going to start feeling bad about keeping money for lessons they keep missing. And, of course, students who don't come to regular lessons can't make good progress. Chronic lesson skippers almost always end up as ex-students.

The best plan is to deal with the issue directly. Tell parents that as long as they are reserving that particular half-hour (or whatever) time slot, you have to charge them for it because you can't offer it to someone else. Tell them that you feel bad about taking money for lessons that are being missed, but the only times you have available are A or B, and they have to pick one. And of course, bring up the problem that a student who doesn't come to lessons cannot learn.

> **Take Note** _____
>
> Some teachers offer chronic lesson skippers the chance to swap lessons with each other by establishing a "swap list" for interested parents. Parents may arrange such swaps on their own with others on the swap list who have the same lesson length. The originating parent is responsible for telling the teacher. Swaps may be limited to two a year so no one family takes advantage and is constantly putting others on the spot.

Parents sometimes simply don't understand or accept a make-up policy. Keep records of every student's attendance, absences, reasons for absences, and make-ups, including any extra make-ups you give if they ask to change times during the course of a week and you can accommodate them. This little bit of paperwork takes about 5 minutes at the end of every teaching day. All you have to do is jot down the date and a note. For example: February 2; lesson missed for soccer; make-up given on Friday, February 4.

That way, if you have to confront a parent about scheduling and make-up issues and they insist that they haven't really missed all that many lessons, you have an exact record of attendance.

When It's Time to Let Go

Sometimes educational or business problems are unsolvable. No one likes saying good-bye to a student, but the reality is that by the time you get to the end of your rope, the student—or the parents—might be there, too. Maybe not with you specifically, but possibly with the whole process of taking music lessons.

If you are thinking about dismissing a student, establish a multistep process. For example:

1. Start with a parent-teacher-student conference in which you review student progress and expectations. To make students responsible for their own learning, ask them to tell you what their goals are and how well they think they are doing.

    Next, ask parents about issues or concerns they may have.

    Finally, it's your turn. Be sure to offer any praise that is due, but state that there are problems that you feel must be addressed in order for the student to make progress.

2. Set a probation period during which any stated issues must be addressed and/ or resolved. A probation period may be a month or, at the outside, two months. That's usually enough time to see some sort of turnaround. You should set specific, quantifiable goals that are reasonably achievable. In other words, the goals should have more to do with effort than with mastering a challenging piece or simply setting the bar higher. Meeting a minimum number of practice hours, memorizing a certain piece, playing a scale or etude with the metronome at a certain speed and with no mistakes are examples of objective goals. Write everything down, and have the student sign it.

The parents need to be on board with the probation period. Be prepared for a wide range of responses from parents. It is even possible that you might lose the student right then and there. The parents may well feel that if it has come to this, it isn't working out, and they should just try another teacher.

3. Ending the period is simply a matter of reviewing whether the student has done what he or she agreed to do. Some teachers prefer to do this in person. Others send a letter outlining the precise terms of the probation and the ways in which the student (and/or parent) is still not living up to the responsibilities.

You can always leave the door open for the student's return. If anything is ever certain about children, it is this: you can't quite predict what they are going to do next. Music is a powerful force, and after a break, they may well want to try again. If you have handled them tactfully and kindly, you may see them walk in your door sometime down the road with a whole different attitude.

The Least You Need to Know

♦ If student practice issues are ongoing and not remedied by the usual bribery, step-by-step instruction, and encouragement, have students sign a practice contract.

♦ Sometimes students fool teachers into thinking they can read notes and rhythms when they are actually playing by ear. Double-check skills by having students learn music on their own.

♦ Misunderstandings with parents about business issues are often the result of inattentiveness and forgetfulness. Address the issues by referring to and reviewing the studio policy.

♦ Before terminating your teaching relationship with a student, establish a probation period during which the student improves in specified ways or performs specific behaviors.

Part 4

A Career That Grows and Changes

Understanding and evaluating new materials, continuing your education, hosting student performances, and using digital media are all ongoing aspects of a music teacher's job that contribute to continued growth, renewed energy, and student satisfaction.

Starting with modern pedagogy, I explore what modern teaching methods offer and how to choose among them, use them, and supplement them for students of various levels. I also explore the digital age and how it is revolutionizing teaching studios. You can use much of this digital equipment to support student performance, and in the performance chapter, I cover both traditional recitals and other opportunities to share music with the community. I finish by talking about the process of continued renewal that is so important to a teacher's growth and satisfaction.

Chapter 15

Modern Pedagogy

In This Chapter

- ◆ Beginning method books
- ◆ Curricula for the intermediate student
- ◆ Curricula for the advanced student
- ◆ Using contemporary music to teach musicianship skills, including technique, theory, and improvisation

Pedagogy is the art of teaching, and it's not new. Johann Sebastian Bach's wife, Anna Magdalena, collected pieces by her husband and other musicians to create a music book for her children. Beethoven's student Carl Czerny made a career out of writing pedagogical exercises for piano students. The Spanish guitarist Ferdinand Sor created volumes of guitar exercises that are still used today. And famous composers such as Schumann, Bartok, and Kabalevsky wrote whole volumes of music for children.

But the preponderance of formalized published method books that proceed step by step is a relatively new invention in the art of teaching. For the new teacher, it is both a blessing and a curse. It's a blessing because method books set forth a path for new teachers to follow. It's a curse because there are many different methods, and sometimes they all seem to contradict each other.

Navigating the Method Books

The instinct for many beginning teachers is to try to remember how they were taught, and then repeat that process with their students. But before you run out to purchase the same volume of beginner music you were trained with, consider two things. First, you (as someone who became a music teacher) probably had greater than average aptitude for your instrument. This means that the method book you used so easily may, in fact, be fiendishly difficult for your students. Also, pedagogy, like everything else in life, changes with time. The methods and ideas that were in vogue when you began taking lessons may have been improved upon, or even supplanted, by later research that applies cognitive psychology, elementary education, and child development to music pedagogy. In fact, you may have learned as well as you did despite your method book rather than because of it.

The Madness of Methods

Types of methods available today depend on the instrument you are teaching. For popular instruments such as piano and guitar, dozens of method books compete for a large, lucrative market. With less popular instruments, there are fewer choices.

Generally, choices include books for preschoolers, for beginning children, for beginning adults, and for accelerated students. "Teach yourself" books (not to mention Internet sites) are also popular. Some of them are solid and pedagogically sound (although self-learning methods actually tend to work better for intermediate and advanced students who have the basics down and the skills to progress on their own). Some of these books contain fantastic exercises and make excellent supplements to a formal course of study, especially in the areas of improvising and playing with backing tracks. Others have a slight whiff of snake oil, with their promises of fast progress and easy learning.

Wise Words _____

Attend publisher showcases at your local music store. I've seen many of my favorite pedagogical composers and editors for free at these. They are sent by the publisher to tour music stores and promote a particular line of books, usually a new method or repertoire series. However, many of the most popular composers spend the first half of their time promoting that material and then focus on their own music for the other half. Even if you're not interested in the particular method, you can pick up good pedagogy along the way. And often you get freebies or substantially discounted materials just for coming.

—Janna Williamson, music teacher, Wheaton, Illinois

With less common instruments such as, say, trombone or tuba, the market of potential purchasers is much smaller, the number of publishers competing is smaller, and you won't have as many choices. The upside is that while there are plenty of books titled something like "Play Piano Today Without Even Thinking," the equivalent is not yet in print for the oboe.

Regardless of what instrument you teach, you need to examine the potential method books carefully to understand why they present the material they do in the order they do. You also need to match these methods to the ages, abilities, and learning styles of your students.

Pedagogy and the Method Books

The first thing to understand about method books and "learn to play" series is that there is no one right way to teach or learn to play music, and no single best answer or correct method. The most experienced teachers will readily tell you that even if they wrote a method book, they wouldn't use it with every student. Each student learns differently, and while most teachers have one or two preferred methods, they also have back-ups (for siblings or classmates who are too competitive to be in the same series), as well as alternate methods for students who for some reason do better with a completely different approach.

Additionally, teachers may use different method books for different age groups and musical interests. You might use one or more methods for the 4- to 6-year-olds, a different one for the 7- to 10-year-olds, and other methods for beginning teens, classical players, and students interested in pop or jazz.

Although a few books on the market seem hastily thrown together, beginning method books are mostly based on careful applications of pedagogical principles, many of them developed in the latter part of the twentieth century, when university pedagogy teachers began to study how people learned music. This translates into sequenced learning materials labeled by levels. These levels do not, however, necessarily translate to consistency. Many methods go about the business of teaching music in radically different ways so that a student cannot always move from Level 1 in one series to Level 2 in another.

Choosing the Method

New piano and guitar teachers may find themselves completely befuddled by the number of choices on the market. But even if your instrument has only two or three commonly used starting method or exercise books, you'll have to carefully evaluate how one goes about presenting the many difficult and confusing concepts involved in making music to a student. In making your choice of a method book, consider the following:

- Is it an ear method or a reading method? The Suzuki method, for instance, is an ear-first method, popular with teachers of very young violin students. Most piano beginner books stress reading first. What ages are your students? Are you comfortable teaching rote methods with ear work? Is this approach common on your instrument? Why or why not?

- If you plan to teach an ear method, how and when will you incorporate reading into the program? Does the method make that transition (or teach teachers to make that transition) or will you be on your own?

- How does the method you are considering approach music reading? Do we memorize notes? Do we memorize "Every good boy does fine"? Do we use landmark notes and then figure out nearby notes by counting up from the notes we have memorized? Do we start on middle C? Do we use intervals? Part of the decision of how to teach reading music depends on the instrument. The piano, for example, is very visual and lends itself to spatial placement by figuring out one note based on the note next to it. Not so violin, or saxophone, or trumpet.

- How does the method present rhythm? Fast notes first, or slow notes first? (There are good arguments for each approach.)

- Speaking of counting, how do we count? *1* for quarters, *1-2* for half notes, or *1-2-3-4*? Or *Ta-Ta-titi-Ta*?

- Does the method introduce dynamics and articulation right away, or does it wait until notes and rhythms are secure? Again, there are good arguments for both approaches.

- Does the method introduce key signatures and sharps and flats right off the bat, or do we learn them slowly over a period of years?

If this all sounds completely overwhelming, go to your local music store and take a look at what's in stock. Ask what their most popular method books are. Popular doesn't always mean good, but at least it's a place to start. You might also network with other music teachers, either locally or online, although you need to be very careful. The loudest voices (particularly online) aren't always the best ones to listen to. And sometimes people who post online have an unrevealed financial interest in a product.

Many publishers have starter kits to introduce teachers to their materials; it doesn't hurt to ask if one is available. (You can check online or call.) They have teacher discounts, too, so be sure to sign up for that as well. The starter packs may give you some sample repertoire, a few pages of the introductory books, and an overview of the course. You'll have to read through the sales hype, of course, but you should be able to get a feel for the course's basic educational priorities and structure.

In addition, some publishers offer teaching videos (on the Internet) demonstrating how to teach their method. (You might notice that the students are all well dressed, look well behaved, and seem to learn every skill with no problem at all!) The assumption is that teachers visiting the site will learn from the videos how to teach that particular method, and will then go out and buy it.

Other publishers make teaching videos available for a price (sometimes quite a high one), which means that you have to be fairly certain you want to use that method before making the investment. And still others give detailed presentations and master classes around the country at various music teacher conventions, conferences, and even music stores.

Ideally, once you've decided on a starting point, you'll buy the complete sets of one or two method books and read through and work through them one at a time. What is being taught? In what order? Does it make sense to you? How might you modify it? Is anything missing? How might you supplement the books? Is the music appealing?

Wise Words

Let us stop the teachers' superstition according to which only some diluted art-substitute is suitable for teaching purposes. A child is the most susceptible and the most enthusiastic audience for pure art; for in every great artist the child is alive—and this is something felt by youth's congenial spirit. Conversely, only art of intrinsic value is suitable for children! Everything else is harmful. After all, food is more carefully chosen for an infant than for an adult. Musical nourishment which is "rich in vitamins" is essential for children.

—Zoltán Kodály (1882–1967), music educator and composer

You'll probably notice that some methods enable you to "turn the page and teach." The learning sequence is not only spoon-fed to the student, but it's spoon-fed to the teacher as well. You turn the page to Lesson 2 and see a half note and how to count it. The song has half notes. The theory book involves drawing half notes. The technique book has clap-back and rhythm exercises involving half notes. You turn to Lesson 3 and find a whole note. And on it goes.

For beginning teachers, these methods can be much easier to use than methods that leave teachers scratching their heads wondering what to make of a rhythm game on page 12 followed by a chanting game on page 13, followed by a rote exercise on page 14.

Most teachers don't get a really good sense of a method book until they've used it and developed their own rhythm for teaching it. There is, after all, a personal component to all of this. You may find a method that seems to meet all your teaching criteria, yet somehow the kids never really take to it. Maybe they don't like the pictures. Maybe they don't like the music. Always remember, students are more apt to practice material they enjoy. Choose a pedagogically correct but boring method book at the risk of student disinterest.

All-in-One Versus Mix-and-Match

Some teachers prefer an all-in-one approach. They buy one Level 1 book for a student, and that book contains all of the author's recommended curricula for that level—performance pieces, technique exercises, music theory, reading exercises, and so on.

However, many experienced teachers find that all-in-one methods are both too rigid and too confusing. Some students are perfectly able to follow the flow and logic of the books, but some are not. It might seem logical to the method book author, for example, that he present the key of G and then the key of F because they each have one accidental. But a fair number of students hopelessly confuse the two. Or perhaps the author presents the C, F, and G scales, but the teacher has found that she prefers starting the study of scales on the black note scales, or that she prefers presenting all the similarly fingered sharp-key scales in order, and leaving F until later.

Experienced teachers, of course, are more than happy to tear out unwanted pages of the method book and use them as fire starter. But beginning teachers sometimes feel tied to the page, fearing that if they don't present a particular concept the way the book presents it, they will miss something important. This is an experience issue.

Facts and Stats

In late 2009, a search at Amazon.com for the words "how to play piano" (within quotation marks) returned 1,816 results. Similar searches for other instruments yielded the following results: guitar 1,437, violin 386, flute 240, clarinet 62. Clearly, any music teacher has a big project ahead when it comes to evaluating teaching materials.

A more flexible solution is to choose a method that offers several books per level. In this case (particularly in piano, sometimes in guitar, and less commonly in other instruments), the method book author presents a basic core lesson book and then makes available several supplemental books. The more popular the instrument (and the more popular the method), the more supplements available.

Often the method book author strongly recommends the use of one or more of the supplements, or even says that the use of certain supplements is essential. In other cases, the lesson books may be fairly complete, but the supplements give a teacher extra material to deal with particular student challenges.

Most mix-and-match method series have a core lesson book, a technique component, a theory component, and a performance repertoire component, as well as other books in various styles, including duets and Christmas music. Some students (and their parents) find keeping track of multiple assignments in this many books confusing.

You can also supplement your chosen method with material you make up, rote exercises, your own theory instruction, and even supplementary books from outside the method.

Intermediates: Beyond the Method Books

Most method books are published in series of several levels, usually progressing through the beginning and elementary levels, and ending somewhere in the intermediate zone.

The intermediate level of most instruments is a long period. Most students enter the intermediate level with a few years of lessons and a reasonable amount of practice. How long it takes to progress to the advanced level, however, is another matter entirely. Some move through intermediate repertoire and skills quite quickly. Others remain intermediate level players forever, never quite developing the fluency and independence of a truly advanced player. And there's no problem with that—for most instruments, there is quite literally an infinite amount of intermediate repertoire, including countless volumes of popular songs. Students at this level can accompany school choruses, play in the school orchestra, or even play in a rock band.

Many teachers abandon the method books somewhere in the intermediate years. Indeed, in some instruments, the method books don't go much beyond the elementary stage. However, developing an effective teaching curriculum by choosing all your own repertoire and technique materials is a difficult task for a beginning teacher. For some instruments, you'll find graded collections of intermediate repertoire. Some of them even enumerate the specific technical skills taught in each piece, or put the pieces in some sort of order of difficulty.

For the student, the transition to "real" music may be tricky. While method book pieces are carefully written to present new elements in a structured, controlled order, real music—music that was not written to teach someone something, but to be an artistic piece in its own right—is much messier. Students may find themselves fighting with two or three unfamiliar elements at a time. Grading these materials and figuring out which pieces a student can do is tricky. It's especially tricky because some students can make comfortable leaps from one concept to another, and other students need material presented to them in small, orderly increments. As a teacher, you need to know both the repertoire (and how its required skills break down) and your students (and how they learn new skills).

> **Take Note**
>
> Perhaps the best thing a teacher of intermediate students can do is to develop a skills list for the instrument and collect repertoire pieces that teach, refine, and reinforce each of these skills. In a notebook, list the skills. As you teach new pieces and encounter new repertoire, record their names on the list next to the skills they teach.

In addition to covering the range of techniques you deem essential, your selection of repertoire needs to cover the basic groups of musical styles. This means varying the music assigned among baroque, classical, romantic, and modern works, and also covering the range of styles in each of those periods.

Popular Music

For many students, the intermediate level coincides with middle school, when students begin to develop tastes of their own. This is the age when kids start bringing in music to lessons and asking if the teacher can help them learn it. We talked about popular music as a motivational tool in Chapter 12; it can be a student saver.

As a pedagogy tool, popular music deserves more respect than it usually gets from music teachers. Learning popular music from sheet music is, it turns out, an unexpected challenge. First of all, very little popular music is originally intended for solo instruments. It's almost all band based (assuming it isn't sampled, in which case you're going to have a real challenge on your hands). On piano, this means that the stretches, reaches, and fingering for your student may not be ergonomic, depending on the skill of the arranger. On guitar, the song won't sound at all the way that it does when a whole band plays it.

Out of Tune

Many editions of popular music come with the assurance that they are "Easy Piano." For most students, these versions are playable after four years of lessons, not the one or two years many people assume from the "Easy Piano" designation. This leads to frustration when, after two years of hard work, a student feels that he can't play even an "easy" piece. Be sure you look at and evaluate the music students want to play. You may need to simplify and arrange songs so they are playable by beginners.

But the most important benefit from popular music is its rhythmic difficulty. The rhythms can be much more complex than any an intermediate classical player is learning, including syncopations, changing time signature, triplets alternating with duplets, and swing. Reading popular music challenges a student's rhythm skills. No matter what you may think of the latest pop anthem, it's worth teaching it for this reason alone. Plus, never forget: students practice what they like. If it gets them to their instrument, it's a success.

Pop songs may also offer the opportunity to talk about arranging music, playing in ensembles, and working out basic harmonizations. If your student has a friend who plays another instrument or sings, you may have an opportunity to do some collaborative work.

Technique for Intermediate Players

Most instruments have a canon of technique exercises that are appropriate for the development of different skills at different levels. For wind instruments, there are breathing exercises. For string students, there are bowing exercises. And all instrumentalists have to learn scales, chords, and arpeggios. In addition, you can make up exercises to address particular technical issues, but be sure to write them down; otherwise, students will practice them for a week and forget about them.

The intermediate years are a time to instill a more sophisticated practice regimen that includes the regular study of technique drills, perhaps as a timed warm-up.

Take Note

A good way for students to practice difficult fast passages is to alter the rhythm. In a passage of running sixteenth notes, have the student alter the rhythm to play each group of two as a dotted sixteenth followed by a thirty-second note. Then reverse the rhythm and play each group of two as a thirty-second note followed by a dotted sixteenth.

The goal of technique, of course, is not to make students mindlessly run up and down scales. It is to give them the tools for fluency on the instrument, which means the mastery of all basic movements and keys. One way to reinforce this is to point out where technical issues appear in music—scale runs, double octaves, arpeggios, and so on. The natural next step, of course, is for students to isolate these technical elements and work on them when working on a piece that contains them.

Pedagogy for Advanced Students

It's difficult to say exactly when students cross that invisible, indefinable line between intermediate and advanced player. It is a matter not just of technique, but also of fluency. Advanced students can learn on their own. They now speak the language of their instrument; they can venture artistic judgments and solve problems. Advanced students are ready to start studying major works of literature. Consider this as a measure: advanced students should be capable of putting together a plausible audition for entry into a respectable college music program.

Of course, not all advanced students go on to major in music (nor should they!). In high school, of course, students have no idea what they are going to do with their lives. The prospective music major may surprise everyone by applying to medical school; the premed student may audition for a symphony orchestra. But to have gotten this far, the student has both talent and a commitment to musical education. The music teacher's job is not to turn the student into a music major, but to make the student the best musician he or she can be in the time they have together.

Repertoire for Advanced Students

At this level, method books are a distant memory. It's as if the teacher and the student are in a little boat in uncharted waters, surrounded by thousands of waves, each of which carries a different piece of music.

An advanced curriculum needs to encompass major works of the various historic styles, along with some encore-style pieces that are appealing and fun to play (and don't take six months to learn). Some instruments have more signature pieces that "everyone" plays than others. You want your student to have a good solid repertoire of some well-worn warhorses and audience or competition favorites. But it's also worth exploring your instrument's literature for less well-known gems. Some instruments have richer repertoire than others, especially for solo performance, so your success in this area will certainly depend on whether you teach tuba or piano!

If your instrument has a rich chamber or collaborative repertoire, you should also encourage students to take advantage of any group performance opportunities available. This is particularly important for string players because they have such a rich repertoire of string trios and quartets.

It should go without saying that the annual course of study needs to have some repertoire from each historic period, and if you teach an orchestral instrument, students should also know their instrument's signature symphonic solos.

At the advanced level, listening becomes a critical learning skill. Live concerts and recordings both offer opportunities to listen and learn, to compare interpretations, and gradually to come to understand what true mastery of the instrument means. If you have several advanced students, a group performance class in which students play for each other and discuss the music is an invaluable way to expand students' knowledge of the repertoire for their instrument and have a chance to discuss issues of interpretation and style.

Take Note

As a music teacher, you are training not only tomorrow's musicians, but also tomorrow's audiences. Student discounts are available at many concert venues in your community. Just ask! And then make sure you tell parents and students about performances.

Technique for Advanced Students

Technique involves not only how quickly and cleanly a student can play, but also other aspects of control, including dynamics, correct finger placement, the ability to move fluidly between positions, and the ability to achieve musical goals even when technical difficulties present themselves. At the advanced level, some teachers prefer to teach technique directly from repertoire or from artistic etudes. However, most teachers also require a certain amount of technical drilling, if for no other reason than that scales, arpeggios, and variations of exercises are generally required in college study. The demands can get trickier as the student becomes more advanced. Have them play scales over more octaves, in thirds and sixths. Start arpeggios on different notes and play in different inversions, with sevenths added; play modes over related chords, and so on.

Arm weight, finger pressure, posture, correct breathing (and not just for wind players and singers)—all of these play a role in technique. The teacher needs to visualize a sort of platonic ideal for each kind of technique, and then apply it to the particular student, whose hand shape, muscle control, speed, agility, hand size, and coordination may well render what is achieved somewhat differently than what is ideal. The teacher needs to know when that is working, when it's not, and how to correct it.

Alternate fingerings and the ability of the student to conceive of and implement different reasonable fingerings and bowings (for string instruments) is also an issue at the advanced level. Concert-level repertoire is not fingered, or is fingered sparingly and sometimes idiosyncratically, and students need to learn to figure out this important challenge on their own without giving in to favoring their weak fingers or taking the easy way out by pedaling to cover an awkward move in a legato passage.

Be creative with exercises. Have students do exercises in jazz rhythms, or in altered keys and modes. The point of scales is not only to be able to run up and down the instrument, but to feel at home in these keys and to be able to use them for improvising and for making music.

Music Theory and Ear Training

If you have an advanced student who is planning to study music in college, basic theory and ear training must be part of your curriculum. Fortunately, today most beginning and intermediate method books include at least some components of theory and ear training, so this shouldn't be new to your student.

Piano students have a leg up as far as music theory is concerned. First, in the last 20 years or so, there has been a massive change in introductory piano methods, with most of them including far more information about chord types, key signatures, and musical form than their precursors did. Second, pianists have been making and seeing chord structures for years before they enter a college music course. And it helps that the piano is a harmonic instrument with a clear visual structure.

Unless you work with your students on theory, students on single-line instruments tend to have a harder time with theory. They may learn key signatures and basic scales and modes, but harmony is not something that many instrumental teachers stress—to the detriment of students who have to figure out what various chord forms are for the first time in a college classroom. Note also that most college music programs require instrumental majors and music education majors to pass a basic piano skills class. So some piano lessons are a valuable element of a prospective instrumental music major's training. Once a student is introduced to the piano, some of the music theory and harmony studies more easily fall into place.

However, instrumental students excel (and piano students have difficulty) in college ear training. Instrumental students have to make their notes and then play them, and they have to tune their instruments. Pianists point and play, and they call a tuner when necessary. Hence the unfortunately too-often-true stereotype of the piano major who can't play "Happy Birthday" by ear. The fact that instrumental musicians so often play in groups (and pianists so often do not) gives instrumentalists a head start in this important area of study.

Take Note _____

To learn ear training, ask students to write out the melodic and harmonic lines to their favorite pop songs. Have them pick and transcribe one song every week or two. This will give music majors a head start and will develop ear-training skills that students can apply to a lifetime of recreational music making.

Teachers should consider these issues when preparing students for college music programs. A teacher who feels lost in ear training and theory should take a university-level course, preferably before taking on the responsibility of teaching advanced students. Quite simply, there's no excuse today for a piano major who can't figure out how to play "Happy Birthday," or an instrumentalist who can't improvise over scales, modes, and altered scales.

The importance of both theory and ear training goes beyond simply preparing a student for more tests and tasks. Theory is a crucial tool for all musicians (and, make no mistake, there is nothing theoretical about it). A pianist who understands how to make chords and construct a basic accompaniment can read thousands of songs out of a fake book and sit in with bands on a moment's notice. A saxophone player who understands a blues scale or a violinist who knows how to put together a fiddle tune can similarly join in with musicians and have fun—and even get work in studios and live gigs.

Jazz and Improvisation

There has been, and remains even today, a deep rift between the world of classical and popular music. Jazz occasionally jumps the chasm, here considered art music, there considered popular. But for the most part, the teacher who coaches a Brahms clarinet quintet is not teaching Benny Goodman, and the piano teacher who teaches a Beethoven sonata is unlikely to move into blues improvisation. This is unfortunate. Too many fine classical musicians wish that somehow they could figure out how to just sit down and have fun with their instrument, and too many pop musicians wish they could read and get their fingers from place to place a little more smoothly.

One challenge, of course, is that many teachers are not bilingual in music. They speak classical, or jazz, or pop, but they don't necessarily speak music. Rectifying this sometimes takes additional study (see Chapter 18) and an open mind.

For students, being able to play in several different idioms has advantages of many different levels.

- ◆ It's fun and motivating for the student.

- ◆ The skills of jazz and pop improvisation include theory and aural skills.

- ◆ Experience playing with a band is both fun and educational as students learn to work in ensembles, rehearse, and listen to each other.

- ◆ Fluency in different styles gives the student the ability to work as a musician, or to sit in as a recreational musician with confidence.

Fortunately, for advanced students who are able to learn on their own with only a little guidance, there are many fine jazz method and play-along books. Exploring these can be a project for teacher and student both.

The Least You Need to Know

- ◆ When starting to teach, evaluate the most popular methods and choose one or two with which you feel comfortable.

- ◆ Look for methods that are consistent with your pedagogical preferences, such as note reading and rhythm, but be sure the music is appealing enough that students will want to practice it.

- ◆ Teachers of intermediate and advanced students frequently keep a list of skills and make sure the repertoire they are teaching addresses those skills.

- ◆ Use popular music and jazz to teach music theory, complex rhythms, and improvisation.

Chapter 16

Teaching in the Digital Age

In This Chapter

- ◆ The benefits of digital keyboards
- ◆ Using play-along CDs as a teaching tool
- ◆ Equipment for recording and amplifying
- ◆ Software and online resources

These are not your grandma's piano lessons! Or guitar lessons, or violin lessons.

MP3s, iPods, synthesizers, YouTube: today's young musicians have more tools and toys available than ever. The teacher who ignores these resources does a disservice to herself and to her students.

Technology and music are now inseparable, as evidenced by the growing number of university programs that have a technology element, sometimes even combining music degrees with engineering degrees. Digital recording technology allows even a young child to make a CD (and copy it, and try to sell it!). Television and movie scores are composed and often partly or even wholly performed on synthesizers and computers. And the Internet offers a wide ocean of learning tools—some good, and some not so good.

Teaching music is in no danger of being replaced by technology (all attempts to the contrary notwithstanding). But although technology can't replace a teacher, it can help teachers by suggesting new approaches to concepts and by offering new ways to inspire and motivate students.

Keyboards

One of the most obvious technological innovations to have an impact on the music teacher—note that I said "music teacher," not just "piano teacher"—is the digital keyboard. Electric pianos first came on the popular music scene in the 1960s. Almost immediately, they were roundly denounced by classically trained pianists. Electric pianos, we were told, were little more than toys, unfit for even the youngest beginner to practice on. Indeed, even today, it's not hard to find piano teachers who shudder at the mention of these "imposters."

It's true that, for a pianist, digital pianos are not substitutes for acoustic instruments. They lack the voice, feel, resonance, and overtones; the sound is completely different. To become a pianist, a student needs to play a piano, not a keyboard. But digital pianos (today's version of the old "electric pianos") can be enormously powerful tools, not just for piano teachers, but for teachers of all instruments—and for students as well.

Why Have a Keyboard?

Simply put, you should have a keyboard because keyboards can do a long list of things pianos can't do.

For piano teachers, keyboards can serve as a second instrument, and can be used for two-piano pieces or for demonstration (so the teacher doesn't have to reach over the student and play from the side, which is not only inconvenient, but can cause stress problems in the shoulders and back). Having a keyboard as a second piano is a great choice for anyone whose home (or budget) isn't big enough for two pianos.

Teachers of all instruments can use digital pianos for jobs ranging from accompanying, to composing, to teaching music theory, to helping students arrange original compositions. From a musical perspective, a digital piano can open students' ears to all sorts of possibilities. A synthesizer with a split bass will highlight differences between registers. And students interested in composition can experiment with various voices and rhythm tracks and come up with their own fully orchestrated pieces.

For piano students, the issue is trickier. There's a lot of misinformation in the world of piano sales—not surprising, when you consider that even a bargain-basement acoustic piano retails for around $3,000, and a decent digital piano with 88 weighted keys and a solid pianolike action runs at least $1,000. Acoustic piano salespeople (and many piano teachers) tell parents that it is impossible for children to learn on a digital piano. Meanwhile, digital piano salespeople say that the playability of a $1,000 digital keyboard is better than that of a cheap acoustic piano. Both have valid points (and, indeed, a digital piano is a far better choice if the other option is a battered old acoustic that can't hold tune and whose keys stick in the summer).

Take Note _____

What's the difference between a synthesizer and a digital piano? Basically, they overlap. A synthesizer has more voices, including rhythm tracks and the capacity to split the keyboard so the bass plays one voice and the treble another. A digital piano has fewer voices, and they are mostly typical keyboard sounds: organ, vibraphone, harpsichord, piano, electric piano. A digital piano may also have a better "real piano" feel and sound.

But either way you look at it, parents are looking down the throat of perhaps $1,000 in piano lessons (that's for the first year alone), plus the cost of the instrument, and they may not even be entirely sure whether Jeffrey is going to like the piano. No wonder, then, that parents are relieved when Aunt Mabel donates a rickety old spinet or Uncle Ned has a cheap keyboard he's willing to let Jeffrey use. For this reason, many piano teachers accept keyboards as a viable at-home practice tool at least for the first few months to two years.

So if we accept that we're going to have students using keyboards, we might as well take advantage of what the keyboards have to offer. And that turns out to be a lot.

Students who practice early in the morning or late at night can use earphones so that no one else can hear—or be disturbed by—the sound. Or, for sensitive teens, the earphones allow them to practice privately, regardless of the time of day. Digital pianos also lend themselves to certain tasks. For example, the student can record a left-hand part and practice the right hand over it, or vice versa. Or the student (or teacher) can record one part of a piano duet on the keyboard, and the student can practice the other part over it.

Keyboards sometimes make sense for very young students. Their height is adjustable, so the student's legs don't dangle from a too-high bench. The student will even be able to reach the pedals! The action of virtually all digital pianos is much lighter than the action of all but the cheapest upright pianos, which means the notes are easier for tiny fingers to press down. Of course, as time passes, the student needs to develop finger strength on a full-size, fully weighted instrument, but for a 4-year-old, a more manageable keyboard makes the same kind of good sense that a child-size guitar or violin does.

Finally, learning how to use a digital piano and its flashy cousin, the synthesizer, are important skills for a piano student. So much of today's keyboard playing is done on digital instruments. Rock bands, wedding groups, even church musicians rely on keyboards much more than on acoustic pianos. The ability to make the most of the keyboard by changing voices, splitting the keyboard, playing two keyboards at the same time, and using foot pedals for volume control or effects are important performance skills that keyboard players are likely to face in the real world. Children love these buttons and knobs; why not capitalize on that interest and use it for learning?

Choosing a Keyboard

What kind of keyboard to purchase depends on who is going to be using it for what purpose.

For a traveling instrumental or vocal teacher who needs a keyboard to teach theory and provide basic accompaniments, an inexpensive 61-note model is a convenient choice. Many of these keyboards are actually well-equipped synthesizers with extensive banks of sounds and rhythm tracks.

Beyond that, a digital piano to be used as a piano substitute should have 88 weighted keys, which means that the keys offer some resistance when pushed down. Don't be seduced by descriptions such as "grand piano hammer action" on a digital keyboard. If you want or need true grand piano action, get a grand piano. You won't really find that action on a keyboard. In fact, the resistance of keyboards varies from feather light to the equivalent of an acoustic upright piano. On a digital keyboard, the more resistance, the better. Finally, the piano should have a sustain pedal.

If the keyboard is to be used mainly for piano work, then spend the money on a keyboard with a better piano sound and feel, and leave off bells and whistles such as 1,000 different voices and 100 preprogrammed rhythm tracks. If, however, the keyboard is to be used mainly for composition and arrangement, look for a synthesizer with lots of voices, even if the extra sounds and options come at the expense of better piano feel. It's possible to get both, but good synthesizers that also have a good piano feel are at the high end of the price spectrum.

> **Out of Tune** _____
>
> Never buy, use, or permit a student to use a keyboard that is not touch sensitive. No exceptions. "Touch sensitive" means that the notes sound at different volumes when pressed down with varying amounts of finger pressure. Only the very cheapest digital pianos don't have touch sensitivity; these instruments are worthless, even potentially harmful, for a rank beginner, and pretty much useless for anyone else because they lack any capacity for dynamics.

Keyboard Learning Features

Not all instruments and add-ons sold as teaching-learning technologies work. And some work with some students but not with others.

Some keyboards, for example, come with built-in "learning" software that purports to teach students how to play by having them follow a moving light, or by showing the note they are playing on a grand staff while they are playing it. However cleverly they are marketed (usually something about "fun" without the "tedium of learning to read music"), they tend to work mostly as an invitation to the student to experiment with buttons and keys. This is not a bad thing; it's just not the same as learning to read music. Having these extra "learning" tools can actually discourage the note-recognition process that needs to occur for children to learn to read music. Reading music is an active process, not a passive one. Passive learning aids that direct students to follow along familiarize but do not teach.

Play-Along CDs

Play-along CDs address the biggest downside to private music lessons—the "private" part. Students spend a lot of time playing and practicing alone. It's difficult enough to coordinate private music lessons for a full-size studio of some 30 or 40 students. To try to arrange regular weekly group sessions for ensemble practice is nearly impossible. But students need to develop ensemble skills.

Benefits of Play-Along CDs

Play-along CDs close the gap by introducing the idea of playing in time with others. To be able to play with a CD requires the application of ensemble skills such as these:

◆ Keeping up with the rhythm

◆ Counting measures when you're not supposed to be playing (and then coming in at the right time)

◆ Keeping track of what you are doing while you are keeping track of what everyone else is doing

◆ Learning to make a mistake, keep your head, and jump back in so quickly and smoothly that no one knows you've made a mistake

◆ Listening to what others in the group are doing

◆ Listening to harmonies and to cues from drummers and bass players

◆ Adjusting dynamics to fit into the group

The newest thing about play-along CDs is the "CD" part. Play-along LP records (yes, that long ago!) have been used for advanced students learning concerti for decades. Back then, if a cheap record player spun at just the wrong speed, the tuning would be off. Starting and stopping accurately at the same place on a record player was virtually impossible. The best the student could do was guess where to set the needle down, then run to pick up the instrument and try again. But playing with these recordings was often the only way the student had to practice his part in context. Because of these difficulties, only advanced students used the old play-along LPs. But with CDs, play-along tracks are practical for students at all levels and have been incorporated into many beginning method books, as well as in scores of "learn on your own" books and separately sold CDs that allow players to jam with and solo over accompaniments in various styles.

Play-Along Tricks and Issues

The old classical play-alongs (many of which are now available on CDs) had—and still have—some other problems as well. The performances are "real" performances with solo tracks removed, meaning that they were recorded with a conductor, an orchestra, and a soloist, and they have all the ritardandos and accelerandos of a real classical performance. As a result, these play-alongs work best for pieces in which the orchestra and soloist play together for most of the piece; in long solo cadenzas, it can be almost impossible to finish at the right time because the original soloist and the student will invariably be playing the cadenza differently. Nonetheless, as frustrating as they are, these CDs at least give players the chance to feel how their part blends with the orchestra. And it gives the soloist a chance to practice scrambling back in to keep up with the orchestra.

> **Out of Tune**
>
> CDs often come with beginning method books, but young children sometimes find playing with CDs confusing and therefore simply "forget" that part of the assignment. If you use play-along CDs for practice assignments, be sure parents are aware of the need for a CD player or an iPod and agree to make one available. And ask them to remind young students to do that part of the assignment.

With jazz and pop CDs, there are fewer accelerandos and ritardandos, so the process is less frustrating. A stable tempo makes for a much smoother interaction between player and CD. Indeed, in many cases, the backing tracks are done with synthesized rhythm parts that keep a steady beat no matter what.

Computers, Software, and the Internet

It's a whole new world out there. Kids who want to hear the new hit song from the latest vampire movie don't have to wait endless minutes for it to come up again on the Top-40 radio rotation. In seconds, they can download it to their iPods. And they don't have to beg a ride to the local music store to find the score for it, either. If Mom is willing to lend her credit card, a savvy music student can download the sheet music nearly instantly.

Educational Software

Educational software can supplement music instruction with exercises and games that offer a fun way to reinforce note reading and theory skills. Be aware, however, that software that looks like an educational program to a teacher can be turned into nothing more than a click-as-fast-as-you-can game by a video-savvy grade-schooler. Games that reward students for speed while not penalizing them for mistakes are guaranteed to be abused and misused. All you have to do is put one of these "How many notes can you get right?" games in front of a child to see that the child's strategy will be to simply click away at as many notes as possible.

Another problem with software is that if you own it, then your student has to work with it on your computer. This requires having a dedicated student computer and a space for them to work, and it requires that you build computer lab time into your schedule. Some teachers do this and feel that it adds value to the program they offer.

Given the cost of music lessons, instruments, books, play-along CDs, and recital fees, you're not likely to be able to sell many parents on extra money for software downloads that may be used only a few times. However, if you do a computer search for "free music learning software," you'll come up with many pages of options. Be aware that far too many of these are "train yourself into perfect pitch" programs (which are neither necessary nor particularly successful—in most cases, people either have perfect pitch or they don't). But many good relative-pitch ear-training programs, as well as music-reading games, are available.

Often free programs are "intro level" sample programs, designed to get you to pay for more comprehensive downloads. Try the free samples first, and if you like them, you can check reviews of the upgrades on music teacher discussion boards or music educator websites and publications to see if the additional investment would be worth it.

Notation Software

Music notation software makes it possible to write finished-looking sheet music on the computer and then print it out. For a teacher, this means being able to write out exercises or arrangements for students (although it can be a time-consuming process until you get pretty familiar with the program).

Take Note

Full-fledged notation software can be expensive—up to $600 or so. To get your feet wet, try out some of the free notation software available for download on the Internet. These are sometimes teasers to the "real" versions (for which you have to pay). Experiment with them so you know what features you like and need. Then spring for the upgrades as necessary.

Software is also available to translate notes played on a digital keyboard into music notation via the computer (although corrections frequently have to be made in notating precise rhythms). These programs do their best to apply standard notation conventions, but they aren't perfect. Often the choices the computer makes with respect to beaming, ties, and rhythmic groupings seem a little goofy. Nonetheless, given the fact that the choice is to write out scores by hand, the notation software is certainly an improvement.

Students learn to read and write music better if they have to do it by hand, or at least put the notes on the right lines and spaces on a computer, rather than simply playing a phrase on a piano and having the computer do the work of notating it. But notation software *may* encourage them to compose.

Note that if you own computer notation software, it's for your use; you can't copy it and give it to your students. According to computer licensing rules, they have to buy their own, although they can use yours if they use it on your computer. The more complex and expensive the program, the more it can do (including transposing, adding chord symbols or guitar tab, and writing in different clefs).

Online Learning Resources

In addition to educational and notation software, thousands of websites have music education material. Free lessons (written and audio) are available all over the Internet purporting to show students everything from how to hold a guitar to how to make a chord. Many contain excellent information and advice; some are merely useless. There are also plenty of paid sites, which charge a subscription or per-lesson fee. Online music instruction is a new and growing field, although most people find that they do need a "real" teacher to sort out the complexities of music notation and technique. However, some students do benefit from on-line lessons, particularly when it comes to learning a special lick or riff. For the moment, at least, for most students, these lessons serve more as a supplement to traditional lessons than as a replacement for them.

Facts and Stats
A 2009 search at Google.com on "how to play the …" (within quotation marks) returned the following results: guitar 280,000,000 sites; piano 2,970,000; violin 108,000; drums 949,000; flute 287,000; trumpet 267,000; tuba 42,300; bassoon 20,900. Although Google results change continually based on their changing metrics for searches, the fact remains that there are a lot of sites for music students—and many more sites for more popular instruments.

While you may have little need to surf the Internet looking for absolute beginner lessons on playing the guitar, your students might wander around, perhaps looking for a favorite lick or technique or the chords for a favorite song. Keep an open line of communication with students about extracurricular music explorations so you can help if they wander into a website that gives inappropriate or even dead-wrong advice.

Sheet Music

Free sheet music and, for guitarists, TAB (tablature) is available all over the Internet, but there are several problems with it. Problems might include the following:

◆ Some of the music is copyright protected, and its distribution on the Internet is, plain and simple, illegal.

◆ Some of the music is just plain wrong: wrong notes, wrong rhythms, wrong chords, wrong riffs. This is especially true on user-generated sites on which anyone can post what he or she thinks the chords are to any given song.

◆ Some of the free music that is legitimately in the public domain, such as classical pieces, are available for free only in very poor editions. A great deal of scholarly editorial work goes into producing an edition of, say, a Beethoven sonata. You won't find scholarly editions, with correct articulation, ornaments, and choices of notes in disputed passages for free on the Internet because the scholarly editions are copyrighted.

The Internet is also a source of music to download for a fee. This is a great option when a student comes in saying, "My friend Johnny is playing this really cool piece and I want to play it, too." Frequently, a quick Internet search is all it takes to locate the sheet music for sale. If you are not familiar with the piece, of course, you'll have to evaluate whether your student can play it. The best situation is when there is a sample page available so that the teacher can see the level of the music she is buying for a student. Even so, sometimes the first page or so is nice and easy, and then when the music arrives, it turns out that the entire middle section is many levels higher.

YouTube and Song Downloads

When asked to give advice to students, virtually every great musician says, "Listen." Listen to everything. And now, "everything" is available.

While stuffy old music teachers might be rifling through their CD collections (how quaint) or their LPs (which have acquired the status of cool antiques), it's possible to push a few buttons and see five different performances of a Rachmaninoff concerto, the entire Van Cliburn competition, and performances ranging from an amateur sitting in her living room playing at an upright to the latest, hottest rock groups.

The Internet gives our students a resource we never had—the ability to listen to many different performances of the same piece, back to back. Kids can download favorites to their iPods or cruise YouTube for different works from a composer they like. You can listen with them and pause the performance to talk about certain aspects, such as choices the performer made about tempo, interpretation, and so on.

On YouTube, students may also find how-to videos that supposedly teach certain skills or songs. Many of these lessons teach by rote, which is fine if a student really wants to learn a particular song. As a teacher, though, try to make sure you know what your students are up to and what they're learning. You may be able to use their interests in a variety of ways, from learning more about chords and improvising, to music theory, to playing with others. And it may give you other ideas for directions in which to take their lessons.

 **Out of Tune**

The Internet remains a dangerous place for children, and many parents do not allow pictures of their children to go online. Never post a video online of a child's performance without the parent's written permission. This goes for recitals and public performances as well.

PA and Recording Equipment

Public address (PA) equipment and recording equipment are not standard items in most private teaching studios. However, some sort of basic equipment is useful for all students. It can be as simple as a handheld digital recorder or even a cell phone. If you teach popular music, jazz, and contemporary (nonoperatic) singing, and if you plan to have your students "play out," some basic PA and sound equipment is necessary. Having it makes the difference between being able to offer your students this opportunity—or not.

PA Equipment

PA equipment depends on the instrument and style of music. Built-in keyboard speakers may be adequate for very small spaces, but you'll generally need an amplifier for larger spaces. For other instruments, amplification may or may not be necessary, depending on the venue and the instrument (vocals, harps, and classical guitars need amplification; trumpets probably don't).

Take Note _____

Everyone's cables and music stands look alike, so mark all your PA and recording equipment, as well as music stands. Colored tape wrapped around your cables is easily visible. Or use those little sticky address labels sent to you by charities. Transport your electronic gear in a gig bag, and keep in it a list of everything you normally use, including an extra power strip, extension chords, and a light for reading music on dark stages.

If you need to amplify, depending on your instrument, you'll need a microphone or a pick-up, cables, and an amplifier or a PA system. The PA system includes a power supply (a piece of equipment that powers the system), a mixing board, and speakers, which are available in various combinations. For larger ensembles, you'll need monitors (which are really just speakers) so that the various musicians can hear themselves. Think of your PA equipment as an evolving need. Start small; you can always trade up.

Recording Equipment

Recording equipment can be as simple or as complex as you want it to be. With today's capabilities, it is possible to record a student performance on a cell phone, which may be all you need to do to talk about a student performance with that student after the fact. However, a small digital recorder offers better sound, and with video, your student can put the performance on YouTube if he or she so desires.

With a microphone, a computer, and some free downloadable software, you can record on a computer, then copy the results onto a CD to distribute to family and friends. This can be a great summer or holiday music project.

Wise Words _____

I use a Zoom H2 Handy Recorder to record pieces that my students have prepared. This gives them an audio progress report. Cassette tapes have become outdated and my students did not have cassette players at home any more. This recorder is small and fairly easy to use, at a price of under $200. It records digitally to a small memory card like those used in digital cameras. The files may be recorded as either .mp3 files (which are perfect for e-mailing home to a student for their computer or iPod) or .wav files, which can be uploaded to a website.

—Marci Pittman, music teacher, Chico, California

A step up is a portable recording studio (a dedicated recording device that can handle multiple tracks). For about $400, you can get a system that makes high-quality audition CDs and almost-professional-sounding recordings of multi-instrument ensembles.

Do you need all this stuff? Probably not. Is it useful? As learning curves have become more manageable and prices have come down, more teachers have invested in at least rudimentary recording equipment.

From a teaching perspective, the most useful thing for recording equipment is to let students hear themselves and discuss the performance in detail with them. *Warning:* you may have to do this a few times before students learn to listen critically. At the outset, they are bound to be inordinately pleased with themselves.

The Least You Need to Know

- Keyboards are relatively inexpensive (compared to pianos) and can handle a whole range of studio tasks, from teaching theory, to accompanying, to serving as a second piano.

- Play-along CDs are excellent teaching tools for group performance, particularly in the areas of jazz, pop, rock, and improvisation.

- Digital learning resources include teaching sites, notation software, and educational games.

- Some basic recording and PA equipment enables students and teachers to record CDs and play out in public venues.

Chapter 17

Performance in the Twenty-First-Century Studio

In This Chapter

- ◆ The benefits of student performances
- ◆ Coping with stage fright
- ◆ Putting on a rewarding recital
- ◆ Adjudications, auditions, and competitions
- ◆ Performance opportunities in your community

Anyone who has studied an instrument probably has a memory of the first piano, violin, guitar, or bassoon recital. Whether in an elementary school auditorium, the summer camp talent show, or a scary-looking recital hall with a big black grand piano, most of us music teachers can conjure up the feeling of that first performance. We may have performed a thousand times since then, but sealed inside us are the memories of slippery, sweaty fingers; fluttering tummies; and trembling knees.

Somehow music lessons wouldn't be the same without that childhood ritual. Parents want it. Teachers dutifully assign performance pieces, print up programs, and find venues. And students expect it. Some endure it, some enjoy it, some excel at it. It is a sort of rite of passage.

Today's teachers have more options when preparing students for performance. We can offer the traditional venues, of course. But with PA equipment being affordable even for small studio owners, it's possible to hold a music recital in a coffeehouse or have a band of students playing at the church picnic. And this helps us communicate the important message to students that music is a lifetime skill, a way to express feelings and communicate, and an art to be shared.

Benefits of Student Performances

There's a long list of reasons to encourage students to perform. There are also, of course, reasons not to put students on stage before they are ready. But for most students, the pros of performing far outweigh the cons.

Perhaps first and foremost, performing takes the student's music out of the studio and out of the context of a teacher-student situation, and puts it where it belongs—in front of people and being shared. Performances also raise the ante by setting both a standard and a deadline. Virtually all children (and adults, too) work much harder knowing a performance is coming up. To prepare a piece so that it can be reliably played with few, if any, mistakes, stops, lapses, and glitches requires a level of practice far beyond what a normal student does if there is no performance on the horizon. With a performance in sight, you can't just phone it in.

Performances can be huge emotional rewards for students who love music and are working hard. The chance to shine in front of peers, to play a really cool piece that others will aspire to play, to be placed in that honored last spot, reserved for the hardest piece on the program—all of these recognize the committed student's work and achievements.

It's inevitable that students compare themselves to one another and that students swell up with pride as their accomplishments are recognized. But performing music is about more than that. At its heart, performing means sharing the music that a student has chosen and worked on. In real life—in the world beyond the childhood music studio—live performances are experiences of community between an audience and a performer. Whether singing around a campfire, sitting in a coffeehouse, going to a rock concert, listening to a chamber ensemble, or hearing a church choir, live performances are community experiences. Being part of such experiences at an early age shows students that they have the ability to connect with people through their music.

Should Participation Be Required?

While the vast majority of students benefit from performing in public, a few do not. As a teacher, you must decide whether to require participation in the events you hold and how to handle the few holdouts you will inevitably encounter.

Interestingly, it's not always your youngest beginners who are most reluctant to perform. Some of them, in fact, are eager to get on stage. There is something to be said for encouraging a young child to play before a friendly group of adoring family and friends before he is even old enough to worry about goofing up. In a small-scale recital that takes place in the teacher's studio, or in an environment such as a child-friendly classroom or a comfortable coffee shop, the nerve issue can be minimized.

Take Note _____

Even if students refuse to perform, try to require them to attend recitals. They can act as ushers, and they can join in the group bow at the end of the performance. Who knows? Perhaps they will be inspired to participate next time.

Nonetheless, just as there are always a few children who hide in the back of the classroom during show-and-tell, there will be a few who are scared of playing in front of others. Or they refuse for their own reasons (which may have nothing to do with fear and everything to do with a power struggle with Mom). There's no reason to try to force a clearly reluctant child onto a stage, especially in the beginning years, especially if he or she is clearly not prepared to perform. Sometimes bribery with cookies works; sometimes it's best to just wait another year.

Teens are the other group who can be reluctant performers, often out of self-consciousness (and sometimes sheer silliness). Sometimes a teen really is almost pathologically shy. It may be possible to get these kids to play in a community service setting, such as a nursing home, where they feel that playing is a way of contributing to the community. But some students would rather quit than call attention to themselves by performing. If that's the case, there's nothing to be gained—and potentially a lot to be lost—by requiring such a student to perform.

Preparation and Stage Fright

One of the most effective ways to encourage student performances is to make them as nonthreatening and fun as possible. That can seem to be an impossible task, given that stage fright is inevitably a part of the mix.

We can't eliminate stage fright altogether. But we can minimize it. Not surprisingly, the people who are less prone to stage fright are (usually) the students who are truly well prepared for their performance. So our job as teachers is to be sure students are adequately prepared, whether they are playing a solo at the Christmas concert, accompanying a school choir, performing with a rock band, or playing in a competition.

> **Wise Words**
>
> The week before my mandatory spring recital I always hold a recital rehearsal in place of regular lessons. Students come on their normal day they have lessons, but they meet as one group and perform for each other as if it was the recital. This is also when I go through recital etiquette, performance etiquette, and performance anxiety. The kids are more prepared, and the recital seems to go more smoothly with this process.
>
> —Jennifer Foxx, music teacher, Goodyear, Arizona

Unfortunately, students very early on in life pick up the habit of cramming, which doesn't work for most things, and certainly doesn't work for music. Even some parents step in, informing the teacher that their child "always manages to pull it off at the last minute." It's your job to educate both parents and students that musical performance simply doesn't work this way, and that operating in this manner shows disrespect for the other ensemble members, the conductor, the audience, and the music.

As the teacher, you can reserve the right to dictate whether your students can or cannot perform in public, enter contests, or perform at your recital. This sounds draconian, but as the teacher, you should have a far better idea than the student of whether the student is or isn't ready to play a piece.

One way to deal with an overconfident, underprepared student is to allow him to perform. Some students need to learn from their own experience. Reserve this strategy for a low-pressure event, where failure won't be a disaster or humiliation, and reserve it for students who are emotionally strong enough to deal with repercussions of a bad performance. (Most students who are strong-willed enough to go onstage with a half-baked piece against their teacher's wishes can deal with the mostly predictable outcome.) Of course, once in a while a student pulls a rabbit out of a hat, and then you have to make a convincing argument for why this can't be expected to happen every time.

> **Take Note** _____
>
> Use group classes to prepare students for performances. Have them practice walking to the stage, playing without making faces or stopping when they make a mistake, then bowing. An effective game is to have members of the group try to distract the performer into making a mistake. Some necessary ground rules: no touching the performer, no getting between the performer and the instrument, and only one "distractor" goes at a time. Distractors can bang doors, turn lights on and off, and make funny faces. Kids like this game so much they beg to play it, so use it for a reward.

Memorization is another preparation tool, regardless of whether you require students to perform from memory. (In the early years, you can reduce stress by not requiring students to memorize, and you will be pleasantly surprised by how many, in fact, do end up preparing their recital pieces to the point of memorization.) The conventions are different for different instruments and types of performances. Solo pianists must memorize; accompanists do not have to. Chamber musicians don't; concerto players do. Solo violinists do; symphony players don't. In rock bands, it is considered completely uncool to play with sheet music in front of you (although if you look closely, you'll see that more than a few professional rock stars have computer screens discretely set up to feed them chords and lyrics).

No matter what the convention, a memorized piece is more secure. So although you may permit a student to use music at the performance, you might also require that the piece be memorized in the lesson. Playing passages with the eyes closed is also an effective exercise. Students may look at you with disbelief when you request this, but they will be equally surprised when they realize how well they did and how well they know the piece.

Dealing with the Results

Sometimes the performance doesn't go as planned. Even the best-prepared students sometimes fall apart from nerves. Little things might go wrong, such as a student who expected to play second has to play first because the first student didn't show up. Or a student has a memory lapse or a technical breakdown.

In a low-pressure situation such as a house recital, teach kids to stop after a misstep at the beginning and say, "I'm going to start over." This can really break the ice because other students can see that a mistake is not the end of the world. Obviously, this doesn't work in formal competitions, but in a beginner's recital, it can be a smile-saver.

A poor performance can be an opportunity for further education, or maybe even a wake-up call. Students learn the difference between being prepared and being overconfident. They learn that they ultimately survived the experience (perhaps even getting back on track and finishing with flourish). And they can try to analyze what went wrong to prevent it from happening next time.

The Studio Recital

The most common venue for a child's performance is the teacher's annual studio recital. Not all teachers hold annual recitals. And by contrast, some hold two, or even more, recitals per year. The decision is a combination of how the teacher feels about performance in general, about performance in light of other learning goals, and about the value of performance to students of various levels.

Different Types of Recitals

At its most basic, a recital can be simply a gathering of several families at a teacher's home, assuming she has a living room big enough to seat everyone. Students take turns playing their pieces, and the event ends with a period of socializing and some treats, possibly provided potluck-style by participating families. This is a good option for teachers who are just starting out and have small studios.

For larger studios, recitals are often formal events, held in a public space such as a school, church, synagogue, or community facility. If you teach at a music school, you can probably host a recital at the school's facility, or you may join with other teachers and mix a few of your students with a few of theirs. This can offer some nice variety, especially if you team up with teachers of different instruments.

In some communities, music teachers host joint recitals for their most advanced students. Participating in one of these "all-star" events is a real honor for the students who represent your studio.

Recital Planning Basics

Before you can choose a space or a time, you need to have an idea of just what type of recital yours will be. Do you have 5 students, or 35? In the first case, you might get creative at home. For example, have a Halloween party where everyone comes in costume and plays scary music. Or have a holiday party featuring holiday songs and a sing-along. If your studio is on the larger side—too large for your home to accommodate—you will undoubtedly need a larger space, and you may even need to decide whether you need to do one recital or two.

Facts and Stats

In a mixed group of varying ages and abilities, a roster of 20 to 25 students makes for a recital program of just over an hour. Try to keep recitals under 75 minutes. Most people (especially young children) don't want to sit still for longer than that. With advanced students, whose pieces can easily run 10 minutes or longer, you'll need to factor in more time, especially if you have anyone with a huge warhorse to display. Conversely, 30 beginners playing 1 minute songs can easily be scheduled into a single recital.

If you have too many students to fit into one recital, split the roster into two recitals. You can split them into groups by age and ability so that young students have one recital and older students have another. Or you can mix and match. Breaking them up by age makes it more likely that friends will be sitting together, which makes the event feel more social. It also eliminates the problem of older beginners being out-played by a talented youngster (something older children can be sensitive about). But having the younger kids see what lies ahead is exciting and inspiring, too. You'll have to make the decision based on the ages and levels of students in your studio.

You can either do the recitals on two separate days or plan to run two recitals back-to-back with an intermission in between (realizing that most families will not stay for the full two-part recital). The advantage of the first plan is that families get a choice of days, so if they have a conflict, they can still participate. The advantage of running the recitals back-to-back is that people can stay for the whole event, if they choose, and you can consolidate the preparation, planning, recital rental fees, and refreshments.

Give Me Some Space!

Finding space for your recital depends on which instrument (or instruments) will be playing and how many people you need to seat. A rock band isn't going to be appropriate in a church, and you don't need a concert hall if you have only five students.

Start with a preliminary headcount. Over time, you will develop a fairly good sense of your families. Some families will show up for a recital with only the student and one parent in tow. Others will bring along an entire claque of uncles, cousins, grandparents, and siblings. Just for starters, figure at about four seats per student.

One key issue related to finding recital space is finding a facility with a suitable piano. This is important even if your main instrument is not piano because most recitals involve at least some accompaniment. For instrumental recitals, an acoustic upright may be acceptable (assuming it is in tune). Keyboards are also a practical solution for accompanying all but the more advanced students.

The issue is much more problematic for piano recitals because most piano teachers strongly prefer having a good grand piano for students to play. (And many advanced students and their families are disappointed if the recital space doesn't offer a good instrument.) But the cost of renting a grand piano for an evening (not to mention transporting it and tuning it) is prohibitive. So piano teachers must either find space with a playable instrument or make do with a digital piano.

Does it really matter? It depends on the type of recital you are planning, the level of your students, and their repertoire. Our studio, for instance, holds a very informal mixed instrument recital in a local coffeehouse, which we rent for an evening. The instruments we teach include piano, guitar, and bass. In addition, we sometimes have guest performers join us. At a recent recital, a sibling of one of our students performed on harp, a friend of a guitar student joined in on saxophone, and musician colleagues joined us, backing up our students in a rock band. Plus, we might rope in a parent to play percussion.

Our coffee shop recital is a family favorite, especially around the holidays, when we add a sing-along component. It has a friendly feel, lots of cookies and brownies, and none of the terror associated with the typical student recital. So it's a great introduction to performance for a young student, and we feel that that is a fair tradeoff, even if we have to make do with a digital piano. But we also hold special invitational recitals and jams in our home (which can seat about 30 audience members) for students who have reached the level where they need a proper grand piano to perform on.

Some other ideas for recital spaces include schools and colleges, synagogues and churches, community centers with pianos, and small recital facilities in your town. Some businesses even have appropriate spaces. Get creative in your community: talk to people at the various social clubs (Rotary, Lions, and so on). A hotel or an inn with a good piano might be a possibility during the off-season, especially if you happen to have a personal contact.

Economics of the Recital

The cost of hosting a recital ranges from virtually nothing to a few hundred dollars. In small informal recitals, many teachers simply ask student families to contribute via a potluck treats table. For larger recitals, there may be a hall rental fee, which is when costs start to add up.

To defray costs, some teachers charge a separate fee for recital participation. Be aware that unless you have made it perfectly clear, both in your written studio policy and in repeated conversations, that you expect all students to participate in the recital, a fee might discourage participation.

If you don't charge a separate fee, the cost of the recital needs to be factored into your expenses when you are setting your prices (see Chapter 5). If you treat recital costs as expenses, they are, of course, a tax deduction.

Another choice, although not a common one, is to charge an admission fee to the recital. Teachers who do this point out that audience members often have to pay to attend student theater productions or dance recitals. But most teachers feel uncomfortable about charging parents to see their own children perform. Because unrelated strangers are not likely to pay money to watch a succession of children playing recital songs, an admission fee seems to send the wrong message.

You may, however, want to advertise your recital if it is being held in any sort of a public space. First of all, the ad acts as a general public message about the existence of your studio. Unless one of your students happens to be a local child celebrity, you probably won't get much of a walk-in audience, but you may attract some people who are interested in checking you out as a teacher.

Programming

Helping students choose selections for a recital can be tricky. Very young beginners can probably wait until about three or four weeks before the recital to start thinking about what they are going to play. At the beginning levels, students learn their pieces very quickly (and get bored with them just as quickly), so there's really no need to spend a month on "Old MacDonald." Start reminding students of the recital about five weeks ahead. By three weeks out, they should have a couple of songs chosen that they think they can play. The next couple of lessons can be devoted to making the pieces recital-ready and secure.

With intermediate students, you need more time, at least six to eight weeks between choosing a recital piece and having it ready to perform. Intermediate pieces (depending on the student and the instrument) can take three weeks to learn, and then there is memorizing (if you require it), getting rid of glitches, finalizing dynamics and articulation and phrasing, and getting it up to performance standard. And advanced students, of course, may work on their pieces for several months.

> **Take Note**
>
> Always plan in advance who will go first and prepare that student for the special job. Choose your most self-confident devil-may-care student to lead off the recital. It can be a beginner or an intermediate student. Most teachers prefer to save the advanced players for later in the program.

The difficulty of preparing recital repertoire is one of the reasons some teachers shy away from more than one recital a year. At the intermediate and advanced levels, preparing for performance takes a lot of time—frequently more time than students are willing or able to practice.

One solution is to dial down your expectations for a recital. Students do not have to play the biggest, flashiest piece they are capable of. In fact, often it's the big flashy piece that sounds like nonstop noise, and the beautifully played pieces that catch the audience's attention.

Many teachers program students in order of difficulty, starting with young beginners and progressing upward. This works if all your students fall into a neat line in terms of both age and ability. But that is not usually the case. You are bound to have an 8-year-old who is playing at a much higher level than a 13-year-old, a fact that will be lost on neither of them.

Some teachers mix up the order, starting with a strong younger intermediate, then having a few beginners, then perhaps a beginner teen followed by some younger intermediate, an intermediate teenager, then a young advanced player, then some older, more accomplished players.

Adjudications and Contests

Another way for students to gain performance experience and to receive informed feedback is to participate in competitions or in judged events in which students are evaluated according to preset standards appropriate for their level. Both are somewhat controversial among teachers, who disagree about how objectively musical performance can and should be rated, and whether competitions are appropriate for artistic events. However, many teachers feel that the chance to be evaluated by a third party is valuable.

Being Involved in Adjudications

Adjudications are noncompetitive events in which students prepare a selection of repertoire and perform level-appropriate technical and sight-reading work as required by the event. A judge or a group of judges grades the performers.

Many adjudication programs are offered in the United States and in Canada. In the States, state music teacher associations hold a variety of "festivals" in which students can audition for all-county or all-state ensembles, or can be evaluated according to standards established by committees of professional music teachers. In Canada, the Royal Conservatory of Music offers a comprehensive graded program of examinations in most instruments. Additionally, instrument-specific programs are available. Probably the largest in the United States is the nationwide program managed by the Piano Guild.

These programs can be good ways for teachers to double-check their curriculum and their students' progress against a general standard. Most of the programs include a combination of repertoire, technique, and fundamentals (which could include theory, scales and arpeggios, sight-reading, chord progression, and other basic skills).

Typically, the audition takes place in a classroom or private studio, attended by the judge or judges. The experience ranges from nerve-wracking to educational, sometimes both, depending on how much emphasis and importance is placed on success. In many programs, judges are encouraged to be positive and reassuring, to the point that grades range from "good" to "superior" and, as in Lake Woebegone, all the children are above average. Some teachers feel that this is reflective of a sort of self-esteem-induced grade inflation and don't participate for that reason. Other teachers feel that it keeps things positive and upbeat.

Out of Tune

Never criticize judges in the presence of your students, even if you completely disagree with their evaluations. Students need to learn that music is a subjective endeavor and that they will be evaluated by critics, conductors, and audiences according to very different standards. As in a sporting event, the judge's words are final, and a student who complains about unfair judging will get a reputation as a poor sport.

Many teachers feel that these events are motivators for students, who will work that much harder to achieve the extra points from memorizing a certain number of songs or reaching a certain grade. It can also be good for students to hear another teacher's feedback. In the early grades, the judge's feedback will almost always mirror the primary teacher's on essential issues such as rhythm, dynamics, and other fundamentals.

At more advanced levels, judges may emphasize something the teacher has decided not to focus on. For example, the teacher of an intermediate student who has had ongoing rhythm problems may decide to hold off on working with accelerandos, ritardandos, and fermatas. A judge, not knowing this, might criticize a student for not using these expressive devices. Nevertheless, this can be an excellent learning opportunity.

The Competition

Competitions exist at virtually all levels of music, from elementary school through graduate school and beyond. They are another way for students to gain performance experience. A typical contest might have a preliminary round and then a final round. Prizes may include scholarships, performances, or even the chance to record a CD.

Musicians and music teachers have conflicting views of musical competitions. From an artistic viewpoint, some teachers consider competitions to be anathema to creativity. Certainly, it is difficult to rate two performers if they are closely matched in level, play similar repertoire, and offer sensitive interpretations.

But competitions can motivate students, even those who have become complacent. The local stand-out pianist who always is selected to accompany the school choir or play a solo with the jazz band may be shocked to find herself in a room full of other pianists her age who can play the exact same level of material, and then some. It can be a real wake-up call to move from a small pond to a slightly larger one, but for students who are serious about music, it's an important step.

With competitions, issues of judging, including favoritism and different tastes, are exacerbated. One judge may respond favorably to a dynamic and crashing performance of a mistake-riddled warhorse, appreciating the effort, the difficulty, and the student's enjoyment of a piece. Another judge might prefer a sensitively rendered easier piece for its musical qualities, phrasing, and maturity.

Like it or not, competitions are part and parcel of a musician's life. In the end, music competitions are a lot like sports—the referees make the calls and the gracious competitors stay silent about the judging and congratulate the winner.

Group Performances

Group performances are important but are often neglected by private teachers, especially teachers of piano. It is so important to remember that the vast majority of music is performed with other people, and that includes piano players. Until recently, there was a good reason that pianists were deprived of this opportunity. Simply put, you can't carry an acoustic piano to your friend's basement to jam along. But with today's keyboards, that problem is eliminated. If students are interested in performing with others, an inexpensive keyboard puts that opportunity at their fingertips.

Developing Skills for Group Performance

Developing student skills for group performance is a challenge for the private music teacher. Often students learn about group performance skills when participating in a school ensemble. Private music teachers should always encourage such participation. The student will be exposed to different music, and nothing makes a student learn to count better than having to keep his place in an ensemble. Students who resist counting for years snap to it when they realize they didn't come in when they were supposed to and the conductor is looking straight at them.

To prepare students for group performances, private teachers should use duets as much as possible. Trading eights and call-and-response exercises are good—even better if they are played in strict time. For teaching improvisation, keyboard and guitar players need to know as many chords as possible, as well as how to cheat the ones they don't know. Everyone (keyboard and guitar players, too) needs to know scales, including pentatonic and blues scales and, later, modes. If students will be playing with horn players, everyone needs to know the basics of transposition. If the horn player brings in a song written for B-flat instruments, the pianist and guitarist need to know what that means for their C-instruments.

Performing in a group also requires learning how to rehearse. There needs to be an understanding that students participating in a group performance have to commit to the group, just as they would commit to a sports team.

Jams

An informal, nonthreatening way to introduce students to group playing is to host jams. To make this work, you need a book with either sheet music or chord charts or lead sheets (depending on how you teach and who is playing what). Familiar three-chord songs make a great starting place because if people lose their place, they can generally find their way back in. Similarly, songs with a repeating chord progression offer an easy entry into the world of jamming.

> **Take Note**
>
> A song circle is a round-robin sort of group performance in which participants take turns choosing and leading songs. Although advanced players can often follow along without chord charts or lead sheets, students usually need them, so be sure participants bring music for the songs they are going to lead.

You also need a variety of instruments and a couple players who can hold things together. In our studio, my partner, David, plays guitar and bass, and I play keyboards and can bang along on a guitar or on percussion instruments. So with my students on piano, I might play drums or guitar (or a backup keyboard), and David might play guitar or bass. And with his guitar or bass students, I sit in and comp chords or bass lines (as appropriate) on keyboards.

Community Performance Opportunities

Your local community may offer a wide variety of opportunities for your students to perform. The sad truth for a musician is that there are tons of opportunities to play out, as long as no one is worried about getting paid. But that's a happy truth for students, who grow tremendously each time they play in front of an audience, regardless of the venue or the size of the crowd.

Nursing Homes

Nursing homes are a fantastic way to get students performing. This is a win-win on so many levels. The residents love seeing children, the students get the chance to do something that obviously is appreciated, and the audience is noncritical.

Performing at a nursing home doesn't require an advanced level of skill, but students should be able to play recognizable songs securely. Some audience members will be able to appreciate more advanced performances. Others, however, may start singing or clapping along, which can be distracting to a student.

Preparation can include games that prepare students for distractions. The teacher should also discuss what students are likely to see: older people in wheelchairs, people who have trouble communicating, people who can't walk or who may be strapped into their chairs. The experience of performing for people in a nursing home can truly underscore the importance of music and its value as a source of joy in people's lives.

Just as with recitals, attention span is an issue for a nursing home performance. Discuss your program with the activities director, but generally, the program shouldn't go more than about an hour.

Open Mikes

Open mikes are a great opportunity for advanced students to perform. You'll want to check out open mikes in your community to get a sense of how they run and how friendly they are. Some are warm and fuzzy, with room for everyone. Some are more professional, with a higher level of players. And there are also some cutthroat open mikes with a clique of regulars, who may or may not be generous to newcomers or to students.

At an informal open mike, all you need to do is show up with your instrument. If you (or your students) play piano, you will most likely have to perform on a keyboard; most venues for open mikes don't have acoustic pianos sitting around. Check ahead of time to find out whether there is a keyboard on stage, or if they want you to bring your own. *Warning*: theirs might be completely different from yours, and it might have an action that makes you (or your students) cringe. But for pianists, those are the rules of the game—you play what you have to.

If there are a lot of players, playing may be on a first-come, first-served basis. You may have to sign up at the beginning of the night, and you may not even get a chance to play if you don't arrive on time. In those cases, players will often be limited to two or three songs (and, no, one of them can't be 20 minutes long). Then there are the open mikes where almost no one shows up and you can stay on stage until closing time.

Try to match your students to the level of the gig, and don't bring ten at a time! Playing out is a reward that students should earn, and they should be capable of playing at the same level as the regulars before you introduce them to this kind of venue.

Involving Students in Your Gigs

If you are playing at the community level (assuming your community isn't West 57th Street in New York City), you might be able to involve students in your gigs. If you're playing at a coffeehouse or another local venue that is appropriate for students (that is, *not* an establishment where alcoholic beverages are sold), you could have students be your "warm-up" act. Make sure you check that this is okay with the venue; not every manager wants to have kids up on stage. But some proprietors will welcome your students (for a couple of short songs), especially if they bring along audience members of family and friends. These numbers matter to a small business proprietor.

Take Note

Once you have a group that can play in time and in tune, look for opportunities to play in your community. Be creative! A group of guitar students can serenade at the local farmers' market, the annual town festival, the firemen's fundraising dinner, or the bandstand in a local park.

You can also ask more advanced students to come up and join you on stage for a couple songs, but you'll have to make a judgment call here. If you are playing professionally, the student needs to be able to hold his or her own in a professional setting.

The Least You Need to Know

♦ An annual recital is a chance for students to show what they've learned.

♦ Stage fright is natural, but you can minimize it with proper preparation, including a "practice recital" before the public event.

♦ Adjudications and contests can be valuable performance experiences for students of all levels.

♦ Recitals don't have to be formal events. They can be held in informal situations such as the teacher's home or in a coffee shop or classroom.

♦ Group performances teach important ensemble and rhythm skills and can be a way to encourage reluctant solo performers to play on stage in their communities.

Chapter 18

A Career to Last a Lifetime

In This Chapter

◆ Your musical and pedagogical education

◆ Professional resources available through organizations, universities, and the Internet

◆ Renewing your energy and preventing teacher burnout

◆ Keeping your love of music fresh and growing

A colleague says, quite simply, "I can't think of a better life than this."

And why would she? We music teachers get to spend our days sharing the love of our art with people ranging from preschoolers to seniors. We see them progress, we see some of them excel, and we see them fall in love with music, just as we did. The work is always interesting, plus, we get to run our own businesses, set our own hours, and work at home (if we choose).

But it's not always easy to keep it fresh. How do we stay energetic the five-hundredth time we teach the same song in the beginner primer, and correct the same predictable mistakes (quite possibly the exact same ones we corrected with the same student the week before)? How do we learn about new developments in pedagogy that might help us get over or around some of the roadblocks we keep running into? How do we continue to grow?

Networking and professional development are important in any career, but in a field in which teachers work one-on-one with students—rather than with peers—these activities are essential. Because we work alone, we have to seek out these opportunities.

When the Teacher Becomes the Student

Learning music is a lifelong process. That's true for music teachers as well as for music students. Sitting in the student's chair means remembering what the learning process is like. In addition to helping you develop and refresh your own musical skills, experiencing the learning process gives you empathy for your students as you remember, first-hand, what it is like to struggle with something for the first time and never quite find enough time to practice.

Continuing education can take the form of a weekend seminar at a local music school, a national conference with famous composers and educators, a community college class, or private study.

Organizations and Conferences

Many organizations provide professional development for music teachers. Organizations range from the multi-thousand-member MTNA (Music Teachers National Association) to small groups of music teachers in your community—something along the lines of the Pleasant Valley Music Teachers Association. The MTNA certifies teachers who meet their standards of performance and teaching experience. Although parents don't usually require certification, it is certainly a mark of professional accomplishment and a way to increase your skills. In Canada, the Royal Conservatory of Music certifies teachers who meet their standards. Organizations may be instrument specific, such as the National Guild of Piano Teachers, or they may be program specific, such as the Suzuki Association of the Americas. Or organizations may be open to all music teachers, regardless of instrument or teaching method.

National organizations and their statewide chapters usually have annual conferences. These are good places to learn about newly published teaching methods, to see demonstrations by the authors on how to teach them, to hear new repertoire, and to take workshops on specific topics—everything from teaching a special needs child to organizing a "monster piano concert" (where multiple pianos and pianists are on stage at a time).

Facts and Stats

In Canada, the Royal Conservatory of Music (RCM) offers a program of auditions and evaluations for beginners all the way up through teachers. It reaches some 500,000 participants in Canada every year. Its publications, including graded repertoire books, are available for purchase in the United States and Canada. In the United States, the recently revitalized National Conservatory of Music of America (NCMA), like the RCM, offers "course syllabi, published series, and support tools across 27 disciplines." NCMA's National Music Certificate Program holds American students to rigorous standards similar to those of the RCM.

Private Lessons

As a music teacher, you certainly don't have to be a concert-level performer, but your playing and musicianship skills are important, particularly when your students start reaching the intermediate and advanced levels. When you begin to teach, your skill level may be more than adequate to teach beginners and maybe even traditional intermediates and advanced students. But several years down the road, your students may request a song in a style you know little about. What then? And what about when your reputation grows and you start getting calls from returning adults, from intermediate high school transfer students, from students hoping to major in music? Can you teach them?

Advancing students require more advanced teachers, particularly if you think a student has the aptitude and interest to major in music. If this is beyond your experience, you need to either brush up on that experience or pass the student on to a more advanced teacher. Local networking should identify those teachers in your community who are qualified to work with preprofessional students.

 Take Note

If you don't have a college music background, meet with a local university's music department chairman or a teacher of your instrument to find out what the audition requirements are for your advanced students. Also ask about expectations in music theory and ear training. Although this information may be available online, actually making the connection and having the conversation can be a valuable exercise for you and for your students down the line.

All of us, of course, can stand to brush up on our skills. For the already accomplished music teacher, it can take quite a bit of searching to find the right coach. Some of us are at a level where we need to work with bona-fide professionals with concert credentials. One place to look, either for a teacher or for a recommendation, is at a local university or college. Even if music faculty don't teach privately, they are likely to know of other professional-level instructors in the area. Your local music teachers' organization or the state chapter of a national music teachers' organization may also be able to help.

Another issue is style. Many music teachers were trained in the classical tradition and aren't comfortable with popular idioms that require improvisation. Yet to connect with today's students, we often need to branch out to a completely different musical idiom. Music teachers with strong classical skills often need just a little bit of coaching to learn enough to show students how to use blues scales for improvisation or how to work through a fake-book rendition of a favorite song. In addition, these forms of music can open new doors and invite some fresh air into your teaching and into your own creativity.

Finally, you could try learning an entirely new instrument. From a business perspective, learning an instrument that is related to your principal instrument is always a good idea. If you pick it up quickly, you may be able to add that instrument to your teaching repertoire, at least at the beginner level. Or an instrumental teacher could brush up on guitar or piano and then use those instruments to accompany students, at least in lessons.

Or you could really branch out, just to keep yourself fresh. Go ahead and learn something completely different that you've always wondered about playing.

College Programs

As a private music teacher, you will only rarely be asked if you have a college degree in music. But while the degree is not necessary, the knowledge often is. As a teacher, you may decide to finish a degree in music, either working on a Master's degree or simply taking classes in subjects that interest you. Colleges and universities offer a wide variety of music programs as well as education programs.

 ◆ **Performance degrees**—These include Bachelor of Music, Master of Music, and Doctor of Music degrees. The course of instruction includes solo performance, as well as ensemble, orchestral, and accompaniment (depending on the instrument), along with music theory, music history, and ear training. The emphasis is on repertoire and musicianship.

- **Bachelor of Arts in Music** —This more general degree trades some performance requirements for more work in theory and history, and it allows the student more time to pursue electives in liberal arts and pedagogy.

- **Music education degrees**—Both Bachelor's and Master's degree programs trade some performance requirements for pedagogy requirements, including supervised student teaching. Music education majors also must learn multiple instruments—at least one in each of the basic instrument categories, plus piano. Music education degrees are the best entrée for jobs into school music teaching.

- **Bachelor's degrees with majors in music technology, recording, and engineering**—Majors (and minors) in music technology and engineering are good options for those interested in recording. These skills are highly desirable in a music studio because they allow the teacher to make effective use of current computer programs, MIDI technology, and various kinds of home recording equipment to make student CDs and record recitals.

- **Education courses**—Music teachers may also find specific courses in the education department useful. Classes in cognitive psychology, early childhood education, and special needs education offer strategies for teachers, regardless of instrument (or even field of study).

Teacher Resources

Beyond formal training and organizations focusing on professional development, teachers can do a lot on their own. Books and magazines are available, of course, on topics ranging from pedagogy, to time management for the self-employed, to jazz improvisation. In addition, the Internet has revolutionized professional development by making unlimited resources available at the touch of a button. The only trick is to know where to look and to be able to evaluate the value of what you are reading or watching.

Websites and Blogs

Websites range from sprawling, multi-thousand-page sites to personal sites maintained by individual studios. Sometimes an individual starts a website with the intention of simply communicating information about the studio. She may then augment it with useful information for her students: how to practice, how to prepare for performance, how to audition. Sometime down the road, the site may grow into a resource visited not only by that teacher's students, but also by other teachers and students.

Other websites are more professional. Some may have obvious or not-so-obvious ties to instrument manufacturers, publishers, or products. Some may provide plenty of free information but offer other, for-a-fee services as well. One example is www. Practicespot.com, which offers free information on everything from how to record a professional studio answering machine message to how to get kids to practice (its original focus). It also offers music teacher–specific templates and website hosting so teachers can create their own turnkey studio website.

Blogs are interactive websites. Typically, the blog format is dynamic, with changing information in a most-recent-post-first format. Many teachers use blogs to communicate their ideas about music and music teaching. Blogs tend to have a personal viewpoint and a personal feel. Most contain a section in which others can leave comments, a list of links to other blogs and web resources, and archives indexed by topic and by date so you can go back to a favorite blogger's site and look for what they have to say about coaching a chamber quartet or preparing a student for a college audition.

Online Forums

Online forums are basically discussion groups on the Internet where teachers can share information, post questions, and discuss their experiences. Some are available on private websites, and some are available on big public websites such as Yahoo! Groups (although the specific forum you want to join may be private or may require you to apply for membership). To find a forum, simply go to the hosting website (such as http://groups.yahoo.com) and type "music teacher" in the search field. The search results will display a wide variety, no doubt, of available discussion groups.

Out of Tune

Never discuss students by name on an Internet forum. You have no idea who is lurking. Plus, if the forum is public, the students or members of their families could discover your comments if they Google their name (as many people do, just to see who's saying what about them).

Forums can be great places to pose questions that need immediate answers because someone is almost always willing to pitch in, or at least to express an opinion. And you can get a lot of different perspectives on a problem. You can also get a lot of misinformation and wrong answers, or answers that may reflect the writer's strong prejudices about certain issues. So read critically and thoughtfully to distinguish good information from bad.

Each forum has its own rules of engagement, as it were. Some are moderated; some are not. If you are new to online forums, you should realize that there are etiquette (netiquette) rules in these communities, just as there are for other types of social interactions and forms of communication.

♦ Listen before you talk. Before you jump in and start pontificating, read what others have to say and get used to the tenor of the conversation.

♦ Be more polite than you would be in person. The other forum participants don't know you, and they can't see or hear you to figure out whether you're being serious, sarcastic, mean, or what. So maintain a polite, somewhat formal tone.

♦ Don't promote your own products or services on a board where commercial activities aren't allowed.

♦ Express yourself, but don't argue. Contribute when you have something to say, but be prepared to listen to others' opinions as well, even if those opinions differ from yours. Keep an open mind and avoid arguing. If you must disagree, give sources so the readers can better evaluate the issue for themselves.

Remember that on the Internet, anyone can write just about anything, true or false, well thought out or not. It's a fabulous resource, but only if you read critically and make your own judgments and decisions.

Staying the Course

Part of your continued growth as a teacher includes applying the new things you learn while retaining the excitement you had when you taught your very first student. It also means taking time for your own musical development and leaving yourself plenty of time to recharge your creative batteries. Being a happy teacher requires taking the long view—this is a career for a lifetime.

Student Attrition

Understand that attrition is something that every teacher encounters. The simple fact is that you will lose every single one of your students. Students move, they decide they like Cub Scouts better, they refuse to practice, they need after-school tutoring, they break their arm and never come back, they switch to English horn, they get on the junior Olympic ski team, they get sick and tired of working so hard, they become bored, they get involved with drugs, or they graduate high school. Whether it takes months or years, you *will* lose every student eventually.

It's difficult not to feel as if you've failed when you lose a student you've worked hard with, especially if you feel that student was really getting somewhere. And it's especially hard to take if that student moves to another teacher. Take note of the students you lose and the reasons. If you see a pattern emerge, do something about it. But also note how long your students are staying with you. And remember that if you are connected with your local community, if you are advertising effectively and networking, another student will soon call to take the old one's place.

Teacher Burnout

Sometimes it just simply helps to vent with someone who knows what you're going through. When your prize student leaves because he'd rather play soccer, when little Richie can't find middle C after two years, when you just don't know how to handle the parent who comes in with a screaming baby and insists on sitting in on the lesson, talking to other teachers can help you brainstorm solutions—or at least you'll feel better for having had a sympathetic and understanding listener.

We teachers also burn out if we have too many of the same level and age of students all at once. Say that word gets out among the parents of second-graders that you're the go-to person for music lessons. You get calls from the parents of a stream of 7-year-olds. Teaching a dozen beginning 7-year-olds back to back is not everyone's cup of tea, and if it isn't yours, you'll find yourself dreading the start of your workweek. Or try this scenario: your Tuesdays and Wednesdays are full of bored teenagers whose main creative outlet is spewing excuses for not practicing.

Recognize what's going on and realize several things. First, children grow. Next year, your second-graders will all be third-graders, and most of them will have moved up a level. You'll be in a groove with them, and they will have found most of their fingers at least some of the time. Furthermore, some of your bored teens will graduate and those who are left may rediscover their love of music. Second, you can always decide to take on only a different type of student for a while, perhaps even advertising that "The Mrs. Sunshine Piano Studio is accepting applications from intermediate and advanced players for the fall semester." Whatever rut you feel you're in, there's probably a way out with a little creative thinking, creative scheduling, or creative programming.

Staying Excited About Music

It's important to remember what brought you to music as a vocation in the first place. For most of us, it was a love of music. It's not unusual to forget that we love music when we hear so much noise day after day. Wrong notes, uneven rhythms, clunky dynamics ... in a moment of sheer burnout, a music teacher might be excused for wondering whether the most important requirement for the job is being half-deaf.

Wise Words

I plan my breaks into my studio calendar knowing that breaks refresh me and recharge my spirit. I use the school calendar(s) and plan my teaching schedule out for the school year. My husband and I look over the local community concert schedule in July and purchase our tickets in August for the season. There's nothing like attending a live music concert—energizing and renewing! I also use my musical skills in serving on my church worship team as a vocalist and pianist/keyboardist. It is exciting for me to work with other instrumentalists and vocalists to play and sing skillfully to honor God and lead people in worship!

—Marci Pittman, music teacher, Chico, California

Starting your own new personal music project might be just the antidote to hearing poor Elise butchered yet again, or too many variations of "Twinkle, Twinkle, Little Star." Set a goal to give a concert, play in a rock band, play at an open mike, perform with a jazz trio—whatever will stir your creativity. Put yourself on a schedule, and then follow your own advice: choose a regular practice time and stick with it.

Or forget about performing and focus on having fun. Find a regular group of fellow musicians to jam with. You can set something up just like a book club, except instead of reading and discussing books, you play and discuss music.

Finally, make a point of listening. Listen to old favorites and listen to new repertoire. On YouTube, you can listen to 50 different versions of your favorite sonata, or click around to discover new pieces you might like.

And listen to live music, too, both major artists and community performances. Go to the big concerts to get inspired. And go to community events to be part of the local scene. If you support it, it will support you. Show up at fellow teachers' recitals or at their gigs at the local restaurant.

Taking Care of Yourself

It's very tempting when you work for yourself to work all the time, especially when you like what you're doing. With music teaching, it sometimes seems that there is always one more thing you could be doing. Paperwork, repertoire and method book research, networking, listening, and your own practice can eat up hours at a time.

It's important to protect your personal time. That's true whether you have a family or live alone. Get out some! Make time to exercise, to garden, to cook a good meal.

Take breaks and vacations. Be sure there is at least one day a week when you do no teaching whatsoever. Take some school vacations as your break times. In other words, avoid the temptation to squeeze in make-up lessons. Make time for yourself in the summer as well, either by taking a week or two off or by scheduling long weekends and short teaching weeks.

The marathon runner knows that he can't sprint 26.2 miles. Teaching music is a marathon—a lifetime passion and pursuit. But by pacing yourself and constantly rejuvenating, you will indeed have a career that lasts a lifetime.

The Least You Need to Know

- Music teacher associations exist on the national, state, and local levels to support your continuing professional growth.

- Taking lessons or classes can rejuvenate your musical growth and help you empathize with students.

- Internet resources include opportunities to network with other teachers all over the country (and world).

- Prevent burnout by taking care of yourself. Listen to music, go to concerts, play music with colleagues, and remember why you chose this career in the first place!

Appendix

Resources for Music Teachers

Organizations

- **Music Teachers National Association** (MTNA)
  www.mtna.org

  Provides certification, continuing education, publications, local associations, and conferences for music teachers.

- **The Royal Conservatory** (Canada) and the **National Conservatory of Music of America** (NCMA)
  www.rcmusic.ca
  www.nationalconservatoryofmusicofamerica.org

  The Canadian Royal Conservatory is a long-standing music and arts education program that serves millions of Canadians.

  The National Conservatory of Music of America is based on the Royal Conservatory curriculum. Both organizations provide pedagogical support to music teachers and a comprehensive examination system for students ranging from beginner to college level.

- **National Association for Music Education** (MENC)
  www.menc.org

  MENC marked its one-hundredth year in 2007. It defines itself as the only association that addresses all aspects of music education. It has more than 75,000 members of active, retired, and aspiring music teachers, and it engages in advocacy for music education nationwide.

- **National Federation of Music Clubs** (NFMC)
  www.nfmc-music.org

  Founded in 1898, the NFMC is chartered by the U.S. Congress. It provides opportunities for musical study, performance, and appreciation to more than 200,000 senior, student, and junior members in 6,500 music-related clubs and organizations nationwide, and it sponsors festivals and competitions in which students can compete and perform.

- **Music Education Network for the Visually Impaired**
  www.menvi.org

  An international coalition of parents, educators, and students addressing the needs of music students who have visual handicaps.

- **American College of Musicians/National Guild of Piano Teachers** (also known as The Piano Guild)
  http://pianoguild.com

  The Piano Guild provides a program of diplomas and adjudications recognizing the progress of piano students through various levels of their education.

Music Education Programs for Young Children

The following is a sampling of the most popular programs for young children. All of these organizations provide teacher training and support.

- **Suzuki**
  http://suzukiassociation.org

  Best known for violin instruction, the famous program started by Shinichi Suzuki is worldwide. This organization provides support for Suzuki teachers in North and South America.

- **Kindermusik**
  www.kindermusik.com

  A private for-profit franchise of programs for group music classes for young children, including teachers' materials, training, and support.

- ◆ **Musikgarten**
  www.musikgarten.org

  Musikgarten specializes in training teachers in music and movement for young children from birth to age 9, and in teaching piano to adults.

- ◆ **Music for Young Children** (MYC)
  www.myc.com

  MYC's program integrates keyboard, singing, ear training, sight-reading, creative movement, rhythm, music theory, and music composition. It provides teacher education in teaching its program to groups of children between the ages of 3 and 11.

Books

Agay, Denes. *Teaching Piano: A Comprehensive Guide and Reference Book for the Instructor.* New York: Music Sales Corporation, 1982. A classic two-volume collection of essays by piano pedagogues on all aspects of teaching classical piano to the advanced student.

Blanchard, Bonnie, and Cynthia Blanchard Acree. *Making Music and Enriching Lives: A Guide for All Music Teachers.* Bloomington, Indiana: Indiana University Press, 2007. Inspiring tales and advice on teaching all kinds of music, from the trenches of a private flute teacher.

Jorgensen, Estelle. *The Art of Teaching Music.* Bloomington, Indiana: Indiana University Press, 2008. Philosophy and practicalities of music education.

Klickstein, Gerald. *The Musician's Way: A Guide to Practice, Performance, and Wellness.* New York: Oxford University Press, 2009. First-rate advice for practice and performance for any instrumentalist, from a guitarist and educator.

Montparker, Carol. *A Pianist's Landscape.* Portland, Oregon: Amadeus Press, 1998. Inspirational reflections on a three-pronged music career: teaching, performing, and writing about music.

Newsam, David R., and Barbara Sprague Newsam. *Making Money Teaching Music.* Cincinatti, Ohio: Writer's Digest Books, 2001. A bit out-of-date vis-à-vis the role of the Internet, but contains solid business advice for the home music teacher.

Tunstall, Tricia. *Note by Note: A Celebration of the Piano Lesson*. New York: Simon and Schuster, 2009. A piano teacher reflects about her students and the challenges a private piano teacher faces.

Uszler, Marienne, Stewart Gordon, and Scott McBride-Smith. *The Well-Tempered Keyboard Teacher, 2nd ed.* New York: Schirmer, 1999. Classic advice for piano teachers, focusing on piano pedagogy.

Wooten, Victor L. *The Music Lesson: A Spiritual Search for Growth Through Music*. New York: Berkeley Trade, 2008. Off-the-beaten-track, quirky but thought-provoking advice for getting to the heart of music from a well-known bass player.

Internet Resources

Internet resources change faster than the speed of books, leaving a long wake of dead links behind. The following links have been around for a while, so it's a good gamble they'll still be hosted by the time this book reaches your hands. And they contain some great tools and information.

◆ **www.practicespot.com**

This website has a wide variety of resources for the music teacher and student, from website software for the private music teacher to practice exercises for students.

◆ **www.howtopractice.com**

Comprehensive resource, blog, and website on practice and performance.

◆ **www.toddfamily.com/policies**

This recommended page is part of a website that highlights various family businesses. One of the family members is a music teacher who has amassed dozens of studio policies from a wide variety of teachers. This policies page has been live for many years. Browse the navigation bar on the left to bring up studio policies; you can compare them and incorporate ideas that you think would work for you.

◆ **www.musicteachersblog.com/2009/04/20-online-resources-for-music-teachers**

This website reviews online resources for music teachers.

◆ **www.berklee.edu/assessments/default.html**

Berklee College of Music's website includes a section of sample skills assessment questions similar to those used by the college to place incoming freshmen into various levels of classes in such subjects as ear training, arranging, and music theory. Studying these questions can give teachers and students an idea of what to expect in music classes.

Copyright Resources

Understanding copyright laws is important for music teachers for several reasons. Laws govern arranging music for public performances, recording music, performing music, and posting and/or downloading music and performances on the Internet. Copyright law also limits how much of a piece of music can be copied for instructional purposes, and under what circumstances this is allowed.

The U.S. Copyright Law has a section called Fair Use that sets forth the circumstances under which it is permissible to copy and use someone else's creative work without buying it or licensing it. According to copyright law, fair use is determined by considering the following factors:

◆ The purpose and character of the use, including whether such use is of a commercial nature or is for nonprofit educational purposes

◆ The nature of the copyrighted work

◆ The amount and substantiality of the portion used in relation to the copyrighted work as a whole

◆ The effect of the use upon the potential market for or value of the copyrighted work

Fair use is notoriously difficult to understand and interpret correctly. To help music teachers, the National Association for Music Education—in conjunction with the MTNA, ASCAP Foundation, Copyright Society of the USA, the American Bar Association, and several other interested groups—has come out with a position statement that attempts to interpret the law for music education purposes. To see the complete text, visit the following site: www.menc.org/resources/view/copyright-center.

View the entire text of the U.S. Copyright Law (October 2007) at this site: www.copyright.gov/title17.

Index

Q-R